Reeducation Camp for Liberal Millennials and Gen Z

LIVING UNDER A REPUBLICAN ADMINISTRATION

Jim Wagner

YOUR CAMP DRILL SERGEANT

First printing: December 2017

Reeducation Camp for Liberal Millennials and Gen Z
© 2017 by Jim Wagner

Printed in the United States of America

Published by **WAR**Arts

ISBN: 978-0-9983358-3-4

Dedicated to
all the Millennials and Gen Zers
that I interviewed, both conservative and liberal, prior to writing this book,
and special thanks to
Seth
Derek
Ben
Nelly
Nataly
Gary
Manique
Darya
Yasmin
Sanam
Juliet
Amanda
Charlotte
Jordan
Ty
Ernesto
Martha
Joe
Valerie

CAMP DIRECTORY

INTRODUCTION

ENTERING THE FRONT GATE
OF YOUR REEDUCATION CAMP

Most Baby Boomers, people born between the years 1946 to 1964, and those of Generations X and Y that came sometime shortly after that if you really want to split hairs, believe that you Millennials, the generation from 1982 to 2000, and you of Generation Z, "Gen Z" to sound really cool, born in the early 2000s who are currently teenagers and young adults, have the attention span of a goldfish. They also believe that your liberal teachers have been dumbing you down since the very first day you stepped foot into kindergarten to a point where today you don't even understand the real world around you, and that you think that you can usher in that all-elusive *utopia* (Google the word to know what it means), and then the world will be a perfect place, and everyone will be locked arm in arm singing the 1985 song *We Are The World*. However, the very fact that you are willing to read this book, which is completely void of any pictures (eye candy that is), proves that you're the exception to that of a goldfish, and your "reeducation" will transpire at a faster pace than most.

Now, let me back up for a second before we head over to Cell Block 1 where you'll begin your stay at this fine camp. Let's sort out this generation labeling that everybody seems to throw around rather loosely, and try to make some sense of it.

As I stated in the opening paragraph Baby Boomers are those people born between the years 1946 to 1964. However, according to Wikipedia, Baby Boomers range from "the early-to-mid 1940s and the end from 1960 to 1964." Then after them came Generation X ranging "from the early-to-mid 1960s and ending birth years from the late 1970s to early 1980s." Yeah, I know, these overlapping years seem a bit confusing.

Generation Y, again using Wikipedia as our resource, is the generation from "the early 1980s as starting birth years and the mid-1990s to 2000s as ending birth years." But, wait! This is the same definition for "Millennials" on the same Wikipedia. No, you're not going crazy. Gen Y and Millennials are one and the same.

Generation Z, also known as Post-Millennials, "typically use starting birth years ranging from the mid-1990s to early 2000s, and as of yet there is little consensus about ending birth years." No wonder this generation is so confused about everything! You don't even get ending birth years on Wikipedia. It's just left wide open. So, what has ended up happening is that most young people today are just referred to as "Millennials." I suppose anyone "young" is under 35-years-old. Past, current, or post, you're all "Millennials" to the Baby Boomers; the ones in power right now. I'm a Baby Boomer, and I'll be your drill sergeant during your stay here.

Who knows what the next generation will be called, for we have come to the end of the alphabet. Don't worry. I'm sure someone will coin a term for the next generation, for we human beings love slapping on labels for different groups of people. It keeps us all in understandable categories, or it separates us, depending on the desired goal.

Now that the generational differences have all been cleared up, let's get moving. Grab your personal belongings and follow me.

Most of you 83.1 million Millennials and Gen Zers were expecting United States Senator Bernie Sanders of Vermont to win the 2016 Democratic Party presidential primaries and then go on to win the presidency of the United States, which would have catapulted America into the new age of "Democratic Socialism," whatever that is. But, we'll discuss this in more detail later. Then the punch to the gut came when Hillary Clinton's camp destroyed the old man. So many idealistic youthful dreams were popped like a balloon by the reality that the system was "rigged." We found that out through the DNC, *Democratic National Convention*, emails that were released by WikiLeaks, along with Donna Brazile's tell-all book *Hacks*. With such corruption there was no way that the Democratic Party, "the establishment," was ever going to let you Millennials and Gen Zers "Feel the Bern." The only "Bern" you got was when he crashed and "burned."

Once Bernie Sanders was out of the way the leftist mainstream media kept telling you that First-Lady-turned-Senator-turned-Secretary-of-State-turned-presidential-candidate Hillary Rodham Clinton was going to be the 45th President of the United States, and that Bernie supporters had no choice but to vote for the lesser of two evils. It was either her or Donald Trump. Therefore, all the polls said that her win was guaranteed by a whopping 90%. They were all giddy predicting, "it will be historic to have a woman as President." After all, *We the People* had elected a "black president," and so naturally the next step in progressivism was to have a Madam President. "I'm with her!" they cried reluctantly.

The majority of your schoolteachers, the leftist media, Black Lives Matter, and even Mexican officials for crying out loud, said that real estate mogul Donald John Trump didn't have a snowball's chance in hell of winning the presidential race. Just to make sure he wouldn't have a chance he was labeled as an "abuser of women," "homophobic," "an Islamophobe," "a xenophobe," "a KKK sympathizer," and a dozen other nasty names, but you know what happened? "The Trump" was elected as the 45th President of the United States of America.

"OMG! What happened?" you asked yourself on that fateful day. There were even actual tears and sobbing by many. The leftist media, with their wet cheeks caused by flowing tears and blowing snot bubbles expanding between sobs, were on the air the next day lamenting, "How did we get this wrong?" Then, despite a fair democratic election, and Hillary Clinton conceding to Donald Trump, a lot of you took to the streets protesting and rioting. "He's not our President!" many of the protest signs stated in big bold letters. Let me tell you, that time in recent history was really inconvenient for us grown-ups, both conservatives and liberals alike, when many of your peers blocked streets, freeways, and highways across the entire nation to make a point. Of course, the point was completely lost, because the gripes were all over the map, and finally the police cleared the roads for those of us who had to get home or drive to work.

Back when communism flourished in the former Soviet Union anyone who didn't accept the platform of the Communist Party weren't just ridiculed, but they were sent to a reeducation camp, and there were many of them spread out across the land behind The Iron Curtain. In Russia these camps were mostly in isolated, freezing cold, Siberia. In communist Vietnam and Cambodia they were deep in the jungles. Today in North Korea they are being discovered all the time by our spy satellites. Yes, we spy on other countries, and they do the same to us.

"What crimes landed people in these camps to get 'reeducated?'" you ask. That's a good question. Speaking against the government or their policies would get you a one-way ticket there. Believing in God would get you hard labor with no cable T.V. in your cell or cramped dorm room. Being a homosexual was a sure way to end up in one. Being "too educated" was considered a big threat, because such people could think for themselves, and thus a great danger to the all-powerful state.

Your side has lost, and this book is your reeducation camp experience. In order to live under a Republican administration, you must learn what it means to be a conservative. Now, before you have a temper tantrum like a toddler screaming out, "I will never adopt conservative views or become a Republican!" and "Vive la révolution!" thrown in there, you need to be smart about this. The problem with you Millennials and Gen Zers is that you don't read the classics: Shakespeare, the works of Mark Twain, Hemingway, the Bible, or Sun Tzu just to name a few. Instead you feed your mind with witchcraft laced *Harry Potter*, children killing children in *The Hunger Games*, zombies gorging on the remnant surviving population, or you watch more and more horror movies with people getting waxed so you can fulfill your blood lust.

"So, who is, or who was, Sun Tzu?"

I'm glad you asked. He was a Chinese general who lived 2,500 years ago and wrote the book *The Art of War*. I know you don't like the word "war," because it makes you feel all weird and uncomfortable inside, but bear with me a moment. Remember that your attention span is longer than that of a goldfish, which is nine seconds in case you didn't know. Oh, and that reminds me. My good friend Butch Pierson is a cinematographer for Hollywood. He's one of the best in the business who has filmed countless blockbuster movies and television series. I'm sure you've seen his work, you just don't know he did it. Butch once told me, while I was on location watching him film a movie, that today's edit cuts last three seconds. In other words, there is a different camera angle that flashes on the big screen every three seconds. Not many years ago it was every five seconds, but they shortened it to keep viewers' attention. "That's because each generation has a shorter and shorter attention span," Butch educated me. Audiences must to be constantly titillated with different images every few seconds to keep them interested. Go back to the 1930s and 40s and, OMG!, the camera seemed to have been frozen in place. In reality we only see from one perspective our entire lives – from our own two eyes; one camera angle, so to speak. However, I've digressed. Back to General Sun Tzu. *The Art of War* is mandatory reading for not only all our military officers, but also all the Fortune 500 corporations' executives study this classic book as well to succeed in business. One of the most quoted sentences in the book is, "If you know the enemy and know yourself, you need not fear the result of a hundred battles. If you know yourself but not the enemy, for every victory gained you will also suffer a defeat. If you know neither the enemy nor yourself, you will succumb in every battle."

That does not mean, "Hi Frank, my name is _____," when it comes to the word "know." Duh! It means that you need to study your enemy, think like your enemy, and develop the ability to anticipate what your enemy will do in order to out maneuver and defeat him, her, or them.

In going through this reeducation camp I hardly expect you to drop your naïve progressive ways and become a conservative, but if you're ever going to win the White House, Senate, House of Representatives, and all the other seats you've lost over the past several years, then you had better know all about the enemy – them, us, me. Just wishing something to happen won't make it happen. Unfortunately, milk and cookies, a safe space, or a comfort animal in the face of defeat was not a good start.

"What the hell are you talking about Sergeant Wagner? Milk, cookies, what?"

Let me remind you. After the defeat of presidential candidate Hillary Clinton, besides many Millennials blocking the roads and torching police cars, many of your peers known as "snowflakes," hopefully not you, were so traumatized over Donald Trump's winning the White House that colleges and esteemed universities all across the nation set up "safe zones." There were literally "crying rooms" set aside where students had coloring books, Play-Doh, and milk and cookies laid out on tables to ease the pain of the loss. Other schools took a different approach to the crisis. They allowed students to take some time off to cope with the traumatic event, which meant cancelling classes, despite many students being right in the middle of their exams. One college even rented a pony, a very popular comfort animal, to help the "kids" get through their grief.

Wow! What a contrast between generations. With the Greatest Generation, the generation of World War II in the 1940s, 18-year-old young men were going off to war to fight Nazi Germany, fascist Italy, and Imperial Japan with bullets and bombs. There were no "crying rooms" for them. There were only fox holes, bombed out structures, and hospital beds for them to cry in. For their families the crying was done in the privacy of their homes, and in places of worship. Yet, despite the tears, fears, and unimaginable horror they faced they defeated the enemy, came back home to build the strongest economy the world had ever seen, and they gave their children a better life and country than the one they had been given by their parents.

Here's how this book, your reeducation camp, will work. Now, pay attention! Each chapter will deal with a major topic that is of concern for you Millennials and Gen Zers. Within each chapter are subheadings getting right to the nuts and bolts of it all. In other words, we'll go into the specifics. The Millennials' and Gen Zers' position will be stated first, and then the Republican conservative view on the same position will be explained to you. I'll even throw in some of my own experiences to make things a bit more interesting for you.

By the end of your stay you'll be a Spartan. You'll have become a conservative Republican, and then you'll be ready to go back out into society as a productive contributing member of society and Make America Great Again.

This is the camp motto. Repeat after me, "Make America Great Again."

Remember, you've got to say this to the camp warden if you expect to get out of here after Cell Block 10. You don't want to go through this reeducation camp again, do you? At least we don't execute people like fascists, socialists (the Nazi types, and we'll get to who they were in a minute), or communists if you fail to tow the Party line. You're not going to find yourself in a mass grave if you fail here. Yes, I know, you won't mean it when you say it, and you'll resist on the inside, but you've got to at least fake it when it comes time for your release date. You want to look and sound the part. Then like a Trojan Horse (you should read the ancient story, or at least see the movie version Troy where actor Brad Pitt plays the role of Achilles) to sabotage the Republican Party and take over the country in the next election, and be on the road to your warm and fuzzy utopia, or for what a small percentage of you are after, a land of anarchy (no rules at all). Wouldn't that be fun?

The most you will get out of this Reeducation Camp for Liberals and Generation Z is that you'll better understand the facts about today's issues, because, let's face it, a lot of people from your generation parrot sound bites they hear from their professors and mainstream media, but they have no idea what they are really fighting against. At least by the time you get out of here you'll be able to do as our beloved American author Mark Twain once advised. *Get your facts first, then you can distort them as you please.*

The minimum that you will get out of this reeducation camp is some coping skills. You're going to learn how to be a good sport about losing. I know, I know. You just found out that in real life there are winners and losers. It's harsh, I know. There are consequences to actions. Your teachers used to give everyone a trophy or a participation ribbon when you raced or played school games, but that wasn't the case after the elections, was it?

So, be smart and absorb all that you are going to be taught in this reeducation camp, and may I be the first to say to you, "Welcome."

CELL BLOCK 1

POLITICAL PARTIES

THERE'S REALLY ONLY TWO PARTIES

In the United States of America there are essentially two political parties. They are the Democratic Party and the Republican Party. There are other parties, but they are "wannabes," that is to say they "want to be" a legitimate political party, but few take them seriously.

Two of our founding fathers, Thomas Jefferson (we'll get to him later) and James Madison formed the Democratic-Republican Party. That's right, the two names were once merged. Then in 1828 Andrew Jackson founded the modern Democratic Party making it the world's oldest active party. Hmmmm, that's interesting. History is on your side.

THE DEMOCRATIC PARTY

The Democratic Party started out with the worldview of classical liberalism. That means a strong belief in civil liberties, political freedom, a representative democracy run by the rule of law, and economic freedom. Or, to be more accurate – free market capitalism. Today's Democrats don't believe in half of this list. Bernie Sander's Democratic Socialism changed all that. Even Hillary Clinton jumped on his bandwagon to get "the Millennial vote" after she stomped him into the ground.

Democratic Socialism is basically communism, but without the statues of Karl Marx or Lenin in every American town square. The difference between the two ideologies is that communism believes that the all-powerful state owns everything, and in Socialism the all-powerful state runs everything. Yeah, I know, it sounds like the same thing. The second one just sounds nicer.

I know a little about communism, because in the early 1960s when I was in grade school my classmates and I all had to get under our desks when the Civil Defense siren would go off. "Duck and cover!" they called it. We assumed the proper position for a nuclear strike by the Soviet Union: on the knees and elbows covering the head with both arms and hands. They were like earthquake drills of today. Then when I was a wet behind the ears private in the United States Army in 1980 our drill sergeants would take us to the rifle range to shoot at plastic human silhouette targets painted like Russian soldiers: toting an AK-47, the red star on the helmet and belt buckle, and all. There was no doubt in our minds who the enemy was. Oh yeah, the communists were a big threat all right. It was a scary time. It was the Cold War, and the Army gave me a certificate later on to prove it – *In recognition of your service during the period of the Cold War (2 September 1946 – 26 December 1991) in promoting peace and stability for this Nation, the people of this Nation are forever grateful.* Are you grateful for my service, and the others who have served during this time? You'd better be! There's nothing more conservative than supporting the military.

Forty-five years of living with the constant threat of World War III was stressful, to say the least, but the Soviet Union finally collapsed, and the Cold War was over. We won. We won by being tough and determined.

Ironically, my wife was born and raised in the former Soviet Union. Who would have thought that I'd be marring the "enemy?" Anyway, ask her, or my father-in-law, about what it was like living under communist rule and they have nothing good to say about the system. Nothing! Before 1991, whenever my father-in-law was watching the news from the comfort of his Los Angeles home, and the anchorman mentioned the Soviet Union, he'd yell out, "Soviet Union!" and not in a good way, and then make the disgusting noise as if he were spitting on the ground, "Thewee!" It was clear what he thought about the former country he had lived in.

Since then I have had the chance to work in countries that were part of the former Soviet Bloc: East Germany, the Czech Republic, and Bulgaria. When I asked my colleagues there what it was like living under communist rule every single one of them said, "We hated it. We knew that the West was living better than us even though they (the government) told us differently." Yes, you could find some of the old timers who longed for "the good old days," but that was only because they lost their pensions when communism fell. Communism made countries go bankrupt. It sounds like what happen to Greece recently, doesn't it? Economics is economics no matter where you live on earth.

So, back to the Vermont Senator, turned presidential candidate, Bernie Sanders. Now, bear with me for a second for a quick history lesson. This is very important to know because many young people wanted to hand over their futures to this man in 2016, and they're even hoping he'll run again in 2020.

Senator Sanders was born on September 8, 1941 in Brooklyn, New York. His father, a Jew, was born in Poland and immigrated to the United States a year before the start of World War II. Lucky him. Bernie's mother was born in New York City to Jewish immigrants from Poland and Russia. Unfortunately, many of her relatives who remained in Poland were exterminated during the Holocaust (we'll talk about this controversial word later in your reeducation process) by the National Socialism Party. You might be more familiar with the German acronym from the word Nationalsozialismus (Nazi).

At an early age, while attending the University of Chicago, Bernie joined the Young People's Socialist League. Just the name alone screams out, "communism!" It was part of the Socialist Party of America with the motto WORKERS OF THE WORLD UNITE. Their logo looks like a Soviet propaganda poster.

In the 1960s and 1970s, during the Cold War, Bernie was active in peace and antiwar movements, and he applied for conscientious objector status. Okay, that's fine. It's just a good thing that everyone didn't do the same thing back then or the Soviet Union would have never been brought to its knees.

After graduating from college Bernie moved to Vermont to live the "rural life," and he worked as a carpenter, filmmaker, and writer pumping out leftist articles. Then he set his sights on politics and became a member of the Liberty Union Party, a radical leftist party, along with the People's Party, which had the party platform of free medical care, legalized abortion, legalized marijuana, withdrawal of American troops from all foreign countries ("Sorry West Germany and Japan. You're on your own to face the Russians."), and a bunch of other stuff. Eventually Bernie got elected as Mayor of Burlington. It seemed that he did have some support for his progressive ideas, and he boldly labeled himself as a "socialist." He was 39-years-old at the time.

In 1988 Bernie Sanders married his second wife, Jane O'Meara, and the next day he went to the Soviet Union for his "honeymoon," as he called it. He went there in his official capacity as mayor, but many felt it was his way of protesting the Reagan administration, which was staunchly conservative. It was a very unusual choice for a country to visit, because most Americans had no desire to go to our archenemy's country. Anyway, that same year Bernie Sanders was the first Independent elected to the U.S. House of Representatives. In 1991 he co-founded the Congressional Progressive Caucus, which was a left leaning organization to promote progressive issues.

You're going to keep seeing this word "progressive," so we might as well address it now. Progressivism embraces environmentalism and social justice with the view that the government ought to change as society evolves. In other words, the U.S. Constitution is outdated, and capitalism is destroying the environment and hogging all the wealth for just an elite few. That's what they believe. That's what you've been told to believe.

Now, back to Bernie Sanders. Where were we? Oh, yes, Bernie's political career. In 2005 he entered the race for the U.S. Senate. He wanted to take his socialism to the big leagues. Although he was a socialist he cut a deal with the Democrats that he'd vote their way. No surprise there. Therefore, Chuck Schumer, chairman of the Democratic Senatorial Campaign Committee, endorsed Bernie Sanders along with Senate Minority Leader Harry Reid and Vermont governor Howard Dean. Then in March 2006 none other than President Barak Obama campaigned for Bernie Sanders in Vermont. The top leadership in the Democratic Party had no problems with adding a socialist to the Senate. After all, they were all "progressive" at heart as well.

Hang in there. We're getting close to the end talking about Bernie's history.

Independents have never had a chance at becoming President of the United States, and so Bernie basically ran as a Democrat, and he even called his brand of politics "Democratic Socialism." He just couldn't drop the "s" word. It was deep within his very soul.

When he joined the presidential race Bernie's presence made it look like the Democrats had a real race going. It was kind of weird that Hillary Clinton was the only candidate for a while, and that the Democratic Party was 100% behind her. But, to everyone's surprise, a large swath of the country's population was more left leaning than anyone had believed. I confess, I didn't want to believe it ether. Throw in the promise of "free" everything, and that was a winning receipt for Democratic Socialism. It really caught Hillary and the Dems totally off guard. Who would have thought that this old socialist-communist white-haired guy would have such an appeal to so many – especially the young?

To make a long story short the Democratic Party placed all their bets, and their energy, into Hillary Clinton. Then lo and behold she won at the DNC, *Democratic National Convention*, on July 26, 2016. Boy, were a lot of Millennials pissed off! Wait, "boy" is now a racist term. Some slave owners used to call their male slaves "boy." How about, "Good God, were a lot of..." No, you don't like that one either because of "God" in there. How about... no, let's just forget it. Let's just go with "A lot of Millennials were angry." I'm glad we sanitized that one. Wait! Hold on a second! The Republicans are in control now. We're the victors. We don't have to worry about political correctness anymore. So, I'm not going to either. You're in my reeducation camp now, and not the other way around.

To wrap it up with Bernie Sanders he told his supporters, after his 2016 defeat, to put his defeat behind them and to support Hillary Clinton. To ease his pain, he went out and bought a $575,000 vacation home, and then he formed his own 501(c) 4 organization naming it *Our Revolution*, which is also the title of his new book *The Goal of Our Revolution*. As stated on the official website, the goal of Our Revolution is to "reclaim democracy for the working people." Isn't capitalism great to afford Bernie all those nice things?

You know when a politician has crossed the line when the Chicago Tribune runs the headline *The Democrats have become socialists* published on September 14, 2017 (to be fair it was an opinion column). Nonetheless, ultra-left Senator Bernie Sanders and Senator Elizabeth "Pocahontas" Warren (Democrat - Massachusetts), along with 16 of their Democratic colleagues, rolled out their socialized health-care plan the day before. They basically told the American public that what they need is for the federal government to run health care – all of it! After all, everyone just loves how the IRS has oversight over their personal finances. So, even though socialism was defeated at the ballot boxes in the 2016 elections, Bernie's "revolution" found new support from a few rising-star Democratic senators who have picked up the red banner, and want to wave it around at the upcoming elections: Cory Booker (D-New Jersey), Kamala Harris (D-California), and Kirsten Gillibrand (D-New York). At least the remaining 28 Democratic senators are not quite ready to change their party's name to "Democratic Socialists."

The Democratic Party was the party, most of its members anyway, that didn't want to end slavery in the United States, and who propagated the Jim Crow laws in the South after the American Civil War. Jim Crow laws were laws that kept racial segregation alive and well in the former Confederate States of America.

Fast forward, and in 1932 Franklin D. Roosevelt, the 32nd President of the United States, introduced liberal-progressive policies calling it the "New Deal." It came on the heels of the Great Depression, which was a time of a lot of bank closings and economic failures following the "Wall Street Crash of 1929."

What also helped FDR get re-elected, besides providing lots and lots of government bailout money to fix the economy, was the repeal of Prohibition in 1933. Prohibition was a nationwide ban on alcoholic beverages from 1920 to 1933. First it was a state-by-state ban to promote public morals and health, and eventually it was ratified as the 18th Amendment by the federal government. But, enough people screamed, "Make booze legal!" and so it was. Does this sound slightly familiar?

We had the Financial Crisis of 2007-2009, while President George W. Bush, a Republican, was in office, and along came Barak Obama promising "hope and change." Like FDR he also poured in a lot of government money to bail out the banks and many big businesses. Plus, a lot of people had been whining for years, "Make pot legal!" and so the enforcement against marijuana became weak on his watch - purposely so. On November 6, 2012 Colorado and Washington became the first states in the union to legalize the sale and possession of marijuana for recreational use. Then other states made it legal. Forget the fact that cannabis smoke contains higher amounts of hydrogen cyanide, ammonia, and other nitro-oxide-bad-stuff than cigarettes, and that the effects of "the high" lasts for one to three hours because of the main ingredient tetrahydrocannabinol (THC), which can induce both euphoria and anxiety, that didn't seem to matter to pot heads. Did I mention that it's also a "gateway drug?" That is to say, marijuana is a habit-forming drug that can lead the user to other more harmful addictive drugs, but whatever. I, for one, get high off of life, and not from drugs or booze. I don't need a buzz to enjoy life, but hey, some people do. I get it.

Let's wrap up our crash course on the history of the Democratic Party. From the 1960s and right up until just a few years ago most Democrats described their party as, "the party that helps the poor, and is concerned about civil rights." However, during the Obama Era the newer definition morphed into, "the party that helps the poor, protects women's rights, everyone should marry who they love, and take away the power of the white oppressive imperialistic males." Oh, also add to that list that the Republicans "don't care about the environment, is the party for the rich, and all they want to do is to go back to the past where all the minorities were oppressed." It's gotten rather vicious over the years, but that's what a lot of people actually believe today.

After Donald Trump won the presidential election the Democratic Party had to do a lot of soul searching. After the crying rooms for traumatized students and teachers, protests and riots, and saying that Trump's win was a "white lash," against a sitting black president (this stupid quote was made by CNN commentator Van Jones, a former aide to President Obama, on national television), many honest Democrats said openly, "Maybe we shouldn't have ignored the white men of this country. Maybe we should come a little more to the middle."

Then about a month later, "Naaaaaaah." Many believed that Trump won because they didn't count the votes correctly. So, Green Party Jill Stein demanded a recount in several states even though she only had 1 percent of the national vote. As if a recount was going to somehow show her the winner. Then it turned out that Trump had more votes against Hillary Clinton than were originally counted. Wow! did that ever backfire. When that ploy didn't work the Democrats then said, "The Russians interfered with our elections. Hillary would have won otherwise."

See, it wasn't about Jill Stein. It was about Hillary.

The White House didn't care for four long years that Hillary Clinton had used her own private, unsecured, computer servers to conduct government business, which was highly illegal, and that any foreign agency, including the Russians, could have pulled information from these servers containing American secrets. She was Hillary Clinton after all. Yet, after Donald Trump won the election suddenly Russian hacking was a top priority. The Obama Administration was "confident" that the Russians were behind the interference of the United States elections, and the big man himself wanted a report about it immediately. Basically, he wanted it before the Electoral College casted their final votes for President of the United States on December 19, 2016, which would make the election official and Donald Trump the President of the United States.

Again, you know the history, or you should know the history, and that was that the Electoral College voted for Donald Trump; not just by a little, but by a whole lot: 304 to 227. There were more red states (Republicans) than blue states (Democrats). Hillary had planned on the generally liberal West Coast and East Coast voting for her, which for the most part they did, but she ignored Middle America. Donald Trump didn't. Therefore, his strategy paid off, and he got the job. Anyway, the Russian obstacle didn't work. Which, when you think about it, Donald Trump colluding with the Russians to swing the presidential election his way doesn't make any sense. First of all, who was in charge at the time of the elections? It was the President of the United States Barak Obama (Democrat), Secretary of State John Kerry (Democrat), U.S. Attorney General Loretta Lynch (Democrat) and CIA Director John Brennan (appointed by President Obama). If Donald Trump and his campaign staff had been teamed up with our archenemies, the Russians, then why didn't the Obama Administration put a stop to it before the elections? Such ties would have been outright treason, which would have been a certain prison term for everyone involved. The Democrats held all the power at the time. Second, why would the Russians want Donald Trump in power when he was going to "Make America Great Again," which meant building back up the U.S. military, and thus become a direct threat against Russia and her dreams of expansion. On the other hand, Hillary Clinton was going to be "the third term of President Obama," and continue to show weakness around the globe. If you were the Russians whom would you want for president of the United States? The lead-from-the-front bulldozer guy, or the lead-from-behind gal? The reason Donald Trump and his band weren't arrested was because the Russian narrative, constantly on a loop by the leftist media, was a lie. Of course, the truth finally came out after, and I repeat "AFTER," Donald Trump was elected President of the United States. Former FBI Director James Comey testified under oath before the Senate Intelligence Committee on June 8, 2017 that Presidential Candidate Trump was never under investigation. There was no collusion with the Russians. Case closed.

Several months after the election the whole "Trump campaign Russian meeting" mess surfaced again. This time it was about Donald Trump's son-in-law Jared Kushner, and chairman of the presidential campaign Paul Manafort. Apparently, during the election these two men had a meeting with Kremlin connected Natalia Veselnitskaya. She claimed to have had some political dirt on Hillary Clinton, which any opposing party would want to know about, but after 20 minutes talking to her the Trump team realized she didn't have any information of value, and the meeting ended. No laws had been broken. However, the investigation conducted by special counsel Robert Mueller discovered something we had always known about the Russians – they are the masters of disinformation. However, before you get all worked up about this meeting, it was a set up. This supposed Russian spy Natalia Veselnitskaya was cleared by the United States Department of Justice under "extraordinary circumstances" to lobby in our country; permission that had been granted by U.S. Attorney General Loretta Lynch (Democrat). The Democrats knew full well that this Russian woman, and her entourage, was in our country lobbying against The Magnitsky Act that imposed sanctions on Russia for alleged human rights violations. Natalia Veselnitskaya had met with other Republicans and Democrats alike, but that small detail came out only after the accusations against Jared Kushner and Paul Manafort. Leaving that "small detail" out is what we call "fake news," and we'll get to this subject a little bit later on. The real story was the Uranium One Scandal that had taken place in the Obama administration, but that wouldn't really come to light until almost a year after the elections.

I know that some high-ranking Democrats were hoping that they could use the Russian ploy to say to Donald Trump, "You're fired!" Get it? That was Donald Trump's famous line from his hit television show The Apprentice (2003 to 2011). People learned a lot about business and American capitalism from that show. I certainly did. But, alas, the President wasn't fired. It's hard to fire someone over something that isn't true.

So, from the time President Trump moved into the White House on January 20, 2017 to June 8, 2017 the American people had to go through almost five months of the leftist mainstream media leading many to believe that some of our agents in our intelligence community, our "spooks," were suggesting that President Trump and his staff conspired with the Russians to win the U.S. presidency, which is an impeachable offense. Former FBI Director Comey had it right when commenting on the media's reporting when it came to President Trump and the Russians, "There have been many, many stories based on – well, lots of stuff, but about Russia that are dead wrong." Dead wrong, meaning lies.

Okay, so that's the story of the Democrats. Now, let's take a close look at your new rulers. Oh yeah! Republican Donald Trump is your President, like it or not. He is. Holding up signs, or putting up on your Facebook wall, "NOT MY PRESIDENT," does not change anything. That's why you're in this reeducation camp in the first place. Or, you can move to a foreign country like several celebrities threatened to do if Trump got elected. Canada seemed to be the country of choice for many like Lena Dunham, Raven Symone, Neve Campbell (she's actually Canadian, so we'll give her a pass), Bryan Cranston, Barbara Streisand, Stephen King, Ne-Yo, Chelsea Handler, Larry Flynt, and Keegan-Michael Key. It's the same place a lot of young American men fled to during the Vietnam War to avoid the military draft, so it probably sounded like a good idea to some of these celebrities. Why is it that nobody wants to flee south? Nobody was itching to move to Venezuela.

What about actor and singer Miley Cyrus? She too claimed that she was going to leave the United States if Donald Trump was elected. However, after almost a year after he took office her fans kept hounding her on social media asking her when she was finally going to leave. The 24-year-old responded, and not in a very lady like manner, "I'm not f- - king leaving the country, that's some ignorant s- - t, that's dumb." So, in a word, No. She concluded, "Because that's me abandoning my country when I think I've got a good thing to say to my country. And trust me, I hear every day on my Instagram, 'Just leave already! When are you going to leave?' Well, that's not going to do me any good. Does it really matter where I am? Because wherever I am, my f _ _ king voice is gonna be heard, and I'll make sure of it."

Well, you guessed it. She had been a vocal Bernie Sanders and Hillary Clinton supporter. On her new album titled Younger Now there is a song on it called "Inspired" that was believed to have been written for Hillary Clinton. So, we can understand Miley's disappointment. She was probably hoping that this song was going to be "President Hillary Clinton's" new anthem, but, alas, it never happened.

So, Canada's not an option for you even though your horse lost the race? In that case, KEEP CALM, AND CARRY ON with some information that is going to enlighten you. You might as well relax, you've got years ahead of you under Republican rule.

There. That's better. On to the next subject.

THE REPUBLICAN PARTY

The Republican Party, also known as the GOP, *Grand Old Party*, was founded by ex-Whigs (the political party from the 1830s until the death of President Taylor in 1850), and anti-slavery activists. That's right, it's the political party,

21

which was very strong in the Northern States, that fought slavery all the way up until Abraham Lincoln abolished it in 1865. You probably didn't know that. The blacks today, or shall I say "African Americans," can thank the Republican Party for their ancestors' freedom.

In 1896 President Theodore Roosevelt pushed for anti-trust laws, which promoted fair competition in business that prevented monopolies, and small businesses loved him for that. Yet, somehow Teddy's move also gave Republicans the reputation of being "the party of big business" as well. Over the years this reputation has been twisted into the idea that the Republicans "only care about the rich," and to hell with the poor, but nothing could be further from the truth.

Democrats, like many socialists and communists, believe that there is only one pie, if I could use the pie analogy. In many respects, they are right. Since these political-economic systems (socialism and communism) place so many restrictions on businesses, and they don't reward workers with financial gain, there are often material and food shortages. Workers in such systems say, in private of course, "Why should I work my but off if I get paid the same amount if I do the bare minimum or I am working hard?"

My wife, who is from the former Soviet Union, remembers spending hours in lines in front of stores. There were always shortages in her country, even of the essentials: eggs, milk, bread, et cetera. Sometimes her and her father, after waiting for a long time in line, the store clerks would just close the door and lock it when they ran out of everything. It was tuff luck for those who never got into the store that day. They'd just have to return the next day, stand in line, and try again. To make matters worse sometimes the electricity would go off for hours at a time in everyone's homes, and even for a day or two. The common expression was, "They cut the power to let everyone know who is in power." Few could afford cars in the former Soviet Union, for cars were luxury items, and those who did have them were the higher ups in the communist party. That was just life in the former Soviet Union.

On the other hand, Republicans don't believe in the single pie concept. They believe in baking more pies. And, not just baking as many pies as the market allows, but allowing competition where people can open their own bakeries, and may the better bakery win – in bringing in customers, that is. If baker A is making better pies than baker B, and marking it up the price to a level that customers are willing to pay for it, to make a profit of course, then why shouldn't baker A enjoy the fruit of his or her labors? I don't care how much money Bill Gates of Microsoft made. I have enjoyed using many of his computer programs he has developed. I personally have benefited from his desire to create and make a profit. I don't care how much Steve Jobs made with Apple. I am using one of his MAC computers right now as I write this sentence for you. Yes, it is an old computer, but it's a good one.

To put it another way, *the rising tide lifts all the boats*. When America is prospering economically most people enjoy the prosperity at all levels. Then they don't worry about not getting their slice of the pie, because there's plenty to go around.

Republicans take a conservative stance on issues, and that is why the word "conservative" is often interchangeable with the word "Republican." The main belief is that government (also known as Uncle Sam or Big Brother) should not play a big role in people's lives. "Protect the country, keep taxes low, don't waste taxpayers' money, and allow people to conduct business with as little intervention as possible," is what most Republicans will say.

"Don't tell me how much soft drink I can put into my cup at a fast-food establishment in New York City," like former Mayor Michael Bloomberg (Democrat) tried to bully everyone into doing in 2013, but thankfully the New York Court of Appeals struck down his overreaching idea. "Don't tell the wealthiest Americans that they need to pay their fair share of taxes," like President Barak Obama did, and never once said in his eight years in office what that magic number actually was. At least presidential candidate Bernie Sanders floated the number "90%." That is what the rich in America should give, 90% of their income to the government. For every dollar the rich earns Bernie thought that giving the government ninety cents of it was acceptable. Well, let me tell you, when socialist François Hollande was elected as President of France in 2012 he slapped the rich (anyone making over 1 million euro a year) with a 75% tax on their earnings. Like every socialist who ever tried it many businesses left France. Even their top actor, Gérard Depardieu, left France and went to go live in Russia; taking his money right along with him. Well, as the French economy got worse and worse, and no big surprise there, the "supertax" was dropped in December of 2014. So, France suffered for two long agonizing years, losing tons of euros in the process instead of the economy growing, until the socialists realized that such a high tax was harmful. "Thank God Bernie Sanders was not elected!" many Republicans proclaimed when he was defeated. If a 75% tax did not work for the French, how would have a 90% tax have worked out in the United States? It wouldn't have, is the short answer.

Fortunately for the French people President Hollande was replaced by President Emmanuel Macron on May 14, 2017. I was in France during the presidential elections. I even went to the voting booths with a friend of mine, and when Macron assumed power, with great pomp and circumstance, I was in Paris that day. No, I was not an invited guest to the ceremony. I wish, but I just happen to be there on a business trip, and let me tell you, the French government taxes me 19% right off the top of what I earn there, and then I get taxed again when I declare my income in the United States. Anyway, President Macron learned a valuable lesson when he was Hollande's Minister of Economy and Finance, and that was not to come out swinging against the rich when he assumed power. President Macron did not want to see a mass exodus of the rich and businesses like his predecessor had caused by levying high taxes. President Macron took a more centrist approach. Another good thing about President Emmanuel Macron is that he and President Donald Trump get along quite well.

Anyway, I'm jumping ahead of myself. We'll cover some of these topics later in your reeducation.

Now, like in any political party, you have some members who are more to the right or to the left in their own party than others, just like some of those found in the Democratic Party. There's not just "one type of Republican," as the mainstream media would have you believe, but there is quite a bit of diversity, and even outright disagreement among the Republicans. A lot of key Republican figures didn't want to see Donald Trump elected; namely: President George H. W. Bush, President George W. Bush, Jeb Bush, Lindsey Graham, John Kasich, Mitt Romney, Arnold Schwarzenegger, and the list goes on.

"Yeah, they're just a bunch of old white guys! Who cares anyway?" you say.

Well, may I remind you that Bernie Sanders was an old white guy as well when he ran for president. After Bernie "old is in."

President Donald Trump, a white guy, was not a spring chicken either when he took office. He was 70-years-old. "White" and "old" was only bad, according to the liberals, if the person was a Republican. Do you see a double standard here? There's lots of them that you Millennials and Gen Zers have that we'll discover in this camp. Every minute of the day the gap between the Democratic Party and the Republican Party is widening, because of "logic" like this.

On March 16, 2017, at 9:15 in the evening, Tony Perkins, an advisor to President Trump, and the president of the Family Research Council, said to an audience of four hundred Orange County guests, "The Republican Party has become more conservative, and the Democrats have become more liberal. They are polar opposites."

I know for a fact that Tony Perkins said this quote, because I was one of his armed bodyguards for that evening. That's right, wearing a suit, gun in a pancake holster, the pigtail wire descending from my left ear, the whole Secret Service look; minus the sunglasses because we were indoors. Well, anyway, I wrote the quote down on a piece of paper just after he said it. I always carry a pocket-sized pad of paper and a pen with me, which is a habit going all the way back to my street cop days. Did you just bristle because I said I was a former cop? Oh, don't worry. We'll touch on this subject of the "police" later, which is bound to ruffle your feathers. Anyway, Tony Perkins said a lot of interesting things at the Friends of FRC Annual Banquet in the Hilton Hotel Costa Mesa.

This is why you are here in this reeducation camp. We conservatives don't want you Millennials and Gen Zers to be polar opposites. We want you to see things our way - the right way (pun intended).

THE OTHER PARTIES

Technically there are other political parties in the United States of American: The Libertarian Party and the Green Party.

The Libertarian Party was formed on December 11, 1971. They believe in civil liberties, laissez-faire capitalism (the first part is French for *leave alone to do*, and together the phrase means no government interference), doing away with the welfare state (you don't work, you don't eat – no more EBT cards), and not getting involved in the problems of the world. This last one is pretty hard core. Well, we all saw what happens when the United States "led from behind," as President Barak Obama did for eight years, and the world fell to pieces before our eyes, and our enemies filled the power vacuum. The bottom line is that if you want to keep your goodies coming into this country (cheaper products from Asia, diamonds from South Africa, French perfume, and German luxury cars) then we must be the world's policeman and keep all the shipping lanes open. That means a strong military that the world respects.

The Libertarians are kind of in the middle politically.

The other party is the Green Party, which was founded in 2001. They promote environmentalism (the so called "tree huggers" now calling themselves "eco-socialists," because, after all, you must have the word "socialist" in there). They believe in nonviolence (China, Russia, Iran, North Korea's dream come true), social justice (who wouldn't want that), gender equality, and LGBT rights. New letters are getting tacked onto this acronym all the time. Now it's LGBTQ, "Q" meaning Queer, and I'm sure that more letters will be tacked on the end of it before you are released from this camp.

The Green Party is considered left wing. "Left wing," again, means "liberal," "progressive," "we're tolerant of everyone except the conservatives, and we'll shout them down in a heartbeat. Or, at least we used to be able to do this freely under Obama."

Neither the Libertarian nor the Green Party has managed to make it to the top. To get elected POTUS that is, *President of the United States*, but they have managed to get into the lower levels of government.

After your reeducation you won't want to join either of these two puny parties. Remember Sun Tzu? The Chinese general we talked about earlier. The goal is to eventually defeat your enemies, and you aren't going to achieve that by being a Libertarian or Green. Not in this lifetime anyway.

So, let's get into specific social, economic, and political subjects you thought you knew all about, but you really only knew the half of it. I'll give the typical Millennial's and Gen Zer's position for each subject, and then I'll follow it up with the conservative Republican position. That's what education, or reeducation in your case, is all about – learning.

CELL BLOCK 2

RELIGION

ATHEISM

What does fascism (like that of Mussolini's Italy and Hitler's Nazi Germany in the 1930s and 40s), communism, and socialism all have in common? They hate religion, and specifically Judaism and Christianity.

Karl Marx (the father of modern communism) once said, "Religion is the sigh of the oppressed creature, the heart of a heartless world, and the soul of soulless conditions. **It is the opium of the people**."

Up until recently many religious leaders and political leaders in Europe have tried to have God and Christianity mentioned in the European Constitution, as well as in the Treaty of Lisbon, but most over there across the Atlantic feel it unnecessary to put in the wording even though European culture was greatly impacted by Jesus Christ. In fact, so much so, that our numbering of years is based upon the birth of Christ. Calendar dates in English before his birth are B.C. (Before Christ), and after his birth is A.D. (Anno Domini, which is Medieval Latin for *in the year of the Lord*) used all over Europe. Yeah, I know, a lot of people are now using B.C.E (Before the Common Era) and C.E. (Common Era), which is truly a Millennial and Gen Z thing to do, because its usage started in the early 2000s. The Jews are the exception to the rule, for they had been using the abbreviation VE (Vular Era) as early as 1825, which was fine, and today's Jews are also fine with B.C.E. and C.E. But, going back to the general use, the question is, "What is the Common Era?" The "Common Era," or "Before the Common Era" is still based upon the birth of Jesus Christ. There's no getting around it. Of course, we'd have to completely change our days and calendars if we wanted to completely get away from the God of the Bible. The French tried doing that after the French Revolution. They created the French Revolution Calendar, which began with the first year of the First French Republic, and they got rid of the seven-day week because the seven-day week also has its origins in the book of Genesis (the first book in the Holy Bible). God created the heavens and the earth, and all the fullness in it in six days, and on the seventh day He rested. Many French Revolution leaders were atheists, but the new calendar, *Calendrier Républicain*, only lasted for about twelve years. Their attempt to change history failed.

Right after Donald Trump's presidential victory the American Atheist Organization had a Christmas present for everyone. They encouraged people to have a "merrier" Christmas by skipping church in 2016. The group's national program director, Nick Fish, even authorized a billboard advertising campaign in several major cities with the parody slogan MAKE CHRISTMAS GREAT AGAIN. SKIP CHURCH!

Then they had another billboard aimed at you Millennials. It showed a young African-American teenager texting a friend. The friend's text read, "U going to church this Xmas?"

The girl's response was, "Lol. No way. I don't believe that stuff anymore."

The friend asked, "What'll your parents say??"

The answer was, "They'll get over it :-P"

The headline on the billboard was "Atheist Christmas. The more, the merrier!"

To each their own. But, it's interesting that the American Atheists still have some Christmas in their Christmas. After all, they're still using the word "Christmas." And, why would they celebrate this "merrier" occasion on December 25th? Why not just avoid the day altogether?

The American Atheist Organization has something in common with North Korean's tubby tyrant Kim Jong Un. During that very same Christmas he had the country pay homage to the "Sacred Mother of the Revolution," his grandmother, instead of Jesus Christ. After all, it was he who had banned Christmas in the hermit kingdom. Having a Bible in North Korea, that contains the story of the birth of Jesus Christ, is a mandatory 15-year prison sentence.

Talk about the Grinch who stole Christmas.

Taking Jesus Christ out of "Christmas" (two words together meaning the *Anointed One* coming from the Hebrew word *Mashiach*, and the assembling together in reverence) is like taking the United States of America out of the 4th of July.

Let me ask you a question, and be perfectly honest with me. Do you believe in the tooth fairy? How about the Easter Bunny? How about Santa Claus who rides about in a reindeer drawn sled in the wee hours of the night on December 24th leaving presents for good boys and girls in their homes? Of course not. At some point in your life you came to the realization that these characters were not real. Now that you are both mature and a grown up how much time do you spend a year telling others that these characters are not real? Do you go around telling children, "Trust me, the tooth fairy does not exist. It's really your parents who replace your tooth under your pillow with some money."

Come Christmas time how much of your own funds do you spend campaigning (printing posters, buying air time on radio stations, or purchasing Google ads) to disprove Santa Claus? I would guess that you don't waste your time on it. Why? It's because everybody eventually stops believing in these fictitious characters. Well, technically Santa Claus is based upon the 4th-century Christian Saint Nicholas of Myra (270 – 343 AD), but the Santa Claus we know today, the fat one in a red suit and white beard, is not the one and the same of yesteryear.

So why then do many atheists spend so much of their time, money, and effort trying to convince others that God is not real? These same people don't put the same amount of energy into the tooth fairy, the Easter Bunny, or Santa Claus. Well, if you have never really thought about it before, consider this. Most people who believe in God when they were young continue to believe in God as an adult. Inherently they believe there is a God. In fact, taking it one step further, tens of thousands of adults around the world, who may never have given much thought to God in their youth, come to believe in God every year. According to the Guinness World Records the Bible is the best-selling book of all time with over 5 billion copies sold and distributed. For a character, God that is, who supposedly does not exist, there are certainly a lot of people who want to know about Him.

The reason why many atheists devote a portion of their lives in trying to persuade people to turn away from their belief in God is because they know that this belief determines people's worldview, and worldview is everything. If they can convince people that God is not real, then one does not have to be accountable to Him. One is then left to determine for themselves what is right and what is wrong. If there is no God, especially the God of the Bible acknowledged by 2,000 plus years of Western culture, then one does not have to worry about sins, Judgment Day, Heaven or Hell, and all that good stuff. One can be free of all that baggage.

What atheists never point out is the human compulsion to worship. This is why every culture on earth throughout history has always believed in gods. It is inherent in human beings. Believing in just one God was purely a Jewish thing in man's history, and Christianity is a continuation of that belief. Then 610 years after Jesus Christ the Muslims followed suit, because before that the Arabian Peninsula was polytheistic (the belief in many gods).

In modern times, some cultures indeed tried very hard to do away with God by replacing it with scientific political atheism. The communist Soviet Union was the first state in human history to officially eliminate religion. This came in the form of confiscating church property, persecuting those who believed in God (be it Jews, Christians, or Muslims) to include reeducation camps and execution, and propagating atheism in the education system. Despite ruling with an iron fist for 69 years the reds never succeeded in completely stamping out religion within their borders, and when the Soviet Union collapsed in 1991 there was a religious revival afterwards. Surprise! Surprise! According to a 2012 survey by Sreda Arena 46.6% of the population of Russia identified themselves as Christians, with almost 60 million members in the Russian Orthodox Church.

In 1949 Mao Zedong established The People's Republic of China, and like the Soviets he implemented state atheism; basically, replacing all religious belief with Marxist-Leninist ideology. Seven decades later Mainland China is still communist, but despite the years of persecution religion thrives there today.

Two years after the death of Mao Zedong the Chinese government guaranteed "freedom of religion" in 1978. Apparently, they thought their old leader's way was a bit too extreme. As a result, many people went back to the country's historical roots of Confucianism, Buddhism, Taoism, and even Christianity that traces its history all the way back to the 7th century during the Tang dynasty. There had always been an underground church in China, but with the ban on religion lifted by the government Christian converts grew at a phenomenal rate. It is estimated that 181 million Chinese came to believe in the God of the Bible. Yet, so alarmed by this rapid growth that in 2014 the Chinese government tried to turn the rising tide by forcing Christian churches to remove crosses from their church steeples, closed churches that did not "meet building codes standards," and even tore down some churches altogether. Needless to say, this caught the attention of the world, and it became a PR nightmare for the Chinese government. Therefore, in 2016 General Secretary Xi Jinping promised to "fully implement the Party's policy of religious freedom," but, and there's the big word BUT, "we must resolutely guard against overseas infiltrations via religious means and prevent ideological infringement by extremists."

Define "extremists."

So, what's my point? My point is that atheists may succeed in turning away many from believing in God, but there will always be more people than not who will believe in gods or God, and many more who come to the same conclusion every year.

Is not atheism a belief system? It's a belief that there is no God.

Most conservatives believe that there is a God, and a good majority of them hold to the Judeo-Christian God of the Bible. Jews believe in the God (although they write it like this – *G-d*) of the Old Testament of the Bible (referred to as the Tanakh) while the Christians believe that Jesus Christ (Greek for Yeshua the

Messiah) is the same God of both the Old and New Testament. The Muslims have it wrong thinking that the Christians worship three different Gods, because of the description the "Father, the Son, and the Holy Spirit." There's a word for it, although this word does not appear in the Bible, and that is the "trinity." What this means is that they're actually three persons in one. What? Did that just blow your mind? Okay, let me explain it this way. A man can be a father to his children. He can also be a husband to his wife, and he can also be a son to his own parents. Different people see him different ways, and he relates to different people differently, but he is still just one person. It's a "trinity" so to speak. That's the best way to explain the Trinity of God. He's three in one, but He is certainly not three separate beings.

Believing in a creator, who is sovereign over the entire universe, makes one accountable to Him, whereas atheists determine what is right and wrong in their own eyes. It's all relative to them based upon the culture and the times they live in. This is called "relativism," and as such there are no absolutes. Let's just pray that none of our future presidents ever come to believe in relativism, like some dictators in history have: Hitler, Stalin, Pol Pot, Idi Amin, just to name a few. After all, who says murder is wrong? For those men that I mentioned murder was "relative." Survival of the fittest, and all that Darwinian happy horse shit.

Many on the left in America have great contempt for their fellow citizens who believe in God, especially the conservative evangelicals. President Barak Hussein Obama started his attacks against believers early on in his run for president in 2008 when he said this about working-class voters decimated by job losses, "They get bitter, they cling to guns or religion or antipathy to people who aren't like them or anti-immigrant sentiment or anti-trade sentiment as a way to explain their frustrations."

For some reason, the President linked guns and God together, as if they were mutually exclusive. The statement was to be taken as a negative. I certainly took it as a negative when I heard it.

If you wish to understand most conservatives you need to understand the Bible, or at least understand people's respect for the Bible. After all, Western culture for the past one thousand six hundred plus years (starting at 300 A.D.) was greatly influenced by the Bible: from our laws right down to how we treat women. That's right! You read it correctly. It was the Bible that first declared, "There is neither Jew nor Gentile, neither slave nor free, nor is there male and female, for you are all one in Christ Jesus." It meant that men and women are equal in the eyes of God. That was a pretty radical statement back then, and it still is today in many non-Christian countries. Wherever Christianity took root in a country there is greater freedom for women today. If you don't believe me try taking your next vacation in Saudi Arabia, and letting a woman drive the rental car around the city. Or, stroll through the streets of Tehran with the women of your group as they wear sleeveless shirts and let their hair down. That is to say, not wearing a veil to cover their heads. Oh, and see what happens if they wear a wee bit too much make-up in public. You'll find out real fast how non-Christian rooted societies treat women. One of my Persian female friends, Shireen, was painting anti-United States protest signs back in the days of Ruhollah Khomeini. This was after the U.S. Embassy had been seized, and the American hostages taken. That's right, she was one of many young women who painted the DEATH TO AMERICA! signs for the Iranian demonstrators marching in front of the former U.S. Embassy in Tehran that lasted for years. Well, one day she and a girlfriend were painting away, and Shireen laughed at something funny. A man walked up to her and slapped her across the face and warned her, "Women don't laugh in public." It was at that moment, with tears streaming down her face, that Shireen thought, *I am going to get out of this country!* And, she did. She eventually escaped over the Turkish border, and made her way to the *land of the free and the home of the brave.*

In that same Bible verse that I quoted to you about people being equal, Galatians 3:28, it is quite clear that slaveholders and slaves are also equal in God's eyes.

Slavery has existed for man's entire history, and in almost every culture at one time or another. It was not just confined to "the whites who enslaved the blacks" in the pre-Civil War United States as most Millennials have been taught.

I hate to burst your bubble, but slavery still exists today. Although technically the last country to outlaw institutionalized slavery was Mauritania (a Muslim country) in 2007, slavery was the norm for Islamic State (aka ISIS) until they got their ass kicked in 2017 when Donald Trump took office, and it was in the ugly form of human trafficking (the new politically correct term for slavery). There are an estimated 28.4 million slaves in the world today, which includes children. Yet, in America we still hear more about the black slaves of over a hundred years ago in our history than what is happening in the here and now. Why is that?

Oh, and speaking of slavery in America, you should know that less than 5% of the pre-Civil War population owned slaves, and even a large number of "free blacks" owned black slaves in America. You never hear that from the left, do you?

Wherever Christianity flourished slavery was eventually abolished. President Abraham Lincoln, a Republican, and a God-fearing man towards the latter part of his life, said concerning slavery, "Those who deny freedom to others, deserve it not for themselves; and, under a just God, can not long retain it."

Would he have freed the slaves if he did not believe in a "just God?"

Of course, 365,000 Union soldiers died, and 282,000 were wounded, carrying out Abraham Lincoln's strongly held beliefs, and their own. The freedom of the black Americans, called "Negros" in those days, from slavery was paid for with the precious blood of many. Therefore, no slavery reparations ($$$) to the descendants of former American slaves are required. The price has been paid in full. There will be no check coming in the mail for those of color.

Here's your homework. Google the words "Battle Hymn of the Republic," and check it out on Wikipedia. Listen to the audio. During the American Civil War this was a frequently used patriotic song. It's part of your heritage.

What you believe in is always going to be displayed in your life.

OUR FOUNDING FATHERS

Right around the time of the primaries in 2016 I was checking my Facebook to see how my relatives, spread all over the country, were doing. I was shocked that my nephew Seth, a Millennial, stated emphatically that our nation was not founded upon Judeo-Christian principles, and that our founding fathers were not Bible believing Christians. I love my nephew, and so I had to set things straight.

"Whoa! Hold on there buckaroo!" I wrote. "You obliviously don't know your American history."

Do you believe the same thing? If you do, have you ever visited our capital? Washington, D.C.? Have you gazed upon The Declaration of Independence? It's the nation's birth certificate. The very first paragraph mention's God's hand in our goal to separate from the British Empire:

*When in the Course of human events it becomes necessary for one people to dissolve the political bands which have connected them with another and to assume among the powers of earth, the separate and equal station to which the **Laws of Nature and of Nature's God** entitled them, a decent respect to the opinions of mankind requires that they should declare the causes which impel them to the separation.*

In other words, there are "Laws of Nature," and God made nature. Then God is mentioned in the second paragraph, and when I was in grade school most children could recite this paragraph from memory:

*We hold these truths to be self-evident, that **all men are created equal, that*** *they are endowed by their Creator with certain unalienable Rights, that among these are Life, Liberty and the pursuit of Happiness.*

According to our founding fathers we were "created," and we did not evolve from monkeys. Even more astonishing is that "all men (this includes you women as well, because it refers to "mankind" and not just sexist "men" as the left would have you believe) were "created equal." Yes, there was slavery at the time of its writing, but the intent of this "revolutionary" document (literally) was to provide the political mechanism necessary that would one day do away with slavery. Read *African Slavery in America* written by founding father Thomas Paine in 1775.

Then the rest of The Declaration of Independence lists our complaints against the government, and that "we" are willing to separate either peacefully or through war. The last sentence reads – *And for the support of this Declaration,* **with a firm reliance on the protection of Divine Providence,** *we mutually pledge to each other our Lives, our Fortunes, and our sacred Honor.* "Divine Providence" is 18th century-speak for "God." And, yes, it was the God of the Bible. Then it was signed by fifty-six of our founding fathers. Had we not won the war all of these men would have been executed for treason. Two of the signers would go on to become American presidents.

Back to our tour of Washington, D.C., and now we are standing before of the U.S. Supreme Court building. At the top of the building there are carved relief figures of the world's lawgivers. The one in the middle, in the most prominent position, is Moses from the book of Genesis holding the Ten Commandments. Upon entering the Supreme Court courtroom the two oak doors have the Ten Commandments engraved upon them. Inside the courtroom, on the wall above where the Supreme Court judges sit, are more carved reliefs of the Ten Commandments. Do you think our ancestors were trying to say something to us? Well, the very first Supreme Court Justice certainly did, and quite clearly. Judge John Jay said, "Americans should select and prefer Christians as their rulers." Wow! If he would have said that today half the country would be screaming, "Separation of church and state!"

Have you ever stood inside the Jefferson Memorial? He's one of the signers of the Declaration of Independence, and was the third President of the United States. He's the one who wrote the phrase "separation of church and state" in a letter to the Danbury Baptists on January 1, 1802, but it has been taken totally out of context to justify the progressive twisting of the phrase to now mean the SEPARATION FROM GOD BY THE STATE. Hello! Jefferson was taking the position that America should not have a "church of America" run by the government like there was a "church of England." The government was not to run the church. The First Amendment adopted in 1791 reads, "Congress shall make no law respecting an establishment of religion or prohibiting the free exercise thereof;" The restriction is made on Congress, and it is specifically about law. Nowhere does it say religion should be eliminated from the public square. Well, moving on with the tour…

On Panel One of the Jefferson Memorial is the second paragraph of the Declaration of Independence, which as you know, mentions God. Panel Two starts off with "Almighty God hath created the mind free," while Panel Three begins with "God who gave us life gave us liberty."

Go inside the Lincoln Memorial and on the South Chamber is the quote, "This nation must be one in which all were '…created equal' was the rule of law and practice."

The Washington Monument in front of the White House, Donald Trump's home, has an aluminum apex with the inscription on the East face that reads "Laus Deo," which is Latin for "Praise be to God." Don't even think of defacing it, because it is way too high to reach.

Inside the U.S. Capitol Building one can't help but notice the huge historical paintings in the Rotunda. The first painting is *The Landing of Columbus* who gave God the credit of his discovery of America. The second painting is *The Embarkation of the Pilgrims* showing them observing a day of prayer and fasting led by William Brewster. The third painting is *The Discovery of the Mississippi* by DeSoto. Next to DeSoto is a monk who is praying to God as a crucifix is placed in the ground. The fourth painting is the *Baptism of Pocahontas*.

Before I met with President George W. Bush on January 12, 2009 in the Oval Office of the White House, my wife and I went over to the U.S. Capitol Building the day before. I took photos of each of the paintings in the Rotunda that I just described to you. I saw them with my own eyes. The influence of the Bible on our government is undeniable. I don't know why my nephew said what he said. Wishful thinking, I suppose.

In the Cox Corridor of the U.S. Capitol is a line from the song America the Beautiful carved into the wall that reads, "America! God shed His grace on thee, and crown thy good with brotherhood, from sea to shining sea!"

Who?

God. The one, and the same, of the Bible.

Stand on the sacred ground of Arlington National Cemetery on the other side of the Potomac River where our brave soldiers, sailors, and airmen are buried, and you can't help but to gaze upon a sea of white headstones with mostly the Christian cross carved into them, with the Star of David peppered here and there, all beautifully lined up. Yet, since we are a country that has freedom of religion you'll also find on a few headstones with no religious symbols for the atheists, the Islamic crescent moon and star for the Muslims, the Wicca pentagram star for modern pagans, and some others displayed. Yet, they are the minority.

Those were just a few examples I gave you that our American history was founded upon the belief in the Holy Bible. If you still don't believe me then pull out a coin or American dollar bill from your pocket and read the national motto: IN GOD WE TRUST. It just didn't get there by accident.

"But wait Master Sergeant Wagner!" you interject, "We didn't start inscribing our coins with IN GOD WE TRUST until 1938. So, it's a relatively new thing."

I knew you were going to say that. All non-God-fearing Millennials do in protest. Well, for your information, and you can check this out yourself online with the U.S. Treasury Department, Reverend M.R. Watkinson, Minister of the Gospel from Ridleyville, Pennsylvania wrote a letter dated November 13, 1861 to Secretary of Treasury Salmon P. Chase urging him that the United States recognize the Deity (a 19th century term for the God of the Bible) by inscribing the words GOD, LIBERTY, LAW on our coins least future generations "reason from our past that we were a heathen (non-believing) nation."

Secretary Chase responded to the Reverend's letter, "No nation can be strong except in the strength of God, or safe except in His defense. The trust of our people in God should be declared on our national coins." Then on January 18, 1837 Secretary Chase wrote a letter to the Mint Director suggesting that the motto "be changed so as to read: IN GOD WE TRUST. Congress passed the Act of April 22, 1864, and those hallowed words first appeared on the 1864 two-cent coin.

The 84th Congress passed a law, which was signed by President Dwight D. Eisenhower on July 30, 1956 declaring IN GOD WE TRUST as the national motto, and the following year this motto appeared on our paper money for the first time.

But, if you want to go back further than the American Civil War, look no further than 1814 during the bombardment of Fort McHenry by the British. Francis Scott Key was so inspired by the American flag still flying over the fort in the morning, with American soldiers refusing to abandon their post, that he wrote The Star Spangled Banner, which became our National Anthem. In the fourth stanza he wrote, "And this be our motto: 'In God is our trust.' And the star-spangled banner in triumph shall wave O'er the land of the free and the home of the brave."

It was during the War of 1812, which was fought from June 18, 1812 to February 18, 1815, where we truly became free of British oppression. Don't forget, this was a time when British troops marched into Washington, D.C. and burned the White House to the ground. Americans knew that it was only by the hand of God that we once again came out victorious against the most powerful empire on Earth at the time.

Now, do a little math. We first gained our independence on September 3, 1783 after shedding blood in the American Revolutionary War for 8 years. Then only 29 years later we were fighting for our national life again. So, as you can see, our federal government, run by *We the People*, the majority of them anyway, have believed in God from the very beginning of American history.

It is not a generic god that early Americans had in mind, or some powerful cosmic entity, but the God of the Bible: the YHVH, the Alpha and Omega, The Lion of Judah, the Bread of Life, the Light of the World, the King of Kings, the Good Sheppard, and the other 900 names and titles He has inscribed in the scriptures.

SEPARATION OF CHURCH AND STATE

Nowhere do progressives want religion more out of public life than out of the public schools. Any mention of God receives the instant protest, "separation of church and state!" Unfortunately, most Millennials don't know their American history, and most Baby Boomers for that matter.

When I was a child I remember this verse my sister and I recited before going to bed each night:

Now I lay me down to take my sleep,
I pray thee, Lord, my soul to keep;
If I should die before I wake,
I pray the Lord my soul to take.

"What does this have to do with public schools?" you are asking. Well, it comes from a book called The New England Primer, which was the first reading primer of the American colonies. In other words, it was our nation's first educational textbook. It was the first book a child was given, that and the Bible, to learn how to read. It was first introduced in 1690 by Benjamin Harris, and it remained virtually unchanged up until it fell out of use after the 1930 edition. Our founding fathers would have all read The New England Primer. In his log cabin in Illinois Abraham Lincoln would have learned to read from it.

The New England Primer is how children first learned their ABC's. There were little woodcut illustrations, the letter to be learned, and then two lines of text to the right of each illustration. From my copy of the 1777 edition, a year after the Declaration of Independence was signed, the very first illustration in the book for teaching the alphabet is that of Adam and Eve, the first man and woman created by God. They're standing next to the tree of the knowledge of good and evil with Eve handing the apple to Adam that God warned not to eat of. To learn the letter "A" the text reads:

In Adam's fall
We sinned all.

To learn the letter "B" American students saw an illustration of the Holy Bible with the text to the right:

Heaven to find,
The Bible mind.

To learn the letter "C" it was:

Christ crucified,
For sinners died.

Letter "D" was:

The deluge drowned,
The Earth around.

In today's jargon the meaning of the letter "A" would mean, *because of Adam's disobedience, we are all born with a sin nature.* The letter "B" taught kids that if they wished to enter into Heaven they needed to believe in the scriptures. Letter "C," which shows a cross in the illustration, means that Jesus Christ is the only way to salvation. Letter "D," of course, was the great flood in the days of Noah that covered the entire Earth. Unbelievable! That advice would send most public school teachers and administrators through the roof. Yet, that is part of our heritage. Not just pre-colonies, or during the Revolution, but this book was America's educational textbook for 240 years of our history. And, if you think the alphabet was the only mention of God, think again. No, it isn't. In fact, go to Amazon and order your own copy of The New England Primer and read it. Every child and school teacher in America should read it. After all, isn't it American history? Shouldn't those in the educational field today know their own history? Then you'll see how many people have lied to us that this country was not founded upon Judeo-Christian principles. You will soon discover that many black robed federal judges have lied to us stating that prayer in school is "unconstitutional," for The New England Primer is filled with prayers. If students and teachers read this book like our ancestors did they would also get the warning written in this book, *Oh! don't reject my precious call, lest suddenly in hell thou fall!*

Now, this next part is also going to blow your socks off. Have you ever heard of "The Bible of the Revolution?" Okay then, let me explain it to you. Prior to the Revolutionary War all English Bibles in the colonies came from England. That's where they were all printed. However, after we gained our independence the British placed an embargo on any Bibles exported to America. Therefore, Congress approved the first English-language Bible to be printed in America, back in 1782, known as the "Aitken's Bible" printed by Robert Aitken. In his own words, it was to be "a neat Edition of the Holy Scriptures for the use of schools."

Bibles in schools! The ACLU would be all over this filing law suits, "This is unconstitutional!" even though it was Congress that first reviewed the Aitken's Bible for accuracy, and then upon completion recommended it for the inhabitants of the United States.

It's also pretty hard to say that the Bible, or the very God mentioned in the Bible, is "unconstitutional" since the very first prayer of the Continental Congress, given by Reverend Jacob Duché, stated that our country's destiny was in the hands of none other than "O Lord our Heavenly Father." This humble prayer ends with:

All this we ask in the name and through the merits of Jesus Christ, Thy Son and our Savior."

That's your next homework assignment. Look up this prayer given on September 7, 1774. Oh, and if you want to see some really good movies on this subject, may I suggest God's Not Dead, God's Not Dead 2, God's Not Dead 3 and The Case For Chirst produced by PURE FLIX. These films are all about liberals' twisted interpretation of Thomas Jefferson's phrase "separation of church and state," and how it is tearing the fabric of our society. The story lines are good, the acting is good (Hollywood quality in fact), and at least you'll know the arguments on both sides. Yes, in this reeducation camp you are allowed to watch movies. Conservatives enjoy entertainment just as much as everyone else. So, get a bowl of popcorn and enjoy!

Not only did children have The New England Primer and the Bible as their required textbooks, but also the Ten Commandments were prominently displayed on campuses throughout the land. I remember seeing them in the main hallway of my elementary school as I passed by them each day. That was in the late 1960s and early 1970s. I'm sure they have been long removed since then.

So, what are these Ten Commandments that so many people seem to be so upset about? Why would Americans, for more than two hundred years embracing these commandments, suddenly want to throw them out of the public squares and out of the schools? Let's go through them one by one. You can find them in Exodus, that's in the Old Testament of the Bible, at the beginning of chapter 20.

1. You shall have no other gods before Me.

2. You shall not make for yourself an image in the form of anything in heaven above or on the earth beneath or in the waters below. You shall not bow down to them or worship them; for I, the Lord your God, am a jealous God, punishing the children for the sin of their parents to the third and fourth generation of those who hate me, but showing love to a thousand generations of those who love me and keep my commandments.

3. You shall not misuse the name of the Lord your God, for the Lord will not hold anyone guiltless who misuses his name.

4. Remember the Sabbath day by keeping it holy. Six days you shall labor and do all your work, but the seventh day is a Sabbath to the Lord your God. On it you shall not do any work, neither you, nor your son or daughter, nor your male or female servant, nor your animals, nor any foreigner residing in your towns. For in six days the Lord made the heavens and the earth, the sea, and all that is in them, but He rested on the seventh day. Therefore, the Lord blessed the Sabbath day and made it holy.

5. Honor your father and your mother, so that you may live long in the land the Lord your God is giving you.

6. You shall not murder.

7. You shall not commit adultery.

8. You shall not steal.

9. You shall not give false testimony against your neighbor.

10. You shall not covet your neighbor's house. You shall not covet your neighbor's wife, or his male or female servant, his ox or donkey, or anything that belongs to your neighbor.

Remember, Congress approved the Bible as a school textbook, and these Ten Commandments were printed within those pages in black and white. Therefore, most colonists, and then later on most early American citizens, agreed with these commandments, and the First Commandment being, *You shall have no other gods before Me*. It was just collectively accepted that the God of the Bible was the God of America. The colonists did not just suddenly appear in a vacuum ignorant of the world around them. They knew all about Islam, Buddhism, Hinduism, and tribal religions in Asia and Africa. They were very much aware that many Indian tribes among them were pagans.

"Were there unbelievers in the beginning of our history?" you may be asking yourself. Of course, there were. They had criminals and pirates, but most of the founding fathers, and the women that supported them, were undeniably God-fearing believers. Now, don't get all bent out of shape because of the term "God-fearing," and yes, I purposely capitalized the letter "G" to indicate the God of the Bible just as it is found in America's first English dictionary, the American Dictionary of The English Language by Noah Webster 1828. This is a healthy type of fear. It's a deep respect, balanced with love. *After all, He is the God in whose hand is your breath. Daniel 5:33* So, yeah, I'd say that someone who has control over every breath that you take is someone that should be reverently feared.

Now, I can understand why many of today's schoolteachers and administrators loath the Ten Commandments, especially the First Commandment. They don't want God ruling over them, and they certainly don't want to be accountable to Him. *Give us Barabbas!* We conservatives understand this. We get it. That's what freedom of religion, or freedom from religion, is all about. But, with that said, I wish that many of today's schoolteachers and administrators would simply be honest with themselves, and the public, and simply say, "Yes, our founding fathers built this nation upon Judeo-Christian beliefs, but today we do not want the God of the Bible in our lives. He will not rule over us any longer!" Wouldn't that be so much more honest then hiding under the blanket statement of "separation of church and state?" The liberals always quote those five words, but they never give the definition of these words in the context in which they were written.

The interesting thing is that you cannot break the other nine commandments without first breaking the First Commandment. You shall have no other gods before Me, and thus if you put God first in your life you would not want to go against Him by breaking the rules that He has established, and sin is exactly that – violating His laws. When a man asked Jesus, "Teacher, which is the greatest commandment in the Law?" Jesus replied, "Love the Lord your God with all your heart and with all your soul, and with all your mind," as recorded in Matthew 22:36-37. This is known as the Shema, which is Hebrew for "hear." It comes from the book of Deuteronomy 6:4-9, which is three books past the book of Exodus. It is the central prayer in the Jewish prayer book, the Siddur, *order*, and it is the very first scripture that a Jewish child learns. The Shema is also written down and placed inside of a mezuzah, a tube-like object, which you may have seen fixed to the doorpost of a Jewish home, business, or a gate. Okay, I realize that I'm starting to get way too theological for you here. I don't want to lose you, so let's keep counting the commandments.

The Second Commandment, *You shall not make for yourself an image*, makes perfect sense. In other words, you should not put anything else in your life first but God. Anything else in His place will lead to emptiness. Yet, people do it all the time. When God is not first in their lives people try to fill this spiritual emptiness with money, power, sex, idolizing other people, sports, education, you name it. This commandment was designed to set people's priorities straight. Of course, if the God of the Bible is not your God, then by all means, "if it feels good, do it." You must fill that void with something.

The Third Commandment, *You shall not misuse the name of the Lord your God, for the Lord will not hold anyone guiltless who misuses his name*, is probably the most misunderstood commandment out of the ten. Many people think it means not to make flippant statements like, "God d- - n it!" or "Jesus Christ!" which you shouldn't do, but the real intent of the original Hebrew is not to do evil in the name of God. In other words, do not misrepresent Him. The book *The Ten Commandments: Still the Best Moral Code* by Dennis Prager clarified this commandment for me. If you want a fascinating read, and you want to really blow your mind, then make this book your next extracurricular reading assignment. Hardly any of your peers would ever touch this book, so you'll have something new and unique to discuss with them.

Now if you were to read the passage in the original Hebrew it reads, and I'll use the English words to avoid confusion, "Name of YHVH, God of you, for the misuse, for not He will hold guiltless, YHVH, who he takes name of Him, for the misuse."

YHVH is the actual name of God, although nobody knows how to pronounce it, because the vowels were never put into it, and the Jews never spoke this word. Yet, in the passage the name of God is used twice. In technical terms, these four consonants are called the tetragrammaton. Okay, I can see that we are getting too deep again for you. So, let's get to the point shall we.

Crusaders murdering innocent people, and using the name of God to do it was misusing the name of God. On the other hand, Crusaders fighting enemy forces may have been justified; slaughtering noncombatants wasn't. The Europeans were facing their own form of ISIS in those days. You can't throw out the baby with the bath water when it comes to history. Skip forward a few hundred years and priests of the Spanish Inquisition torturing other people just because they disagreed with the Catholic church's version of Christianity was misusing the name of God. Catholics and Protestants killing each other for hundreds of years isn't exactly what Jesus had in mind when he said, "Love your enemies." When Hitler marched on Europe, and he had his soldiers murder millions of people, it would have been better if the words, GOTT MIT UNS, *God With Us*, had been removed from the belt buckles of the German soldiers before they did their evil deeds. And, I'm pretty sure when men and women strap on bombs to their bodies and detonate them in the middle of a bus, train, or crowded shopping mall, and saying that God is behind it, it's most likely not something God would condone. Yes, the God of the Bible advocated violence in certain circumstances in both the Old and New Testament, and He Himself took the lives of some people who disobeyed Him, both in the Old and New Testament, but the reasons are very specific, and they must be viewed in their context. So, if people are going to do evil acts, then don't drag God into it. No wonder so many people today hate God…

The Fourth Commandment seems like a pretty good deal to me. The God of the Bible wanted His people to rest one day out of the week. The reason He had to tell his people to "chill out and relax," including employees, foreigners, and animals, is because most people won't. History has proven that most ancient cultures pushed themselves seven days a week. In the Roman Empire there was no such thing as a day off during the week. You just worked until you dropped. Even today many people voluntarily work themselves seven days a week to "get ahead" in life, but they are burning themselves out doing it.

The Fifth Commandment, *Honor your father and your mother, so that you may live long in the land the Lord your God is giving you*, sounds like the natural thing to do. Yes, there are a lot of jerk wad parents out there, but most of them are loving and caring of their children. Of course, "honor" means to have a high respect for someone. Those who have a high respect for their parents usually have a high respect for other authorities above them: the police, the local government, the state government, the federal government, and yes, in many cases, even God.

The "nuclear family," as they used to call it dating back to 1947, was the foundation of human society. It was married heterosexual parents raising their children. It worked for our almost 6,000 years of human history. But, today, OMG! if you believe in the nuclear family they, the liberals, want to nuke you.

The extreme left has never liked parents having control over their own children. The whole purpose of the Hitler Youth (Hitlerjugend) before World War II was used not only to make the youth more dependent upon the Nazi government than their own parents, but it was also used to draw children away from the churches. This is historical fact. I know, because I've studied it in Germany. I've visited many museums in the "Vaterland," and they are shamefully honest about this dark part of their history. I've got photos of their propaganda, artifacts, and photos of photos.

Now, turning our attention back to the extreme left. When my wife was a little girl in the former Soviet Union she went to a boarding school where the government made it very clear that children's loyalties were to be stronger to the state than to their own parents. Communism was their god. Karl Marx, the father of communism, wrote in The Communist Manifesto, which we will study in more detail a little bit later in your stay here, that both religion and the traditional family had to be abolished. Coming up to more recent times, Hillary Clinton's book *It Takes a Village* insists that society should meet all the needs of a child rather than the parents, just like Karl Marx advocated. I wonder if she still thought that when President Donald Trump took office? Did she want the Republican village raising this new generation? Probably not. It takes a village only if society is progressive.

On the Black Lives Matter website, under the navigation button BLACK VILLAGES, it states, or at least it did at the time of the writing of this book, "We are committed to disrupting the Western-prescribed nuclear family structure requirement by supporting each other as extended families and 'villages' that collectively care for one another, and especially 'our' children to the degree that mothers, parents and children are comfortable."

Does this all sound familiar? "Disrupting the Western-prescribed nuclear family" and "villages." Well, I don't know about you, but one village that is not working out so well is the City of Chicago. In 2016 there were 762 murders there. That's more than a 50% increase than the year before. Oh, and I didn't even mention that there were 4,368 shooting victims in all. Most of these shootings were black on black. Let's compare that to the U.S. fatalities in war-torn Afghanistan the same year. In 2016 we lost 15 military personnel over there. So, it was statistically safer being a combat soldier in the dusty villages of Afghanistan than in the streets of Chicago. Even two years of our military personnel being "advisors" over in Iraq and Syria to fight ISIS had brought about 27 servicemen killed, and 16 wounded that same year. And, I haven't even given you the black on black statistics in New Orleans, Philadelphia, Washington, D.C., Detroit, et cetera. The big war is here in our own country, and it is due in large part to the breakdown of the "nuclear family." Yet, where is the outcry from the left about those black lives lost? You didn't hear much about it, because in 2016 these cities were run by the Democrats: Mayor Mitch Landrieu of New Orleans, Mayor Jim Kenney of Philadelphia, Mayor Muriel Bowser of Washington, D.C., and Mike Duggan of Detroit. In police work we'd call this "a pattern."

Black Lives Matter may desire for African-Americans to disrupt the "Western-prescribed nuclear family," but I have news for them, the same family structure exists in Asia, the Middle East, Africa, and the rest of the planet. The nuclear family is not just a Western tradition. You're smart. You can already guess what kind of society Black Lives Matter wants.

Most people generally accept the Sixth Commandment, and that is *You shall not murder*. You'd be pretty upset if someone murdered you or someone you love, wouldn't you? However, who says it is wrong to murder? You?

Here we go, back to Adolf Hitler. Why not? The left uses him as an example all the time in vilifying Republicans. Some on the left even compare President Trump to Hitler. Pfffft! Anyway, Hitler thought it was fine to bomb and invade innocent countries, plus try to exterminate the Jews. The Russian leader Joseph Stalin is reported to have had anywhere from 34 to 49 million of his own countrymen murdered. My wife's uncle was one of those casualties. Former Los Angeles police officer and Reserve naval officer Christopher Dorner thought he was justified in murdering 4 people and injuring 3 others during his rampage in the month of February 2013. Because he had been fired from the LAPD he wanted to kill as many cops as possible, and even family members of cops. I remember this incident because I was directly involved in the manhunt for him when I was a soldier with the California Military Department stationed at Joint Forces Training Base. Unbeknownst to us, Dorner had stayed on our base for two weeks writing his hate-filled manifesto just before the shootings. Some of my men had seen him come through the gate a few times before the rampage. After all, he had the proper identification. I may have seen him a time or two while supervising the front gate, but I don't recall. It was the biggest manhunt in Californian history. Some people just don't see murder as a sin. Fortunately, our history is based upon European culture, and European culture was based upon the Bible, and the Sixth Commandment, God's law, states that murder is wrong. It just so happens that the conscience of many non-believes also lines up the same way. After all, the Bible states that we were made "in His image," and so it stands to reason that we have an inherent knowledge of good and evil, but the line can be crossed by free will.

And, no, you cannot "murder" an animal. Eating animals is "killing," and not murder. Self-defense is also not murder. Fighting other soldiers in a war is not murder. The Bible makes the case for killing under certain circumstances. I guess you'll just have to read the Bible so you'll have everything in the right context. Remember, "get the facts." You should read the Bible anyway, even if you don't believe it, to at least have more intelligent arguments, and to understand Western history, and your culture better.

You shall not commit adultery, is the Seventh Commandment. Nothing gets people into more trouble than sleeping with someone else's spouse. Even liberals know this. So, why isn't this commandment allowed to be posted anymore in most courthouses? If people followed it there would be a lot less cheating and less ugly divorce cases.

The Eight Commandment is *You shall not steal*. Any company in America tells you this policy if you want to work for them. It also really sucks when someone steals something of yours. I had that sinking feeling one morning when I found that someone had broken into my truck and took a bunch of my stuff, not to mentioning screwing up my door lock that I had to fix. So, if you don't like people stealing your stuff, then what is so wrong with this commandment? Why wouldn't we want children to embrace this concept in schools? If everyone followed it, we'd have less theft.

Commandment Nine is *You shall not give false testimony against your neighbor*. This doesn't mean just in a court of law, "Do you swear to tell the truth, and the whole truth," it also means not gossiping about someone or trying to destroy their reputation or character. Just imagine if gossip was eliminated completely from our society. Well, God could imagine it, and He told us that we shouldn't do it. Which brings me to a joke.

During a luncheon, there were three church pastors who decided to confess their weaknesses to one another. The first pastor said, "I told a little white lie to my wife the other day. I told her that I was going to visit a sick person in the hospital, but I really went to go play golf." The second pastor said, "I am physically attracted to a lady in my congregation, and it is all I can do to avoid lusting after her." Then the third pastor said, "I have a real problem with gossiping, and I can't wait to get out of here."

The final commandment, the Tenth Commandment, states *You shall not covet...* and goes on to give a laundry list. The word "covet" doesn't just mean wanting something, but having a great desire to have something that belongs to another person. If you act upon your covetousness you could very well violate one or more of the other commandments. Jesus made a profound statement when He said, "You desire but do not have, so you kill. You covet but you cannot get what you want, so you quarrel and fight. You do not have because you do not ask God."

Again, imagine if everyone did not covet other people's things. They just went out and got their own. How many wars have been waged over territory? How many people have been robbed or killed over gold, money, and possessions? How many bosses have been sabotaged because someone under them wanted their job? Wow! The Ten Commandments makes perfect sense. Yet, why are they so offensive to so many people in our society? Do you think that if we mounted them back up on all the walls of our public schools that we'd see a drop in school shootings, assaults on teachers, and other mischievous activity? If students came to believe them, then yes, we would see a dramatic positive difference. It certainly worked in the past. Just go to Wikipedia and type in *List of school shootings in the United States* and you'll see the dramatic statistical jump in school shootings from the time when the Ten Commandments and public prayer were in the schools, and then the spike each decade after they were removed from the schools. No, it was not just the written words on a plaque or a few words that were mumbled in the morning that kept a lid on violence, but it was what was in people's hearts that kept the violence down in former generations. It was the meaning behind the Ten Commandments, coupled with school prayer, that acknowledged a creator who requires law and order to keep people's dark side in check. Remember, *In Adam's fall, We sinned all.*

Everyone has his or her own worldview. That is to say, a collection of beliefs about the world. Religion, or lack thereof, undeniably plays a key role in shaping one's worldview.

Now that you have been reeducated, when it comes to the importance of the Bible to many conservatives, you can better understand why they take some of the social and political positions that they do on issues.

Oh! and let me add one more thing for clarification. It has to do with the phrase "separation of church and state." We get the English word "church" from the Greek word *kuriakos*, which are two words mended together meaning "Lord" and "belongs to." In other words, "those who belong to the Lord." In the first century A.D. the word "church" was not synonymous with a "building," but the "body of Christ;" i.e. the believers. Therefore, our founding father Thomas Jefferson had his theology and politics spot on. "Church" was not to denote the inhabitants of a country, as was the case with the "Church of England" in his day, for such a "church" was a manmade distinction. If one were not in the Church of England, one was a second-class citizen. Therefore, rather than imitating the former government that had ruled over us by replicating a "Church of the United States of America," which would have caused the same divisions and intrigue that the British Empire had experienced, the new American government did away with the manmade distinctions when it came to religion, and allowed every citizen to be "one nation under God." The idea was not to do away with "the body of Christ" within the government, for almost all of our founding fathers were God-fearing men, but to go back to Jesus' original teachings of the "church." This is exactly the situation Thomas Jefferson refers to in his letter to the committee of the Danbury Baptist association in the state of Connecticut when he wrote "Believing with you that religion is a matter which lies solely between Man & his God, that he owes account to none other for his faith or his worship, that the legitimate powers of government reach actions only, & not opinions, I contemplate with sovereign reverence that act of the whole American people which declared that their legislature should 'make no law respecting an establishment of religion, or prohibiting the free exercise thereof,' thus building a wall of separation between Church & State."

The entire letter, only three paragraphs, can be found online with the Library of Congress titled *Jefferson's Letter to the Danbury Baptists.*

I've learned long ago to go to the source on any subject, and when I kept hearing over and over "separation of church and state," I knew something wasn't quite right by the way the left was throwing around this quote, and so I read the entire letter myself, all of about a minute of my time, and other documentation that provided me with the backdrop as to what was happening at the time in American history to prompt the third president to write the letter. However, now that more and more people are finding out for themselves that Thomas Jefferson was not trying to push God out of the public square, now many on the left want to push Thomas Jefferson out of our collective memory. Why? Because "he owned slaves."

On September 12, 2017 protestors at the University of Virginia covered the Thomas Jefferson statue with a black shroud, and posted a sign on it that read TJ IS A RACIST + RAPIST.

It's scary enough that many of these university students, and those bused in to foment discord on the campus, don't know American history, but it's even more scary they don't know English grammar. Hello! McFly! Thomas Jefferson, or "TJ" as they labeled him, died in 1826, and so their sign should have read TJ **WAS** A RACIST + RAPIST, past tense, and not **IS** A RACIST, present tense. If only they'd spend more time actually learning the basics: reading, writing, and arithmetic.

Anyway, at the feet of the shrouded Thomas Jefferson statue were young people carrying BLACK LIVES MATTER banners and signs. One BLM sign read F_ _ K WHITE SUPREMACY. Another sign read HATE HAS HAD A PLACE HERE. Well, it seems that there is still hate going on at the University of Virginia, and that hate is directed against the founder of their own university – Thomas Jefferson.

If the left succeeds in destroying the reputation of Thomas Jefferson, and dismiss him because he was a slave owner, then the U.S. Constitution is next. You might as well just tear it up or burn it now. Of course, if this is done, then will follow the political vacuum, and what will fill it? I'll tell you what will fill it, and I'll keep saying it as long as you're in this camp, and that is "THE VACUUM WILL BE FILLED BY SOCIALISM / COMMUNISM."

Just three months after the disgraceful demonstration before the Thomas Jefferson statue, in December of 2017, just in time for the holidays, Black Lives Matter of Los Angeles called for holiday shoppers to spend their money only at black-owned business in order to make it a "black Christmas." Of course, there is nothing wrong with blacks supporting black businesses, if only that were the case. However, the group leaders stated that the reason for creating BLACK CHRISTMAS was to "resist white capitalism."

What? American capitalism is "white?" I didn't know that. When I buy a product I just assume that a lot of people, of all colors, helped get it to me, and I'm thankful for each one of them. When I pour milk into my cereal I never give it a second thought as to who milked the cow, who transported it in a truck, and who stocked it in the refrigerator of my local grocery store for me. Do you?

Anthony Ratcliff, a BLM leader stated, "Black Lives Matter and other organizations build a a strong critique and understanding of racism, and white supremacy, and sexims, and homophobia, transphobia, but we have to have as much hatred or vitriol against capitalism."

Black Lives Matters, practically every time they say something, reveal their true colors. It certainly is not black, but communist red.

CELL BLOCK 3

GUNS

BANG! BANG!

"Guns." Scary word isn't it? Well, to a lot of Millennials and Gen Z it is. In fact, it is to a lot of the Greatest Generation and Baby Boomers as well.

For decades now, the Democrats are the ones who have been passing strict gun control: local, state, and federal. They especially get all worked up after a mass shooting incident. Like clockwork, they always piggyback their agenda onto the latest tragedy before the victims' bodies have even been buried. Yet, you will never hear these same people give kudos to gun owners who have successfully defended themselves against criminals. If they did this they'd be giving kudos every day, and sometimes several times a day. Why? Because, if the true facts were known daily then people would see that guns in America do more good than harm.

If it were up to the vast majority of Democratic politicians they would ban firearms all together for private citizens. After the 2012 Sandy Hook Elementary Shooting, the 2016 Orlando Nightclub Shooting, the 2017 Las Vegas Shooting, and other tragic massacres, there were calls for stricter gun control, and some even suggested repealing the Second Amendment. It doesn't matter to them that over 32 percent of Americans responsibly own more than 300 million firearms. They use the occasional mass murder by a lone gunman to prove how "bad" guns are, and how we need to get them out of the hands of wackos, criminals, and terrorists.

Since owning firearms is a right, and not just a privilege, as declared in the Second Amendment of the Constitution of the United States of America, Democrats can't outright ban them, but they have certainly put a lot of restrictions on them as the alternative. Had Hillary Clinton won the 2016 presidential election she would have declared war on the NRA, *National Rifle Association*, and would have had the power to hurt them. So, as part of your reeducation process you should join them. No! Not Hillary's old followers, but the NRA. As I always tell my self-defense students, "You don't have to like guns, you just need to know how to use them." I say this should they ever have to use a criminal's gun, or a terrorist's gun, against him in self-defense. Of course, knowing disarming techniques help, or how to move and take cover if you at out-of-reach distance.

The argument by the left is that guns are dangerous, and that the citizenry is not responsible enough to have them. Only the police and military should have them. Oh, and did I fail to mention that Hillary Clinton has at her disposal armed U.S. Secret Service agents 24/7 for life, and that she has been protected for three decades now. It must be nice. I, for one, carry a gun, because a cop is too heavy to carry, and I can't afford bodyguards.

"Who needs to have an AR-15 for crying out loud?" many Democrat politicians lament. In case you don't know what that is, it is a military style semi-automatic rifle, and I have one at home. It's a fine weapon. It's also used as a hunting rifle by many.

"Why would anyone need high capacity clips?" they also ask rhetorically in horror.

First of all, they're not called "clips," as a dumbass would call them. They're "magazines." A clip is a strip of metal that holds...

Ah, forget it! Look it up yourself.

Now, let's reeducate you on firearms.

First of all, a rifle, shotgun, or pistol is only a tool. That's right, a TOOL. It's a dangerous tool, I'll grant you that, but a tool nonetheless.

If you place a loaded gun on a table, and nobody touches it, then that gun cannot hurt a fly. It's just an inanimate object. It just sits there collecting dust.

That tool sitting on the table can be used for good or it can be used for evil, just like a knife or hammer can. Plenty of people are injured and killed with knives and hammers each year, both accidently and on purpose.

A police officer shooting a criminal who is trying to kill someone is a good way of using the tool. Oh, you don't like the police? Then let me use another example so you don't lose sight of the point. Let's say someone, a complete stranger, is breaking into your home, and he is definitely going to hurt you. Using a gun to protect yourself is a justifiable homicide, a good thing, if you happen to kill him. It would be better if he got wounded and survived, but hey, maybe he shouldn't be breaking into someone's house and breaking the law. Of course, your intention is never to kill anyone, but merely to "STOP" the threat. Unfortunately, when you try to stop someone with subsonic or supersonic projectiles aiming at center mass they tend to die from them.

Now, a criminal or terrorist who picks up the same tool from the table, and uses it, now you have real trouble on your hands. Criminals and terrorists are notorious for using firearms for evil purposes. The funny thing about them is that they don't care about breaking the laws either.

"Well, if we just stopped selling guns at gun stores and gun shows the criminals and terrorists wouldn't have guns to use," you say in protest.

Wrong! Are you that ignorant?

Before I tell you this, take a deep breath. Are you ready for it?

Criminals and terrorists can purchase firearms on the black market even if guns were banned for the next few decades, or even for the next hundred years for that matter.

Guns are illegal in many countries, or heavily regulated, and shootings still occur in those countries. In 2015 France had strict gun control, and they are not even a gun culture like us "cowboys" in America. Heck, you're not even allowed to carry a pocket knife in public in France. But, did that stop some of the worst terrorist attacks in French history? No, not at all. One cannot simply buy an AK-47 in Auchan (a French convenience store in case you haven't been there) or Printemps (a posh department store in the middle of Paris). Yet, weapons are flowing into France everyday through Eastern Europe coming up through Syria. Russian weapons used in the Ukraine conflict are finding their way into the streets of Berlin and Paris. And, there are even worse weapons out there on the streets. Where are the 400 American-made shoulder-fired surface-to-air missiles "taken" from Libya during the terror attack on the U.S. consulate in Benghazi, and our subsequent pull out from that country? They're still missing. One of those babies can take down a passenger jet. That could certainly ruin your vacation.

Trying to stop the manufacture and sales of guns is like pushing your finger into a toy balloon. The air just shifts, and then fills the space again when the finger is removed. Try telling Iran to stop making weapons and supplying them to terrorists. Try telling criminals not to break into people's homes or military armories to steal weapons. Good luck with that.

Here's the reality. No matter how many laws governments pass criminals and terrorists will always be able to get their hands on firearms, and even explosives for that matter. Sure, you might stop the mentally ill person from buying a legal gun with the changing of some laws, or letting a hot head cool off for a 10-day waiting period after the purchase of a firearm, buy you're not going to stop "gun violence." You can try to be like many Brits who want to ban pointed knives in the United Kingdom, because there are too many stabbings each year, but get real! Anyone can make a knife in his or her garage. It's just a sharpened piece of metal. You can even print a gun that fires real bullets on a 3-D printer as well. How are you going to stop it? Are the Democrats going to ban 3-D printers?

When I was a police officer, and then later in my career a counterterrorist agent, and then a military police soldier after that, I just assumed everybody was potentially armed that I came into contact with. I didn't have x-ray vision like Superman, and therefore, in order to stay safe, and go home every night, I accepted this reality and maintained my situational awareness at all times. I wasn't afraid of armed law-abiding citizens, I was worried about the bad guys.

So, why are so many conservatives adamant about "clinging to their Bibles and guns?" It's because, it all boils down to our country's history.

Can you hang on for a little history lesson? Of course, you can. Listen up! Okay, read up then!

When the Original Thirteen Colonies were under British rule we were fat, dumb, and happy. We were a British colony, and that was fine - for a while anyway. However, as America became an "adolescent," so to speak, we wanted more autonomy (self-government in a region). We had every intention of staying loyal to King George III (1738-1820), but our masters on the other side of the Atlantic Ocean didn't always have our best interests in mind. A central government doesn't always know what is best for the locals who are far away.

The whole "no taxation without representation" argument came up over tea coming into the colonies from the East India Company. Tea was as important then as the coffee served at Starbucks is today. A lot of people just have to have their coffee fix in the morning. I sure do. The same was true for tea back then. The tea monopoly, protected by the crown, was considered "equal to a tax," according to colonists, so prices went up, and eventually the colonists blew a gasket. All right, they didn't have cars back then, but they said, "This is BS!" So, then came the Boston Tea Party. A bunch of white Protestant political protestors, called the Sons of Liberty, dressed up like Mohawk Indians, boarded a bunch of ships in Boston Harbor and threw the crates of tea overboard in defiance of the Tea Act. They broke the law. This was the beginning of "the resistance." Oh, excuse me, "Native Americans." I used the word "Indians" didn't I? If this event would have happened in the Obama Era, or even today, the Sons of Liberty would be labeled as "racists," and children and university students would not be allowed to wear feathered headdresses for Halloween either.

The more we pushed for more freedoms to self-govern, the more King George, through his minions, started to push back and oppress our leaders; men who would eventually become our founding fathers. The worse it got the more troops (the red coats) were needed to maintain law and order. Riots broke out, killings happened here and there, and tensions were high. Then, like any powerful State starting to lose control of their power, they stared using heavy-handed tactics. The British government conducted search and seizures of homes and businesses without warrants, soldiers were ordered to take up residents in people's homes without consent, and then finally WAR! It started on April 18, 1775 when 700 British troops tried to confiscate the weapons of a militia at Concord, Massachusetts. "You ain't taking our guns and ammo!" they said. Okay, I'm paraphrasing, but they made their statement loud and clear to the King by defeating the British in the first battle of the war. On June 14, 1775 the United States Army was created. Stand up at attention when you read this! And, on July 3, 1775 George Washington took command of the Continental Army, and continued the fight in Boston. On July 4, 1776 the Thirteen Colonies had had enough of trying to CO-EXIST, and declared independence. That date is on the plaque that the Statue of Liberty is holding in her left arm. Thank God most colonists had firearms, scary "military looking" ones at that, in their homes, for they used them to fight their oppressive government. Without those firearms there would not be a United States of America today. The founding fathers knew this, and thus the Second Amendment was written, which reads:

A well regulated Militia, being necessary to the security of a free State, the right of the people to keep and bear Arms, shall not be infringed.

BOOM! There it is. States have the right to maintain a well-regulated Militia to keep their States free, and people have the right to keep and bear arms (firearms). For sixty years the liberals fought over the comma after the word "state" arguing that the intent of the Amendment gave only States the right to keep and bear arms. However, in the District of Columbia v. Heller case (2008) the Supreme Court of the United States declared that the comma in question divides two different thoughts, and that the Amendment does indeed protect an individual's right to possess firearms for traditionally lawful purposes. Rights come from God, whereas privileges come from governments.

The purpose for citizens to keep and bear arms is not just for hunting or self-defense, but to have the proper firepower on hand in case the United States government becomes tyrannical. Thomas Jefferson, the one that the enlightened students of the University of Virginia want to erase from their collective memory, said, "The strongest reason for the people to retain the right to keep and bear arms is, as a last resort, to protect themselves against tyranny in government." And, this is a guy who became President of the United States.

Why don't those who always quote Jefferson with his "separation of church and state" also quote his support of citizens having guns? And, not just any ol' firearms, but firearms capable of dealing with a tyrannical government. Hmmmm, is there a double standard here? Yeah, it's called "cherry picking."

In the 1920s Germany's Weimar Republic opted for gun registration. Of course, the law-abiding people complied with the law, as they always do, but the communists and Nazis did not. The Nazis eventually came to power in the 1930s and Adolf Hitler used those registrations to disarm and attack his political opponents. Then the self-proclaimed dictator had even stricter gun control implemented, and the eventual confiscation of firearms. Once the German citizens were unarmed the Gestapo (the state police) had complete control of people's lives, and even took millions of lives with very little resistance: the Jews, gays, political dissidents, and Christian clergy who spoke out against the brutality.

In 1920 the communist government of the Soviet Union decreed that any non-communist possessing a weapon would be given a minimum six-month prison sentence. When dictator Joseph Stalin came to power he made possession of "unlawful firearms" a crime punishable by death. Not long after this law had been established came a brutal genocide that lasted three decades. It's pretty hard to resist tyranny when you don't have firearms, and the government does.

Ever since the People's Republic of China was formed there has been the strictest of strict gun control by the communist government. This government does not tolerate dissent of their policies. However, despite their iron fist way of ruling the country, in 2012 the police uncovered 670 secret sites for the illegal manufacture and distribution of guns, and 20,000 suspects were arrested belonging to 360 criminal organizations. It was reported that 160,000 guns and 2,780 tons of explosives were seized during the raids (Xinhuanet News January 16, 2013). There's a lesson somewhere in this.

STOP TERRORISM WITH STRICTER TRUCK CONTROL

During the celebration of Bastille Day in Nice, France on July 14, 2016 a terrorist drove a 19-ton truck on a crowded boulevard for pedestrians only killing 86 people, and injuring 434 others. Then on December 19, 2016 another radical Islamic terrorist drove a stolen delivery truck right into the middle of a square of Christmas shoppers in Berlin, Germany killing 12 people, and injuring 56 others. Then to start the New Year off right a Palestinian ran over four Israeli soldiers in Jerusalem on January 8, 2017. Two months later, on March 22, 2017, a radical Islamic terrorist, driving on the iconic Westminster Bridge in London, jumped the street curb and plowed over pedestrians on the sidewalk portion of the bridge killing four people, and injuring 50 more. During this "car violence" his car crashed, he got out, headed for the British Parliament, you know, Big Ben and all, and stabbed to death a police constable. Fortunately, this monster was shot to death before he carried out further acts of "knife violence." Then another vehicle ramming attack followed on June 3, 2017 when two radical Islamic terrorists drove their rental van into a crowd of people on London Bridge, and when it came to a stop they jumped out and started stabbing as many people as they could in the Borough Market area. Eight people were murdered, and 48 injured; 21 of them critically. But, it didn't stop there. Why let a beautiful summer go to waste? That was ISIS's thinking on August 17, 2017 when two radical Islamic terrorists drove into a crowd of pedestrians in the tourist block of Las Ramblas in Barcelona, Spain: 13 dead and over 100 injured. But, of course, it's not always radical Muslims behind the wheel. Just five days before the Barcelona attack, on August 12, 2017, suspected white supremacist James Fields, 20-years-old, was arrested by police for the murder of Heather Heyer, 32-years-old, for driving his car at high speed into a counter protest group in Charlottesville, Virginia. This event was so horrific, and the ramifications so destructive to our society, that President Trump Tweeted about it, and gave numerous press conferences on it. We'll talk about Charlottesville more when you get transferred to your next cell block.

Of course, the terrorist organizations Al Qaeda and Islamic State had been encouraging vehicle ramming attacks for years, and worldwide there have been a lot of them. So why aren't the liberals constantly screaming every time this happens, "We must have stricter car and truck control!" Why don't we hear on the mainstream American media, "Breaking News. Another truck violence attack!" I'll tell you why, it's the same reason we don't hear the left pleading, "Stop knife violence!" The reason is because trucks and knives are not used to stop tyrannical governments, but firearms are. Socialist, communist, and fascist governments are afraid of an armed population. "Armed" can only mean one thing – firearms.

Now, let's entertain the ridiculous for a moment, even if you outlawed all trucks and knives in the country criminal and terrorist attacks using these tools would continue. Some terrorist would find an old abandoned truck in a barn somewhere, fix it up, and then use it. Some criminal will sharpen a plastic toothbrush, like they do in some prisons (this item is called a "shank") and stab someone with it. Yet, every time there is a crime or act of terrorism in the United States where a gun was used it's always the gun's fault. "Gun violence!" they cry.

When James Hodgkins showed up at a baseball field at the Eugene Simpson Stadium Park in Alexandria, Virginia on June 14, 2017, where over twenty Republican congressmen were practicing for the Congressional Baseball Game for Charity, and whipped out an SKS Soviet Era assault rifle and shot up the place with 50 rounds, wounding House Majority Leader Whip Steve Scalise, a congressional aid, a lobbyist, and two police officers, the first thing the left stated as the source of the problem was, yes you guessed it, the gun. Once again, we were made to believe that "gun violence" was the root cause. There were news organizations that used those exact words – GUN VIOLENCE. What the "fake news," to appropriately use President Trump's term, didn't want to highlight for the American people was that James Hodgkins had a hit list in his pocket, that he had been a left-wing activist, had been a volunteer for the Bernie Sanders 2016 presidential campaign, and openly stated his hatred for the Republicans and President Donald Trump on his social media. To put it simply, he was a domestic terrorist hell bent on political assassination. Yes, he used a firearm to carry out his deed, legally bought I might add, and it was the tool of his choice, but it was also firearms that stopped the situation from becoming worse. For you see, Scalise had two of his armed bodyguards of the Capitol Police with him that day, and had it not been for their brave intervention, the situation could have been the worse assassination in American history. There were a lot of our leaders running around on that field that day. Fortunately, the police officers shot and killed the terrorist before he had a chance to murder everyone on that field.

We will always have knives, and we will always have vehicles. We need them, because they do more good than they do harm. Likewise, we will always have guns in the United States, and for now they are doing more good than harm. Here's a case in point. On September 16, 2016, three armed intruders kicked open the door to a woman's home in Gwinnet County, Georgia, but what they weren't expecting was a 36-year-old restaurant owner, still in her pajamas, moving on them tactically firing a gun. The result was that these three thugs ran out of the house for their very lives. It serves them right. Do you want to see it? It's a hoot. A home security camera caught the action. It's on YouTube under the title *Video from fatal home invasion released.* If the small-build Asian gal had not had a gun, and the intestinal fortitude to use it, the story could have turned out much different - tragically so. So, don't tell me after you see this video that all guns are bad. The only thing that she didn't have, but could have helped her had the bad guys fought back their own guns, was a high capacity magazine.

"Hey, State of California, this is the reason good citizens need more than 10 rounds of ammunition in a magazine that is inside the semi-automatic pistol!"

I'm referring to my State's asinine law that considers "any ammunition feeding device with a capacity to accept more than 10 rounds" to be a bad thing. So, that means that legally I am only allowed to have a 10-round magazine in my Berretta 92F for self-defense instead of the 15 rounds that a high capacity magazine is designed to carry; some even more.

So, in this video the thugs had, between the three of them, a minimum of 30 rounds in their three guns, assuming that they were following the California gun law during their breaking and entering, and not using high capacity magazines. The bottom line is, the crooks had a lot of ammo.

Well, at least I don't live in New York where there is a 7-round limit. I guess in their wisdom that is all a person needs in a self-defense situation, or if the government ever went tyrannical.

The answer to the gun problem, and always had been, is to lock up criminals who use them in the commission of a crime, and then throw away the key. Taking it a step further, is terrorists who use firearms during an attack on American soil should be executed, if found guilty, whether they're an American citizen or not. For if a terrorist is an American citizen then he or she is a traitor to the country, which is punishable by death. A terrorist should not have the protection of the Constitution of the United States of America. The moment they became a terrorist they gave up their rights as a citizen, because they had become a combatant against their own country. But, since we are a fair people they'd still get a fair trial nonetheless, but in a military court at Guantanamo Bay detention camp.

What? You disagree with execution? See, here we go again. It is all about one's worldview. Many conservatives support capital punishment, because it is a Biblical principle.

Anyone who takes the life of a human being is to be put to death.
Leviticus 24:17

Whether you think so, or not, capital punishment is a deterrent. The first execution of 2017 was carried out on January 11, 2017 in the State of Texas. The authorities put to death Christopher Wilkins by lethal injection. He was convicted of killing two men who tricked him. They sold him a piece of gravel telling him that it was crack cocaine. At his trial Wilkins also testified that he killed another man outside of a bar in Fort Worth. Therefore, in the State of Texas, everyone now knows that if you murder someone over a $20 item you will pay for it with your own life.

There's an old Baby Boomer expression you should remember. It goes like this, "Don't do the crime if you can't do the time."

CELL BLOCK 4

RACISM

HATRED BECAUSE OF SKIN COLOR OR ETHNICITY

Welcome to Cell Block 4. The number "4" represents the "four corners of the world." After all, we Americans come from the four corners of the world, including the Native Americans a long, long time ago. However, even though we, the human race, are of the same blood, some people just can't get along with their fellow man because of the color of their skin or ethnicity. One man listens to Hip Hop, and he is called the "n" word. Another man listens to country music, and he is labeled a "redneck." How ridiculous is that?

Racism is defined as a person being against another person of a different race, believing that their race is superior. The law of the land, The Civil Rights Act of 1964, prohibits employment discrimination based on race, color, religion, sex and national origin. In my opinion, racism is the failure to understand others.

When I was a baby in 1962 legal racial segregation existed in the South. There were still some signs on restrooms that actually stated WHITES ONLY, and others marked COLORED. It wasn't just for restrooms, but for restaurants, movie theaters, bus stations and other establishments. However, these signs were rapidly disappearing. That's because just years before my birth the modern civil rights movement began when a black woman, Rosa Parks, on December 1, 1955 refused to give up her seat when a bus driver told her to give it up, even though she was in the colored section, for a white passenger because the WHITES ONLY section was full.

Thank God, for Martin Luther King Jr., an American Baptist minister, who led a years-long peaceful protest against racial segregation, which began with the Rosa Parks incident. It was a long hard struggle, and it even cost the life of this great civil rights icon in 1968, but legal racial segregation was eventually abolished in the United States of America.

Men and women of color were no longer held back. Black comedians became household names like Redd Fox, Bill Cosby, Richard Pryor, Eddie Murphy, and Martin Lawrence. Black singers became idols such as James Brown, Ray

Charles, Michael Jackson, Darvy Traylor, Tina Turner, Whitney Houston, and Byoncé. Blacks in the military received the highest recognition like Clifford L. Alexander Jr. (the first black Secretary of the Army), General Roscoe Robinson Jr. (the first black four-star general), Brigadier General Hazel Johnson-Brown (the first black female general), and General Colin Powel (the first black Chairman of the Joint Chiefs of Staff who was appointed as the Secretary of State by President George W. Bush). African-Americans also took prominent roles in our government such as Carl Stokes (the first mayor of a major city), L. Douglas Wilder (the first black Governor), Robert C. Weaver (the first U.S. cabinet member), Thurgood Marshal (the first black Justice of the Supreme Court of the United States), Condoleezza Rice (the first black female Secretary of State), and Barack Obama (the first African-American President of the United States).

Of course, African Americans are not the only "minorities" in the country. Other people of color rose through the ranks as well, like Rosario Marin who was the highest-ranking Latina to serve in President Bush's Administration. To top it off she was an immigrant from Mexico. I'm highlighting her as an example of "The American Dream," because I was the Team Leader for her protection detail on August 30, 2001 when I was a sergeant with the Orange County Sheriff's Department's Dignitary Protection Unit in California. Yes, I played a small role in American history. I was behind the scenes. I was the "gray man" (a bodyguard term) that nobody paid attention to, but I kept her safe from harm that day. Well, actually, it was that evening. And, me being a white male, it did not bother me in the least that my "boss" was a Hispanic woman. Not only was she my principal (in bodyguardspeak that's the person being protected), but I was even willing to take a bullet for her. So, don't ever tell me that all police officers are racists, because I sure wasn't.

After January 20, 2009 racism had officially ended as far as most Americans were concerned. President Barack Hussein Obama was elected as the 44th President of the United States.

An African-American (although he was half black from his father's side, and half white from his mother's side) had made it to the top position in the country. Heck, in the entire Free World for that matter, and he had only made it there because white voters put him there. The minority votes alone would have never got him into the Oval Office. Thus, because of whites, he became "The Man." This was a derogatory term used for decades by many blacks to describe the white majority government. That is to say, "the establishment" that ruled over them.

When Obama took office I was one of those people who said, "Racism is officially over in the United States." Of course, that didn't mean it was eradicated from the hearts of every American, for racism in some people will always exist, but racism as an American institution was finally over. A great hurdle had been jumped.

Unfortunately, President Obama did not seize the historic opportunity to heal the wounds of racism in our country, but he made things worse. No, more than that. He opened up the almost healed wound, and then he threw salt into it. During the Bush Administration, from 2001 to 2009, I don't recall there being any riots in the United States over racial issues. Well then, let's take a closer look to see if I am right or wrong with my recollection, shall we.

2001 nothing. 2002 nothing. 2003 nothing. 2004 nothing. 2005, ah, wait a minute. That was the year Hurricane Katrina devastated New Orleans by covering 80% of the city with a flood of water. The brunt of the Category 5 hurricane hit the United States on August 29, 2005, and President George W. Bush declared a state of emergency along the Gulf Coast on August 27, 2005. What? He was anticipating a catastrophe, and getting government resources ready days before it actually hit shore? Amazing. That was quite proactive of him. However, in the aftermath of the natural disaster a lot of African-Americans blamed the President for not doing enough to help the African-American communities of New Orleans, when in fact much of the blame was due to Mayor Ray Nagin, a black man, and Louisiana Governor Kathleen Blanco. Of course, a lot of people bought into the leftist propaganda at the time. While giving a concert for the victims of the hurricane Rapper Kanye West stated, "George Bush doesn't care about black people."

Well, we can't really look at Hurricane Katrina as a racial issue, because most of the rioting, looting, and rapes were black on black. It was so bad that the Army National Guard, along with civilian security contractors, were called in to restore peace and stability.

2006 nothing. 2007 nothing. 2008 was, wait for it, Barack Hussein Obama was elected as the first black president of the United States. That does not sound like racial tension to me. How about you? What do you think? Again, a lot of Americans were thinking the same thing that I was back in 2008, and that was we weren't white, black, or whatever anymore, we were finally Americans. The only colors that mattered where RED, WHITE, and BLUE.

So, President Obama came in the White House with no racial tensions to speak of, but he started picking at the scab, if I could use this graphic analogy, and he started doing this rather early on in his presidency. You need to know this history, because we're in the current mess we are in because of it.

It all started on July 16, 2009 when police Sergeant James Crowley responded to a 9-1-1 call of men breaking into, and entering, a residence in a well-to-do neighborhood. It was a crime in progress report – the most dangerous kind to a police officer. The residence was that of Harvard University professor Henry Louis Gates Junior in Cambridge, Massachusetts.

According to the 9-1-1 dispatch recordings, and the police report, Sergeant Crowley arrived at the front door and knocked. When Professor Gates, who was standing inside the residence on the other side of the door, asked what the police wanted Sergeant Crowley explained that he was there to investigate a break-in in progress. When Professor Crowley opened the door he said, "Why, because I'm a black man in America?"

Sergeant Crowley ordered Professor Gates, a few times because of his uncooperative demeanor, to produce a photo identification so that he could verify if the house was indeed his, and that he was not unknowingly talking to some burglar. Professor Gates refused at first, but then produced his Harvard University identification card. Professor Gates yelled at the sergeant, and then told him that he didn't know who he was "messing with." Oh no, here comes the namedropping any second now.

Professor Gates stepped outside, and he continued to yell at Sergeant Crowley accusing him of racism. Sergeant Crowley warned him that he was becoming disorderly, but Professor Gates persisted. After a second warning Sergeant Crowley placed Professor gates under arrest for disorderly conduct.

It was determined that Professor Gates had just returned home from a trip to China, and he found his front door to his home jammed shut. Because he couldn't get it opened his driver helped him by forcing the door open. This is what the witness saw from a distance, and reported what they witnessed to the police.

It turned out that Professor Gates was a friend of President Barak Obama, and the President of the United States of America decided to comment on the incident publicly on July 22nd stating, "I don't know, not having been there and not seeing all the facts, what role race played in that. But I think it's fair to say, number one, any of us would be pretty darn angry; number two, that the Cambridge police acted stupidly in arresting somebody when there was already proof that they were in their own home, and, number three, what I think we know separate and apart from this incident is that there's a long history in this country of African-Americans and Latinos being stopped by law enforcement disproportionately."

STRIKE ONE! for President Obama. That was the beginning of racial tensions.

The President's comment was offensive to law enforcement agencies all across America for a couple of reasons. First, the Cambridge police was accused of having "acted stupidly," when they hadn't. There was probable cause for the arrest. Second, for accusing all of law enforcement for stopping African-Americans and Latinos disproportionately. That was a whopper! According to the Bureau of Justice Statistics the percentage of adult males incarcerated in the United States at that time was 0.7 whites, 1.8 Hispanic, and 4.7 African-American. So, what that means in plain English is that more Hispanics were convicted of crimes and incarcerated than whites, and more than double the amount of blacks had been convicted and incarcerated than Hispanics. One time when I was a cop in Southern California, back in the 1990s, I pulled over a young black man who had been driving northbound on Harbor Boulevard in the City of Costa Mesa. When I approached him the first thing he said to me was, "You stopped me because I'm black!" I answered him, "No, I stopped you because you have a warrant for your arrest," which he did. Oh sure, President Obama later stated that he regretted his comments to the American people, after a ton of people got pissed off at him, and he did some quick backpedaling saying that the incident was a "teachable moment," but it didn't stop him from sticking his foot into his mouth again, doubling down using the racist card.

The next incident came on February 26, 2012 when Neighborhood Watch coordinator George Zimmerman, a 28-year-old Hispanic man, was driving through the Twin Lakes gated community in Sanford, Florida when he saw a young black man walking in the rain. He immediately called the police and said to the 9-1-1 dispatcher, "We've had some break-ins in my neighborhood, and there's a real suspicious guy."

He described the suspicious man as, "just walking around looking about," and "this guy looks like he is up to no good or he is on drugs or something."

The suspicious young man started to run, and George Zimmerman got out of his car and chased him, even though the dispatcher advised against this course of action over the phone. George Zimmerman asked the police to call him back so that when they arrived he could give them his new location.

Some sort of altercation took place between George Zimmerman and 17-year-old African-American Trayvon Martin that ended with George Zimmerman fatally shooting Trayvon Martin. Police arrived five seconds after the shooting, which was approximately 7:17 pm. George Zimmerman was bleeding from the nose and the back of the head from injuries.

As it turned out Trayvon Martin was staying with his father's fiancée at The Retreat at Twin Lakes, which is a 260-unit gated townhome community. Unfortunately, police records indicated that there had been disturbances, suspicious males peeping into windows, and break-ins for a year leading up to the shooting. What exactly happened that evening only George Zimmerman and Trayvon

Martin knew, and one involved party is dead. One witness, who didn't see the shooting, saw Trayvon Martin on top of George Zimmerman on the ground and punching him.

George Zimmerman was not arrested, because the police believing it to be a case of self-defense. Then when this story made national news all hell broke loose. One reason is because NBC edited George's Zimmerman's call to the police to make it appear that he volunteered Martin's race as to why he thought the man was suspicious. However, the unedited 9-1-1 recording revealed that George Zimmerman mentioned race only when asked to do so by the dispatcher. This was the beginning of "fake news."

It didn't take long for many, without all of the facts and doctored video footage, to label George Zimmerman as a "racist," and activists like Reverend Al Sharpton and Reverend Jesse Jackson made accusations to stir the populace up. Al Sharpton said, "Forty-five days ago Trayvon Martin was murdered. No arrest was made." Jesse Jackson referred to Trayvon Martin as "murdered and martyred." These two high-profile black leaders had made themselves self-proclaimed "judge and jury" before all the facts were known.

If that wasn't bad enough President Barak Obama decided to jump into the fray on the side of the activists stating to the American public on March 23, 2012, "When I think about this boy, I think about my own kids, and I think every parent in America should be able to understand why it is absolutely imperative that we investigate every aspect of this… If I had a son, he would look like Trayvon."

What did Trayvon look like? In all the photos they showed on the news he looked like a cute 14-year-old boy wearing a hoodie. He looked like the kid next door. In fact, the hoodie became a symbol of this "murdered and martyred" young man. Other photos the media showed over and over on the air was Trayvon Martin when he was 12-years-old with a friendly smile, but the mainstream media never showed the photos of him at an older age flipping off the camera with his middle fingers simultaneously or the gang look with the backwards baseball cap on his head. Those photos were a bit frightening.

"If I had a son, he would look like Trayvon." What kind of statement is that? It was a statement to pit the races against one another; black against white. Because, at first, everyone thought George Zimmerman was "white." After all, "Zimmerman" is a good German name. How embarrassing it was when the media found out that he was Hispanic. Oh well, the truth about him didn't change the agenda. The "killer" may not have been white, but the whites were still victimizing blacks somewhere in the country. Or so that is what the narrative being pushed was all about.

Well, the second half of the President's comment was indeed incendiary, but the first part was a definite clear message to the American people that the local police and courts were not capable of bringing George Zimmerman to "justice," and so, by golly, President Obama, by using the federal government at his disposal, would make sure that justice would be indeed served.

However, things didn't turn out like the President, activists, and left leaning media wanted. George Michael Zimmerman was acquitted of second-degree murder.

In response to Zimmerman's acquittal the Black Lives Matter activist movement was born. More about them later...

STRIKE TWO! for President Obama.

Two years later came the big one. On August 9, 2014, in Ferguson, Missouri an 18-year-old black man, by the name of Michael Brown, had just robbed a convenience store in broad daylight, which was recorded on a surveillance camera. He had stolen several packs of cigarillos and assaulted the store clerk. It wasn't an armed robbery, but a strong-arm robbery. Along comes police officer Darren Wilson down the street in his police care, and he sees Michael Brown and his sidekick Dorian Johnson walking in the middle of the street liked they owned it. Just as Officer Wilson was telling the two men to get out of the street for their own safety the call of the robbery comes out over the radio. Lo and behold the two men he had just shooed away matched the description of the robbers.

Officer Wilson quickly backed up his police car to block them from getting away. Just as he was about to get out of the vehicle Michael Brown, which the media later called the "gentle giant," essentially dove through the driver's side window, which was rolled down, and shoved the uniformed police officer back into his seat and tried to disarm him of his holstered pistol. I don't know about you, but as a former cop that is a life and death survial situation. Criminals who get a hold of an officer's firearm usually bring about a bad ending for the officer. I can't think of anything more terrifying.

When the firearm went off Michael Brown, in momentary shock no doubt from the loud noise and flash, stopped his attack, backed off, and then tried to flee. Officer Wilson went after him on foot. After all, he was a felony suspect who had just tried to seize a cop's weapon. However, instead of Michael Brown surrendering, like any good citizen would do if the police were after him or her, this "gentle giant" turned around and attacked the police officer a second time. Officer Wilson did what any officer would do under the circumstances, with only mere moments to react to protect his own life, he fired at the hostile suspect who had already tried to take his gun once. The twelve bullets that were fired all hit the front side of Michael Brown's body, with two of them going into

Brown's right arm. One of those bullets killed the attacker. That's what happened according to witnesses and forensic evidence, but that is not exactly what survivor Dorian Johnson said, or how the media reported the incident.

Dorian Johnson, the friend of the robber, stated to the media, and then later gave the same testimony before the grand jury, that Officer Wilson tried to get out of his car, but the door hit them as it swung open and bounced back closing it, and so Officer Wilson reached out of the open window from a seated position, grabbed Michael Brown by the neck, and tried pulling him into the vehicle through the window.

Oh! Come on! This is ridiculous! No police officer in his right mind would pull a robber through his window while in a seated position, especially when there are two suspects involved. Fighting from a car seat is not an easy thing to do, and it would be easy for anyone on the outside to pull away. I know, because I have taught many police departments Seat Defense techniques, and none of them involve pulling the attacker into the car. Anyway, back to Dorian Johnson's lies.

Of course, Dorian Johnson said that his hommie "did not reach for the officer's weapon at all." It was just a "tug of war." During the struggle, when the gun went off, Michael Brown tried to get away. Who wouldn't?

But then, as the story goes on, Officer Wilson got out of his patrol car and shouted, "I'm going to shoot!" and then fired his pistol striking Michael Brown in the back. His friend turned around with his hands raised pleading, "I don't have a gun. Stop shooting!"

This version of the story enraged the black community, and the whole "hands up" account became the symbol of the Ferguson protests by activists placing their hands up above their heads in the surrender position, and then later black politicians started doing it, then black athletes, and sympathizers of all races picked up this hand gesture ad nauseam. Not only was the false narrative of racism by whites against blacks alive and well, because Officer Wilson was white, but the seeds of hatred for the police in general sprouted from this incident having germinated with the previous two national incidents. The slogan "Hands up, don't shoot!" became the rallying cry against supposed widespread "police violence."

To make a long story short, the peaceful protests turned into riots, and there were three waves of unrest over a one-year period. Even the National Guard had to be called in to restore law and order. In response to the unrest President Barak Obama had the U.S. Department of Justice investigate the Ferguson Police Department, and a separate investigation of Officer Wilson. The President sent U.S. Attorney General Eric Holder, an African-American, to Ferguson on

August 20, 2014 to meet with Michael Brown's family. It was clear to the American public that the administration was sympathetic to residents supporting the false narrative. Maybe it was because the White House sent three officials to attend Michael Brown's funeral in St. Louis. Funny, they didn't send any officials to former British Prime Minister Margaret Thatcher's funeral the year before, which really pissed off the Brits. She had had stood shoulder to shoulder with President Ronald Reagan during the Cold War, and deserving of a visit from the sitting President. To top it off President Obama accused the police across America of becoming too "militarized."

Right about this time in history many whites were starting to question the Obama administration's motives. It was as if the White House and the U.S. Department of Justice were exploiting any incident that could be perceived as white v. black racism. It seemed to be a page right out of the book *Rules for Radicals* by Saul Alinsky. The book was sometimes quoted by President Obama; the same book dedicated to the first radical in history – Lucifer. Oh yeah, I'm not kidding. The book is dedicated to "the first radical known to man who rebelled against the establishment and did it so effectively that he at least won his own kingdom – Lucifer." That's a quote right out of the book. In case you don't know your Bible, Lucifer is the angel that rebelled against God, was cast down to Earth along with a third of the angels who had joined him, and became the fallen angel we know today as Satan or the Devil. And, it wasn't just President Obama who seemed to have used this Marxist piece of literature like a playbook for his own presidency, but Saul Alinsky (1909 to 1972) was greatly admired by Hillary Clinton. When she was at Wellesley College in 1969 she wrote her senior thesis titled *THERE IS ONLY THE FIGHT... An Analysis of the Alinsky Model*. You can read it today on the Internet – the original. She interviewed Saul Alinsky herself. And, you wonder why the greater part of the evangelical Christian community did not support President Obama or Presidential Candidate Hillary Clinton. Well, maybe you didn't wonder why. You were just told that the evangelical Christians are just a bunch of religious fanatical right-wing nuts. Anyway, back to the racism issue. Wait! Hold on one second. Before we move on, Saul Alinsky does tie into what we are talking about here. When Hillary wrote her thesis, and submitted it on May 2, 1969, she didn't agree with everything her mentor had to say. Oh no, she had some even more radical ideas than him, and she let it be known when she was running for President when she told Black Lives Matter, "I don't believe you change hearts, you change laws, you change allocation of resources, you change the way the system operate." Now, this was supposedly said in a closed doors session, but it does sound familiar. Where did I hear this kind of talk before, or something similar to it? Oh yes, when she was speaking at the 2015 Women in the World Summit about the right to "reproductive health care," a very caring term for "abortions," declaring that "Laws have to be backed up with resources, and political will. And, deep-seated cultural codes, religious beliefs and structural biases have to be changed." There are those two words again, "resources" and "change." So, in other words, change, change, change. HOPE AND CHANGE. Snopes, citing this same quote from Hillary, makes it seem like Christians were all in an uproar for nothing, but you can watch the video, in its entirety, yourself. Yes Snopes, she was saying "as a demand that American Christians deny their faith." However, we'll discuss abortions when we move you into Cell Block 6. Now, back to racism. I mean it this time.

President Obama had had several opportunities to tell the American people, people of every color under the flag, to put the racial card back into the deck and live in harmony, but it seemed like he was the one dealing the cards after each incident involving a white man that either offended or killed a black. Yet, blacks were slaughtering blacks by the hundreds in his home city of Chicago yearly, and hardly a peep was said about that. Blacks killing blacks was a taboo topic among the Democrats.

Oh, and in case you forgot, or you didn't know, Officer Darren Wilson was cleared of any wrongdoing. It was a justifiable homicide. Officer Wilson had acted in self-defense. The Department of Justice had compiled an 86-page report, which included 40 witnesses that corroborated Officer Wilson's actions. U.S. Attorney General Eric H. Holder Jr. himself called the report "fair and rigorous from the start," and "The facts do not support filing of criminal charges against Officer Darren Wilson in this case."

STRIKE THREE! for President Obama.

These three incidents, case studies if you will, that I've presented as part of your reeducation, were the three incidents that rekindled racism in America. Yet, even though racism was not a factor in any of these incidents, many activists ignored the facts and kept insisting that young black males were an endangered species in this country. Not endangered by fellow blacks, which was the truth of course, but by whites and the police.

So, what is the position on race relations that most conservatives take? I can tell you with certainty that the political right is far less racist than the political left. In fact, when Donald Trump was running for President he said that the most compassionate thing he could do for the black community was to make their lives better, because Democrats had failed them both economically and socially, and that they only showed up every four years just to get their votes. Whereas Donald Trump pressed the African-American community for their votes by reasoning, "You're living in poverty, your schools are no good, you have no jobs, 58% of your youth are unemployed - - what the hell do you have to lose?"

WHITE PRIVILEGE

Who came up with this moronic term? Those who say it, aren't they kind of racist themselves?

The term "white privilege" assumes that just because someone is Caucasian, "white," that they have more privileges than non-whites. That may have been the case in some pockets of the country in the history of the United States, but it certainly has not applied in the last couple of decades. Case in point, Barak Hussein Obama, a black man, was elected as President of the United States in 2008. A person can't get any more privileged than that, and I've already mentioned earlier other minorities who have "made it to the top." Apparently, nothing held these people back. So how is it that blacks are not privileged, and at the same time some are? You can't have it both ways. It's obvious that this logic from the left doesn't fly. Conclusion: white privilege is a false term.

The Hillary Clinton camp constantly chanted the slogan "white privilege" when she was running for POTUS, which is ironic, because she is as white as they come. Maybe she was speaking from her own experience, or self-guilt, because her father managed a successful textile business. She not only attended college, but she earned a law degree from Yale Law School in 1973. Two years later she married Bill Clinton, and not long afterwards she was the First Lady of Arkansas when her husband became governor. When Bill Clinton became the President of the United States in January 1993 she became the First Lady of the nation. Her and her husband were privileged indeed. Now, mind you, there is absolutely nothing wrong with the Clintons being privileged. It's only wrong when you yourself are privileged, act like you are not privileged, and then get people all stirred up against those who are privileged, and use the term "white privilege." Do you see the hypocrisy? I hope so.

It wasn't just Hillary Clinton's staff and supporters that were blaming white America for the racial tensions in the United States, tensions that President Obama had stirred up first, but she was the main culprit during the presidential race. On April 13, 2016 at Al Sharpton's National Action Network Convention, a mostly black audience, she stated, "White Americans need to do a much better job of listening when African-Americans talk about the seen and unseen barriers you face every day." Apparently, she forgot about her former boss sitting over there in the White House when she was the Secretary of State from 2009 to 2013. In fact, I don't recall her giving any such speech when she was living in the White House herself a decade earlier from 1993 to 2001, which technically would have been a time when race relations were worse. But, they weren't worse. The 1990s saw the African American community improving economically. By the time President Bill Clinton left office 51 percent of black employees were white-collar workers. 20 percent of the black labor force, approximately 3 million workers, were classified as professional and technical workers and administrators. Think about this, in 1940 one-third of the black labor force had been in agriculture, but that had virtually disappeared by the late 1990s with only 80,000 African-Americans working as farm laborers and agricultural managers. Also by the late 1990s African-American executives were coming up through the ranks and becoming chief executive officers and presidents of major corporations for the first time, like Richard D. Parsons who served as CEO and chairman of AOL Time Warner, and Kenneth Chenault who was the CEO and chairman of American Express. Hillary Clinton poo pooed my white privilege, but let me tell you, I'd trade my supposed white privilege for Kenneth Chenault's total compensation of $50,126,585.00 any day, and that was just for the year 2007.

Hillary went on to say at the convention, "We need to recognize our privilege and practice humility, rather than assume our experiences are everyone else's experiences." Hmmmm, and you wonder why so many conservatives didn't care if they were called racists, and then voted for Donald Trump. There's nothing like getting slapped in the face with false accusations.

Hillary Clinton not only pushed the white privilege narrative to get black votes, but she even added fuel to the racial fire by saying on July 8, 2016, "Too many African-Americans have been killed in encounters with police."

Hogwash! The statistics, according to The Washington Post for 2015, show that 990 people were shot by law enforcement. 948 of those shot were male. 494 shot were white, and 258 were black. Do you need to see these figures again? 494 whites, and 258 blacks. So, based on raw numbers, wouldn't this next statement also be true? "Too many whites have been killed in encounters with police." Of course, that sentence was never spoken by the leftist media or leftist activists, because it didn't fit their agenda. Truth can be an agenda killer.

How about this statement, which was also never spoken either, "Too many men have been killed in encounters with police." Whoa! That means that that the police are targeting men, and not women! The police must be going out of their way to hunt down men." That's how I'd write it if I were a leftist journalist. Or, could it be that the reality is that more men commit crime than women, and more men attack the police than women. Yes, obviously, this is the case. Numbers don't lie.

Hey, it's too bad that the police had to shoot anyone, white or black, but this proves that the police are not out there hunting down young black males. Again, the left was, and still is, pushing this false narrative. Why?

Reality is reality, and a lot of people, both black and white alike, swallowed this deceitful lie during the Obama administration era and during the 2016 presidential elections, and it somehow morphed from *white privilege* to *white men are enemy number one*. After all, it was "white rage" that got Donald Trump into the White House. According to black author Carlo Anderson, Ph.D., who wrote the book *White Rage: The Unspoken Truth of Our Racial Divide*, the support for Donald Trump was actually a virulent backlash against President Barak Obama, a black president.

Now, if the left wants to chant a more accurate slogan today it should be "American privilege." It has a nice ring to it, and it's true.

Under the Constitution of the United States of America *We the People* all enjoy the same freedoms, and they're not just privileges, but rights. They're in the Bill of Rights. We are all privileged to be Americans compared to the rest of the world. Nobody is going to stop an African-American from pursing the career of his or her choice. Nobody is going to prevent a Mexican-American from attending college. No American LGBTQ is going to get arrested by the police, taken to the top of a tall building, and then pushed off of it like ISIS militants did to some men in Tal Abyad, Syria in 2015, and then posted this cruelty on YouTube for the whole world to see.

All of us, no matter what color we are, are very privileged in America. Therefore, when you are released from this reeducation camp you'll purge this "white privilege" nonsense from your mind. You live in America where a white person or an African-American can become President of the United States. And yes, even a woman... just not Hillary Clinton. Remember that.

WHITE MEN ARE THE PROBLEM

Not only was the term "White Privilege" coined in the Obama era, but another fallacy was propagated by the left just before the 2016 presidential election, and that was that the real enemy in America is "white men." Michelle Obama made that point perfectly clear on October 3, 2017 at the Pennsylvania Conference for Women when she described how she noticed at the State of the Union addresses she used to attend that, "one side of the room it's literally gray and white. Literally, that's the color palette on one side of the room. On the other side of the room, there are yellows and blues and whites and greens. Physically, there's difference in color, in the tone. Because one side: all men, all white. On the other side: some women, some people of color." In other words, all those white men wore conservative attire, but thank goodness on the Democratic side of the room the women, and people of color, spiced things up with colorful clothes. As if what people are wearing in the halls of Congress has anything to do with good governance. Michelle Obama also said that she was "always the most embarrassed" when she had guests with her when attending this event. Although her statements sounds like an airhead saying it, it is anything but shallow. Her following statement follows up on her thinking, and it's truly frightening, "No wonder, no wonder, we struggle. No wonder people don't trust politics. It's that, we're not even noticing what these rooms look like. But, it's not just politics. I mean, I'm sure we can go in any C-Suite," then she chuckled, "in this country, and we would see the same thing happening. So, until we are ready to fight for that, which means that some people have to be willing to give up their seats to make room, or…"

What? Are you kidding me? C-Suite is a corporate term for the top executives starting with the letter "C," such as chief executive officer (CEO), chief financial officer (CFO), chief operating officer (COO), and so forth. Do you get what she was trying to say? By comparing her previous statement about Congress to the corporate world she was stating that there are too many white men running American corporations, and to make them more diverse the people, women and people of color, have to be ready to "fight" to make it so, or some of those white men "have to be willing to give up their seats to make room." For whom? I thought in America you had to work hard to become successful? I thought top corporate positions were for people who could make the company efficient and profitable, and had nothing to do with skin color or gender. Since when did the words "fight" and "willing to give up their seats" come into play in America?

Michelle Obama's comments were both stereotypical and racists. Yet, the crowd she was speaking to applauded her. Obviously, a lot of liberals believed that garbage. It's amazing how many liberals cannot detect reverse racism in themselves.

Contrary to Michelle Obama's opinion, and popular belief among many Millennials and Gen Zers, white males are not the enemy of American society, and anyone still saying that is, again, a racist. That's right, a true RACIST. Racism goes both ways you know. Plus, I already thought we had women running major corporations? What about Indra Nooyi of PepsiCo? What about Mary Barra of General Motors? What about Ginni Rometty of IBM? Meg Whitman of Hewlett Packard? Marillyn Hewson of Lockheed Martin? Marissa Mayer of Yahoo! And, the list goes on. Did they have to have a revolution or have white men give up their seats for them? I don't think so. They earned it, and they deserved it.

Well, okay, perhaps Marissa Mayer of Yahoo! didn't. Her leadership of Yahoo! was disastrous. From 2012 to 2017 Yahoo! cut half of its employees, and she blew it big time by buying the blogging platform Tumblr for $1.1 billion. She was also at the helm when their customers suffered massive security breaches by hackers. The company had once been worth more than $100 billion, but by the time she was on her way out it was worth $5 billion. But, not to worry. Marissa Mayer collected $239 million in compensation. "That's 900,000 dollars every week she spent wrecking the company," Tucker Carlson of Fox News announced on his show on June 6, 2017. So, what was her worldview when she was CEO of Yahoo!? After all, one's worldview dictates who they are. At the 2013 Dreamforce conference in San Francisco she said that her priorities in life were, "God, family and Yahoo! except I'm not religious, so it's really family and Yahoo!" Interesting. Take God out of the equation, and… It just goes to show you that man, woman, black, or white, people are people. You have good people in life, and you have bad people. Race or sex has nothing to do with talent, skills, work ethic, or character.

Hillary Clinton stated many times when she was running for president that she should be elected as POTUS because she was a woman. Well, that is outright SEXIST. She also accused the Republicans of being against diversity. Such comments are RACIST. Not only were her verbal jabs racist, but highly hypocritical. Long after the election had taken place, on September 27, 2017 at a marketing and professional development conference in Boston, former First Lady Michelle Obama jump all over that subject as well stating, "Any woman who voted against Hillary Clinton voted against their own voice." So, in other words, 40% of the women in America who voted for Donald Trump were stupid because they didn't vote for a woman who would all but guarantee unrestricted abortions and give them a leftist government.

Let's look at this logically. The Democratic Party only had three viable candidates running for the office of the president of the United States in 2016: Hillary Clinton, a white woman, Martin O'Malley, a white man, and Bernie Sanders, a white man. Two white men and a white woman. On the other hand the supposed "racist party," the Republican Party, fielded a truly diverse group: Donald Trump, a white man, Ben Carson, a black man, Chris Christie, a white man, Ted Cruz, a Hispanic man, Marco Rubio, a Hispanic man, John Kasich, a white man, Jeb Bush, a white man, Rand Paul, a white man, Lindsey Graham, a white man, Carly Fiorina, a white woman, Mike Huckabee, a white man, Bobby Jindal, an East Indian, Rick Santorum, a white man, George Pataki, a white man, and Jim Gilmore, a white man. That makes 10 white men, 1 black, 2 Hispanics, 1 East Indian, and 1 white woman. Not only were the Republican presidential candidates diverse, unlike the Democrats who only claimed to be, but the GOP gave the Republican base 15 candidates to choose from; not just 3 like the Democrats. Apparently, the liberals were so blinded by their own propaganda labeling the Republicans racists and enemies of diversity, that they never noticed the skin color of their opponents. Yet, even after the election many Millennials and Gen Z continued to label President Donald Trump, and the Republicans, as "racists."

The question now is, "are the Republicans really racists, or was it, and still is, all just leftist propaganda?"

Let's consider some of President Trump's choices for his cabinet and his cabinet-level staff. For the sake of time, let's not list the white males. Here goes: Secretary of Housing and Urban Development Ben Carson (African-American), Secretary of Transportation Elaine Chao (Asian, woman), Secretary of Education Betsy DeVos (white, woman). Three out of 16 secretary positions is not bad. Yeah, I know. Betsy DeVos is white, but I threw her in to prove the President is not sexist as Hillary Clinton made him out to be. For the cabinet-level staff we have: Ambassador of the United Nations Nikki Haley (East-Indian, woman) and Administrator of the Small Business Administration Linda McMahon (white, woman). Two out of eight is not bad either. Now, if President Trump were truly "racist," belief that other races are inferior, or "gynophobia," the abnormal fear of women, then he would have appointed nothing but white males to the cabinet and cabinet-level positions to run the United States government. The fact that you have different races and women in top cabinet positions is proof enough that these two accusations against the President are false. Come on! Admit it! At least in this reeducation camp we don't force you to write and sign a letter denouncing your political party. And, we don't torture until you do.

Oh, and let's not forget President Donald Trump's choice for the top medical position in the country – Surgeon General of the United States. On August 3, 2017 the United States Senate confirmed Jerome Adams, an African-American. Upon his confirmation the Surgeon General stated that his priorities would be "the opioid epidemic and untreated mental illness." After all, the majority of our mass shootings, if it's not from radical Islamic terrorists, are from people with mental illness.

I personally look forward to the day we stop looking at someone's skin color if a person gets a position or not. The only question should be, "Is he or she qualified for the job, and will they uphold the United States Constitution? Only racists look at the color of one's skin."

And, speaking of "white men," it seems that the left is not just fearful of living white men, but dead ones as well. We already had a discussion about students at the University of Virginia covering up the Thomas Jefferson statue with a black shroud, and labeling him a "RACIST + RAPIST," but a year before that incident undergraduates at Yale University did something just as asinine. They launched a petition demanding that the English department abolish the core course requirement to study great historical writers of English literature. Within the petition it states, "it is unacceptable that a Yale student considering studying English literature might read only white male authors." So, in other words, who needs Geoffrey Chaucer? He was only the "father of English literature," and considered the greatest English poet of the Middle Ages. What English major needs to read William Shakespeare? His plays were only the most known pieces of literature in the history of America, second only to the Holy Bible. The same goes for Edmund Spenser, John Donne, John Milton, Alexander Pope, or William Wordsworth who helped to launch the Romantic Age in English literature. They were all a bunch of "white male authors" not worthy of reading.

I almost forgot! What about Charles Dickens? In 1843 he wrote the beloved story *A Christmas Carol*. You know, it's the one about a stingy penny-pinching miser named Ebenezer Scrooge visited by the Ghosts of Christmas past, present, and future. Of course, I know perfectly well why some Yale students would love to have everyone stop reading this book, and that's because it's about Christmas – the holiday many on the left would love to do away with. Although I love the exchange between Scrooge and the spirit of his deceased business partner Jacob Marley, I can see how the left would hate this masterpiece.

"But you were always a good man of business, Jacob," faltered Scrooge, who now began to apply this to himself.

"Business!" cried the Ghost, wringing his hands again. "Mankind was my business. The common welfare was my business; charity, mercy, forbearance, and benevolence, were, all, my business. The dealings of my trade were but a drop of water in the comprehensive ocean of my business!"

It held up its chain at arm's length, as if that were the cause of all its unavailing grief, and flung it heavily upon the ground again.

"At this time of the rolling year," the spectre said, "I suffer most. Why did I walk through crowds of fellow-beings with my eyes turned down, and never raise them to that blessed Star which led the Wise Men to a poor abode! Were there no poor homes to which its light would have conducted me!"

This is English literature at its finest, and it eloquently points to the Christ child.

The petition to abolish white male writers called upon Yale University to "decolonize" the course. That means getting away from studying pre-20th century authors and to "deliberately include literature relating to gender, race, sexuality, ableism, and ethnicity." In other words, English literature history need not include English literature history.

There's probably another petition going around right now, I jest, by yet another group of undergraduates in Yale's World History Department demanding that when it comes to the study of the Roman Empire that the study of the emperors be dropped, because they were "white male emperors." Julius Caesar, Augustus, Tiberius, Caligula, and the rest of them – gone. Bye, bye. No more study of Greek philosophers Socrates, Plato, or Aristotle. No more study of the French Revolution, no more study of the Vikings, no more... hell, let's just drop studying Western Culture all together. That's where it's all headed anyway. Oh, wait, the study of Karl Marx and Lenin stays, even though they were white guys, along with Harvey Milk and Bernie Sanders, both white, because they carried the torch of liberalism. The petition will allow for exceptions, chosen carefully by the propaganda officers who know best.

Oh, brother!

One of Yale University's most famous graduates was William F. Buckley, Jr. In 1951, at the age of 25-years-old, his first book was published titled *God and Man at Yale*. He saw the storm clouds on the horizon at his old alma mater, even back then, when he wrote these words in the preface, "I myself believe that the duel between Christianity and atheism is the most important in the world. I further believe that the struggle between individualism and collectivism is the same struggle reproduced on another level. I believe that if and when the menace of Communism is gone, other vital battles, at present subordinated, will emerge to the foreground. And the winner must have help from the classroom."

Imagine today if the president of Yale University got up to the mike at his inaugural address, and spoke these words, "I call on all members of the faculty, as members of a thinking body, freely to recognize the tremendous validity and power of the teachings of Christ in our life-and-death struggle against the forces of selfish materialism. If we lose that struggle, judging from present events abroad, scholarship as well as religion will disappear."

Well, those words were indeed uttered before the Yale faculty by the incoming president of the university, Charles Seymour, on October 16, 1937. He remained the president until 1951, and evidently his words impacted William F. Buckley, Jr. for in Chapter One of his book it begins with this quote.

My, how far Yale has drifted, just as predicted. When Yale undergraduates set their sights next on 21st century white male writers to be abolished their own William F. Buckley, Jr. will be the first to go.

Oh, and for you leftists, you had better stop using the term alma mater, for it is a Christian era Latin term associated with the Virgin Mary; the one who gave birth to Jesus Christ having been impregnated by the Holy Spirit. *Alma* – nourishing, and *mater* – mother.

Anyway, why don't those undergraduates in English Lit at Yale University just be honest to the student body, and state what they really mean in their petition, which would go something like this, "it is unacceptable that a Yale student considering studying English literature might read only authors of Christendom. We no longer adhere to their belief system, and thus we want to read only modern authors that advocate left wing causes." Instead they use the smoke screen of reverse racism thinking that nobody can see through the lie.

FINALLY, SOME PEACE AND CALM

2016 was a tragic year in American history. 64 law enforcement officers were shot and killed, and many of them were revenge killings for the false narrative that was being propagated by the left that the "police were hunting down black men." What did people expect to happen when many Black Lives Matter supporters went into the streets all around the country in protest chanting "Pigs in a blanket, fry them like bacon!" Obviously, it wasn't everyone in the BLM movement, for there are many good people with good intentions in this organization, but there were enough radicals to be alarming, especially when Micah Xavier, an African-American, ambushed and killed five Dallas police officers, and wounded nine others on July 7, 2016.

Police were present at a peaceful march where people were protesting the police killings of Alton Sterling in Louisiana and Philando Castile in Minnesota; both men were African-American, and the shootings occurred within days of each other. Mr. Xavier was reportedly angry over these two police shootings and open fired on white police officers with an assault rifle and Glock 19 pistol in retribution. So well-armed was the suspect, not to mention being an Army Reserve Afghanistan War veteran, that the only way to end the standoff was for the police to send in a remote-control bomb disposal robot, that was armed with an explosive, and detonate it to cause fatal blast injuries.

President Obama called the Dallas shooting "a tragedy," and then jumped right into the need for more gun control. That was the problem - GUN VIOLENCE. Not the Obama administration for stoking the flames of racism, or people of all colors chanting "Pigs in a blanket, fry 'em like bacon!" but the weapons that seemed to have just jumped off the shelves and killed those five police officers. President Obama's speeches were not worded to heal a racially divided nation, and thus the Fraternal Order of Police, the largest police union in the United

States, made it known that they were not thrilled in the manner that the President handled it. On the other hand, Republican presidential candidate Donald Trump was saying what most people wanted to hear, and that was, "We must restore law and order." The American public was getting sick and tired of the lawlessness permeating throughout the country under Democratic rule. A lot of people backed Donald Trump for this reason, and this reason only. They wanted to feel safe again.

For seven months there had been no racial riots under the Trump Administration. The racial upheaval of the Obama administration had subsided. Law and order had been restored, and finally, there was some peace and calm. The only racial issues of the day were those brought up daily by the leftist media accusing President Trump of being a "racist," and that was because the United States Supreme Court agreed to allow President Trump's immigration travel ban on travelers from six predominantly Muslim countries to go into effect on June 26, 2017. The ban had been defeated before in the lower courts, but concerns for national security eventually won out. Plus, immigration enforcement along the southern border slowed illegal border crossings by 76%.

During these first seven months in office the President had to constantly debunk the racist accusations, which he had been doing ever since he was a presidential candidate stating, "I am the least racist person that you've ever encountered."

You've heard the old expression; *a picture is worth a thousand words*. Well, how about another homework assignment. Why don't you go to Google, and look up some of the images of Donald Trump rubbing elbows with African-American leaders and entertainers over the decades before he was the President: Donald Trump with Mike Tyson, Donald Trump with Jesse Jackson, Donald Trump with Don King, Donald Trump with Michael Jackson, Donald Trump with Al Sharpton, Donald Trump with Oprah Winfrey, and the list goes on, and on, and on. Nobody ever accused him of being a racist when he was a real estate mogul or hosted one of the most popular reality television shows in history. In fact, it was Reverend Jesse Jackson that praised Donald Trump in 1999 for helping the African-American community through Jackson's organization Rainbow/Push Coalition. Jesse Jackson is the same guy who visited communist Cuba in 1984 and stated, "Long live Castro! Long live Che Guevara! Long live Patrice Lumumba!" Fast forward to this supposed "racist" in the White House, President Donald Trump, and he selects Omarosa Manigault as the Director of Communications for the Office of Public Liaison. That's right, this black woman became a trusted advisor to the President of the United States.

"Oh, then she must be an Uncle Tom," the left would chide. Well, for your information she used to be a Democrat, up until 2015 anyway, and she even worked in the office of Al "Our world faces a true planetary emergency" Gore during the Clinton administration.

So, how do you go from being a liberal to a conservative? How does one change their worldview like that?

She turned to God, that's how. God was her priority.

CHARLOTTESVILLE RALLY

All had been calm on the "racism front" until the Unite the Right rally, also known as the Charlottesville rally, took place on August 11, 2017 in Charlottesville, Virginia.

It all started in March of 2016 when Charlottesville's vice Mayor, Dr. Wes Bellamy, requested that the statue of Confederate General Robert E. Lee in Emancipation Park be removed, and the park to be renamed Lee Park. He got his wish, and in June of 2016 the park was renamed, but the statue remained.

Dr. Bellamy is a former high school teacher, and he earned his Doctoral Degree at Virginia State University, thus he is a well-educated man. In 2017 Dr. Bellamy was serving as the president of the 100 Black Men of Central Virginia, with the organization's stated goal of "exploring ways the African-American (AA) males voice could be heard and respected in our school community," and also the Co-Chair of the Charlottesville Alliance for Black Male Achievement, with one of the principles being "the lives of Black boys and young men matter."

Now, I'm not implying anything based on Dr. Bellamy's race or associations, and from my research on him he seems to have done a lot of good for the youth of Charlottesville, but he had to have known that his suggestion of removing the statue was the equivalent of lighting a fuse. But, then again, maybe it was time for someone to speak up.

Mayor Mike Signer, a Caucasian who earned his Ph.D. in political science from the University of California at Berkeley, voted against the removal of the Robert E. Lee statue defending his position by saying, "I believe the Lee statue should remain as a reminder that many Americans were once treated as the property of others, then as second class-citizens." However, he later changed his position.

In February of 2017 the Charlottesville City Council voted to remove the General Robert E. Lee statue from Emancipation Park, a city park, where it had stood since 1924. This decision was very controversial from the get go. Many on the left labeled the Civil War General Lee as a "terrorist," "traitor," and a "racist," while many on right wanted the statue to remain in place to commemorate Virginia's history.

Instead of removing the statue immediately after the vote it just stood there, and as such it gave plenty of time for the opposition to organize and hold rallies at the foot of the statue. First was a "Take-Back Lee Park" rally on May 13, 2017, and then a Ku Klux Klan rally on July 8, 2017. There were 50 Klan members and 1,000 counterprotesters there. Fortunately, the rallies were nonviolent, but the writing was on the wall. Still a month later the statue stood. It stood there six months after the vote. Why?

The organizer of the Unite the Right received a city permit to hold a rally, and rally they did. White supremacists, white nationalists, neo-Nazis, neo-Confederates and a bunch of private militias showed up to protest the removal of the statue on August 11, 2017. Of course, this event was widely advertised, and so counterprotestors also showed up to the park. It was a who's who of leftist organizations: Black Lives Matter, Antifa, Democratic Socialists of America, the Revolutionary Communist Party, the Metropolitan Anarchist Coordinating Council, and others. This mix of groups was a recipe for disaster, which could have been avoided months earlier.

So, the obvious happened, and the two sides clashed with each other, and violently. 14 people were injured in the scuffles, and five were arrested. However, the police let the event continue. The next morning, August 12, 2017 the governor of Virginia, Terry McAuliffe, Democrat, declared a state of emergency. Seven months earlier this same governor announced legal action against President Trump's executive order on immigration (Aziz v. Trump et al.). Within the hour of the governor's order the police declared the assembly to be unlawful.

Two hours later a man who had been in the protest, on the side of the white supremacists, did a vehicle ramming attack against counterprotesters killing 32-year-old Heather Heyer, and injuring 19 others. Police arrested suspect James Fields, an Ohio resident, charging him with the murder of Heyer, and attempted murders of the others. If that was not bad enough, two police officers responding to the incident in a helicopter crashed, which killed them both.

Rally organizer Jason Kessler blamed law enforcement for the violence, because they did not keep the two sides separated from one another.

National Security Adviser H.R. McMaster labeled the act as an act of domestic terrorism, and later that night U.S. Attorney General Jeff Sessions opened a civil rights investigation. President Donald Trump had condemned the violence, but many on the left were outraged that he did not specifically name the right-wing groups. So, when he did just that, he named the groups involved, they said, "too little too late."

But, Trump is Trump, and he voiced what many on the right were thinking, and that is, "There are two sides to a story. I thought what took place was a horrible moment for the country, but there are two sides to a story."

Well, that statement really made the left go ballistic. They wanted to hear that it was entirely the fault of the right, and that the left had absolutely nothing to do with the friction. It seems that the radical left has the right to freedom of speech, but the radical right does not. On one hand it's okay to chant, "What do we want? Dead cops! When do we want it? Now!" but on the other hand it is not okay to wave the Confederate battle flag or the KKK cross in a legally demonstration.

The two stories President Trump was referring to were the radical groups on both sides; right and left. After all, it takes two to tango. "You had a group on one side that was bad, and you had a group on the other side that was also very violent. Nobody wants to say it, but I will say it right now," Trump added.

The result of this "outrage" by the left was that Democratic ruled city governments, and citizens alike, throughout the South wanted to take down all the Confederate statues. Such an event took place on August 14, 2017, two days after the Charlottesville incident, when a crowd of protestors in Durham, North Carolina gathered around a statue of a Confederate soldier that had the words IN MEMORY OF THE BOYS WHO WORE THE GRAY engraved upon the base.

Two white men ran up to the base of the statue with a long ladder, leaned it up against the tall monument, and 22-year-old Takiyah Thompson, a woman of color, shimmied up the ladder as a group of protesters below, predominantly white and black Millennials and Gen Zers, chanted, "You can't stop the revolution!" Then they went right into the chant, "No cops! No KKK! No fascists! USA!"

How did the cops get lumped into this group? Anyway…

One black guy had a professionally printed protest sign that read COPS & KLAN GO HAND IN HAND. Another sign read MAKE RACISTS AFRAID AGAIN. These were the exact same printed signs that were at the rally in Charlottesville. Hmmmm, Durham is 169 miles south of Charlottesville, and over a state line. Do you think that perhaps there were some "community organizers" coordinating these two events? Do you think some money was spent to print up all the signs and get people transported there?

Anyway, Thompson tossed a yellow strap around the head of the statue like a lasso. How she remained perched up there on the precarious thin ledge supporting her 200-pound frame, while both manipulating the thick strap and keeping from slipping, was quite an athletic feat. Once she climbed back down the ladder the crowd below pulled the loose end of the line like a tug-of-war until the statue toppled to the ground and instantly bent into a grotesque heap of metal.

Seconds later a few people broke from the jubilant semi-circle and started spitting on the deformed statue and kicking it.

The next day sheriff's deputies arrested Thompson along with three other activists: Dante Emmanuel Strobino, 35, Ngoc Loan Tran, 24, and Peter Gull Gilbert, 39. Obviously, they had all been traumatically scarred somehow by the Civil War that took place over 150 years ago, and took it out on the historical statue. That said, it wasn't hard to identify the culprits since videos of the event had been broadcasted by dozens of news outlets, as well as all over the Internet. In fact, through the videos taken at the event other participants were arrested, and an array of felony charges brought against them. In American we don't form mobs and tear down monuments. We go to the ballot box to change things. Well, at least that is how it used to work.

It was reported that members of The Black Youth 100 Project were not only present during the vandalism of this historical monument in Durham, but they handled the communications for many of those involved.

"So, who are they?" you ask. That's a good question. I had never heard of them either until I looked them up.

I'll let them answer for themselves. On their website, under the navigation button ABOUT, it states, *"BYP100 is an activist member-based organization of Black 18-35 year olds, dedicated to creating justice and freedom for all Black people. We do this through building a collective focused on transforming leadership development, direct action organization, advocacy and education using a Black queer feminist lens."*

What? "A Black queer feminist lens?" What is that? I thought the same thing.

If you go deeper into the site you'll find that on May 21, 2017 BYP100 "joined Ferguson Action and Black Lives Matter to put out a national call for actions to end state violence against All Black Women and Girls."

You can go to the BYP100 online store and buy your very own T-shirt, baseball cap, or stickers that have printed in big bold letters UNAPOLOGETICAL-LY BLACK.

Now, wait a minute here. Hold on buckaroo! Let me get this straight. A lot of people on the left were angry at the white supremacists at Charlottesville for their slogans and symbols, but it's perfectly okay for the left to have slogans equating the police to the KKK, having T-shirts with racial overtones, and waving around symbols of clenched black fists?

President Trump was right. "There are two sides to the story."

Of course, we conservatives know that for many on the left it was not merely about one-hundred-year-old statues that had remained unmolested during the Obama administration, and at least fourteen presidents before that. The distain for Confederate history was merely the small match to start the much larger forest fire – American history as a whole. For just hours after this ugly incident more Confederate monuments were being vandalized and removed by local governments in the dead of night, graffiti appeared on the Lincoln Memorial, and in Chicago a bust of Lincoln had been burned (the very President that defeated the Confederates and freed the slaves), and many on the left were calling for statues of President Thomas Jefferson, the principal author of the Declaration of Independence, to be taken down in the same disgraceful manner since he owned slaves. Some African-American leaders, like CNN's Angela Rey and civil rights activist Al Sharpon (yes, the very same man found in years of photos schmoozing pre-President Donald Trump), clearly stated that even the Jefferson Memorial in Washington, D.C. should come down. Remember, I spoke about this very same building when you were in Cell Block 2; the one with lots of references to the God of the Bible engraved on those sacred walls. Wow! You've learned a lot of things since then. Of course, Thomas Jefferson helped produce the very document for our *raison d'être*; our nation's reason for being.

So, what would the left like to replace the Jefferson Memorial with? The mob tearing down the Confederate soldier statue in Durham, North Carolina made it perfectly clear by the word they were chanting, "REVOLUTION!" Rising from the ashes would be the memorial to Democratic Socialism. There would probably be a big statue of Bernie Sanders, messy hair and all, in the center of the building with his wonderful quotes on the cool marble walls. The leftist admirers gazing upon it would get all teary eyed when they came to the panel reading, I AM CONFIDENT THAT THE VAST MAJORITY OF PEOPLE WILL UNDERSTAND THAT THERE IS NOTHING INCOMPATIBLE BETWEEN SOCIALISM AND DEMOCRACY.

Things were spinning out of control real fast.

President Donald Trump called it right when he said, "This week it's Robert E. Lee. I noticed that Stonewall Jackson is coming down. I wonder, is George Washington next week, and is it Thomas Jefferson the next after? You really do have to ask yourself; 'Where does it stop?'"

In response to the clashes between the left and the right Missouri State Senator Maria Chappelle-Nadal, an African-American Democrat, posted on her Facebook, "I really hate Trump. He's causing trauma and nightmares." But, what really got her into trouble on August 18, 2017 was writing, "I hope Trump is assassinated."

What? President Trump was causing the trauma and nightmares, and it had nothing to do with radical groups on the right and left coming face to face with a Democratic run police department failing to keep the two sides separated?

She joined the long line of other prominent people who had threatened our sitting President: singer Madonna, comedian Kathy Griffin (the one who held up a fake Donald Trump bloody severed head like an ISIS jihadist), actor Jonny Depp eluding to the assassination of President Abraham Lincoln by actor and Confederate sympathizer John Wilkes Booth. I guess the progressive left are truly "pro-choice," which seems to also apply to people who are out of the womb and running the country. Well, the sentiment seems to be that anyway. It's hypocrisy.

Well, senator Chappelle-Nadal promptly got a visit from the U.S. Secret Service, and many on the right called for her resignation. When she realized the hot water she was in she quickly retracted her statement.

Let me give you some free advice while you're in my camp. No matter what you think about a President, present or future, don't ever make a threat against him or her. Not only will you be investigated by the feds, but you can land yourself in prison. Better yet, respect the President no matter what his or her political affiliation may be. He or she is still the President of the country, and worthy of respect. You don't have to respect the person, but you do need to respect the office. The President, good or bad, popular or unpopular, represents the people of the United States of America. The Lord Jesus Christ once wisely said, "Give to Caesar the things of Caesar, and to God the things of God."

Now, I'm all in favor or removing all Nazi statues in the United States, and – What? There have never been Nazi statues in the United States of America erected in public squares or in the U.S. Capitol Building? Yes, you're absolute right. We've never, as a people, displayed a Nazi statue or monument. There has never been a U.S. military base named after a Nazi soldier that we fought against in North Africa and Europe? So, answer me this, "Why do we have neo-Nazis in America? If Confederate statues encourage right-wing wackos to commit acts of violence against people of color, then what statues and monuments are prompting the neo-Nazis to do the same?"

Duh! It's not the statues, but it's the hearts of people.

Now, when this whole tear-down-the-Confederate-statues thing went down I started asking a lot of my Republic friends what they thought about it, and most seem to agree that the Confederate statues mean nothing to them. After all, it was Democrats who erected these statues and monuments all across the South in the first place. That's right, for years white Democrats in leadership positions wanted the North to know that they had been physically beaten during the Civil War, but not their spirit. A common saying for almost a hundred years was, "The South will rise again!" Yet, the Union tolerated this rebellious spirit as long as it was never backed up by action, i.e. armed resistance.

Conservatives are not emotionally attached to the Confederate States of America. Take down the statues and put them in museums. That's fine. What we will not tolerate is going after prominent figures of the United States of America – the side that won the Civil War. Liberals are crossing the line when they think about touching statues and monuments of George Washington and Thomas Jefferson just because they owned slaves. We cannot overlay our modern culture like a template over theirs. Slavery had been a part of mankind's history for thousands of years. Yet, our founding fathers laid the foundation for slavery to be ended in the United States. George Washington privately expressed his belief that slavery had to be eventually ended. That didn't stop him from freeing his own slaves, but hey, he was slowly getting there. Thomas Jefferson penned the words *all men are created equal*. Okay, perhaps he did not believe that for the negroes, for in his day most men looked upon slaves as property, but his words are true none the less. The U.S. Declaration of Independence may have been signed by him, and other slave owners, but because their ideas were true the document has produced the freest nation in the world. To attack the documents of our founding fathers is to destroy the very foundation of this country, and what is it going to be replaced with? A Democratic Socialist declaration of independence and a new constitution. Nope! We conservatives are going to protect this part of our history. We're going to fight for the preservation of the foundational building blocks of this nation. Our President, government officials, judges, police, and military had better do it also, for they all gave an oath to protect the U.S. Constitution. Anyone of them who does otherwise should become private citizens and no longer remain a part of our government.

Now, when every last Confederate statue and monument is removed from the public square do you honestly think racism is going to stop in the United States? Well, it certainly will take away the anguish many African-Americans feel towards these reminders of the past, which is good, but it's never going to change evil hearts.

If I were to go around the country and ask liberals, "What is the worse "sin" that a person could do in America?" I'd get one of two answers. First, is "racism," and second is, "hate speech," which are synonymous in today's culture.

So, who decided that hating someone is wrong? You? Your parents? The government? If you know anything about history then you know that men have been hating each other since writing was invented. It's recorded for us. So, if we have been fighting and killing each other since time immemorial, then perhaps hating is just part of our nature; our DNA. Why would we attempt to change something that has always been?

Here's the answer. We Americans get the idea that hating someone or mistreating someone because of skin color or ethnicity is wrong based upon our history, our Judeo-Christian heritage, which has influenced Western civilization for over

2,000 years. Did not the Lord Jesus say, "Everyone who hates his brother is a murderer, and you know that eternal life does not reside in a murderer." 1 John 3:15

Murder is the worse crime one can do against another person according to the Bible, and there are plenty more scripture verses to back it up. It makes sense, doesn't it? If someone is not allowed to live any longer there is nothing left for them on this Earth: no more relationships, no work, no play, no eating, no...

Yet, among many liberals, murdering unborn babies because they may be inconvenient or murdering someone because their "quality of life" has been compromised due to age or illness is perfectly okay, but hating someone, oh my, that is the worst thing you can do. To Jesus hate and murder go hand in hand. It doesn't matter how you justify murder, just like one cannot justify hatred. There's no room for either. But, then again, it's all about one's worldview, isn't it?

There's a good book that you can order through Amazon called *Convicted: A Crooked Cop, and Innocent Man, and an Unlikely Journey of Forgiveness* and Friendship by Jameel McGee and Andrew Collins. It's about a black man and a white cop, both of whom clung to the stereotypes that their subcultures had taught them. However, when their worldviews changed, so did their hearts towards one another.

So, here is the solution to racism in our country. STOP BEING RACIST. Love your neighbor.

That's it. It's a simple solution. Everyone with any reason knows this to be true.

Let's go back to the weeks after the terrorist attacks of 9-11 in 2001. For weeks after the attacks there were commercials aired on television with many people of color saying just one thing, "I am an American."

The hyphen "-" was removed for a brief time in our history. It was refreshing not to hear African-American, Mexican-American, Native American, or whatever, just "American."

Always be leery of those people, regardless of their race, emphasizing the hyphens, and those who want to divide us, "US" as in the United States, based on race or ethnicity. You've heard it before, *we all bleed red*. It's perfectly fine to respect and appreciate one's cultural roots, but if it makes you think in terms of "us" and "them," and not *We the People*, then you have a real problem, and you are perpetuating the problem.

Before we leave the subject of racism now's a good time to give you a personal story, like I said that I would do from time to time. I am no stranger to racism. When I was stationed at Fort Benning, Georgia with the communications unit of the HHC 43rd Engineer Battalion (Combat, Heavy) I was the only white guy in the unit, and the rest were black. To my surprise a few of them wanted me out of the unit the moment I arrived. They even went to the sergeant to convince him to put in the transfer to get me out. He asked them, "Why do you want Private Wagner out?" Their answer was, "Because he's white." Well, my sergeant had no intention of stepping into that career ending trap, and he told them, "He stays! And, you better not mess with him."

The story has a happy ending. After a few months of living and working together all the guys in the unit came to like me, and I even learned how to speak jive to get along with them better. "Man, I be trippin at da crib after dat." So, because they could not get rid of me they decided to make me an "honorary black." I kid you not.

When I was working in South Africa there was a time or two that I could see the unmitigated hatred in some of the faces I came across simply because I was white, or they would spit on the ground the moment I walked past them making it obvious the discuss they had for white folk. Of course, in South Africa I really stood out in some neighborhoods. The people there didn't know that I was an American when walking around, and so they just assumed that I had once been on the side of Apartheid that had once suppressed them. A coworker, an Afrikaner (a white person of Dutch ancestry), and I came close to losing our lives one night in Johannesburg just because we were white. Yet, despite my very real experiences of racism against me I do not hold a whole race of people responsible for the actions of a few. I judge people by their merit, not because of their skin color.

TOXIC MASCULINITY

On one hand many on the left are proclaiming that "men and woman are equal," while others are saying that masculinity is "toxic." Toxic, meaning: idolizing male role models of the past, a need for dominance, hatred and mistreatment of women, a tendency towards violence, homophobia (yeah, one must always slip that one in there), and suppression of emotions. They say that such men have "lost touch with modern society."

On November 6, 2017 Professor Colleen Clemens of Kutztown University in Pennsylvania, yes academia once again, tweeted "Toxic masculinity is killing everyone. REPEAT. Toxic masculinity is killing everyone."

She posted this comment after 26-year-old Devin Patrick Kelly went inside the First Baptist Church in Sutherland Springs, Texas during a church service and murdered 25 people, and wounded 20 others with a semi-automatic rifle.

Professor Clemens is the Director of Women's and Gender Studies at the University. So, just imagine what kind of information she is filling people's minds with; especially young impressionable women. Talk about learning to hate men...

"Wait! I thought we were talking about racism? Why'd we jump to the topic of male-female relations?" you rightly inquire trying to mentally connect the dots.

Well, I'll tell you why. Professor George Ciccariello-Maher tweeted that "Trumpism" and "white victimization" was to blame for the mass murder shootings in Las Vegas just a month before the church shooting.

So, don't you see the connection? The dots are connected for you. Both shooters were male and white. Therefore, there can only be one solution, according to the left (although they don't come out and say it so directly), and that is strip all power, and masculinity, from white males. I guess we'd have to start with President Donald Trump first, and then Vice-President Mike Pence, and then on down the line it'd go. Have you noticed that Hollywood has been "masculizing" female action heroines more and more? They are just as powerful and warrior-like as their male counterparts: Lara Croft in Tomb Raider, Sarah Connor in Terminator, Trinity in The Matrix, Jordan in G.I. Jane, and the list goes on.

What exactly would America look like if only women were in power? Hmmmm, are there any examples of this in the world today? Ah, yes! Sweden. This country of almost 10 million people boasts of having the first "feminist government."

To start with, the Swedish feminist government was proud to pledge $600 million to replace money withdrawn by President Donald Trump when he withdrew from the Mexico City Policy, which is a policy for the international funding of abortions. Swedish Climate Minister Isabella Lovin of the Green Party even posed for a photo, with seven other female government officials, to mock the "male-dominated" Trump team that is pro-life, when signing the official document to fund the policy.

So, if we were to use Sweden as an example of what a feminist government would be like in America, it would be pro-abortion.

Let's look at another example. In 2017 several Swedish officials, all women, led by Trade Minister Ann Linde, paid a state visit to Tehran, Iran to sign several memorandums of understanding concerning trade between the two countries. Yet, every one of these European female officials chose to wear the traditional Muslim headscarf while they were in the Islamic Republic of Iran. Their reason for this show of "respect" in wearing the scarves was because not doing so "would have been illegal" in Iran. So much for being the champions of women's rights. Meanwhile at home Swedish society is unraveling with unprecedented sexual assaults against Swedish women; not by white males, but Muslim male immigrants, but the Swedish government labels anyone "racist" if they complain about this plight.

So, based upon this second example, a feminist government in America would be pro-abortion, capitulate to Sharia law, and label people as "racist" if they complain about the problems associated with Islamic immigration. Wait! That doesn't sound like a "feminist government to me," but it sounds exactly like the former Obama administration. It sounds like the majority now within the Democratic Party. Again, and when are you going to finally get it that people are people? You have good people, and you have bad people. How they govern is not based upon their race or gender. It's all about one's worldview.

The bottom line is that there is no such thing as "toxic masculinity." To feminize men, and to masculinize women is a social pipe dream that is only designed to erode traditional Western values. Pitting men against women, and women against men, is originally leftist propaganda, i.e. communism. We'll get a little deeper into this when we talk about Karl Marx. *Plus la change, plus c'est la même chose*. That's French for "The more the change, the more of the same thing."

Wow! That was some heavy stuff! But, here's the good news. You're stay in Cell Block 4 is over. Grab your stuff, because you're moving into Cell Block 5 now. Line up! Ass holes to belly buttons. Forward, march!

CELL BLOCK 5

LAW & ORDER

THE POLICE

Let me give you some insight into the mind of a cop, for I was a law enforcement officer for most of my adult life: a corrections officer, a street cop, a S.W.A.T. officer, a deputy sheriff, a federal agent, and a military police soldier for the last ten years of my exciting career. From my teens all the way up to my mid 50s I've been in the tactical community. That's why I'm the Master Sergeant in charge of your reeducation. I've been around the block a few times. Come to think of it, not just "around the block" here at home, but I've worked in a dozen countries around the world. These eyes have seen people laying in American streets bleeding to death from gunshot wounds, red communist flags waving in foreign streets, to street preachers proclaiming the Gospel on European street corners.

When I first heard the news about Officer Darren Wilson shooting 18-year-old Michael Brown on August 9, 2014, in Ferguson, Missouri I thought, "If the police officer shot this young man in cold blood then he needs to be punished to the full extent of the law." Most cops, like myself, hate crooked cops, along with those who get their thrills out of intimidating or hurting others. However, I did not form an opinion about the case when it first came out, because when the incident first happened not enough details had been released to the public to form an educated opinion. Call me old fashion, but I believe in the old adage, *innocent until proven guilty*.

When the story first broke nobody had heard the cop's side of the story, and CSI investigators were still examining the evidence. Whereas I withheld judgment until all the facts were made known, others did not. Protests began immediately by the ill-informed, which soon turned into riots.

Not only did years of police work prevent me from rushing to judgment, but also my conservative Christian-based worldview kept me level headed as well. I knew what Proverbs 18:17 states, and that is, "The person who tells one side of a story seems right, until someone else comes and asks questions." All the questions in Michael Brown's shooting had not been asked, nor answered.

Over the weeks and months concerning this case I heard the evidence, a piece at a time, presented by the news media, just like everyone else did, and then I finally formulated my opinion based upon my own professional training and experience. The race of the officer and the suspect was irrelevant in the shooting. I said to my family and friends when I had reached my conclusion, "Officer Wilson was justified using lethal force against Michael Brown." I got some pushback from some of the gullible people I spoke to, but I held my ground.

As I told you in Cell Block 4 the vindication of my professional opinion came when the Department of Justice came to the same conclusion that I had reached with the release of their official report, and they had all the facts, whereas I didn't. The shooting certainly wasn't racially motivated or else U.S. Attorney General Eric Holder, an African-American, who had initiated a federal investigation by the order of President Barak Obama, also a black man, would have been all over it. They were itching to give Brown's family "justice."

Oppps! Many people didn't care what the DOJ findings were. Why let facts get in the way? The final report did not fit the racially motivated agenda that was being propagated by many.

From the ashes of Ferguson rose the Black Lives Matter movement. At first BLM was a legitimate grassroots movement wanting nothing more than for the nation to take a good hard look into police violence against black men. They saw a possible problem, and they wanted it fixed. There's nothing wrong with that. However, all the reverse-racism, and the vile hatred for the police, pretty much destroyed their cause in most people's minds.

Well, interesting enough, all the supposed racism in this country that was starting to boil over, and all of the openly anti-police sentiment that was actually getting people hurt and killed, died down after Donald Trump was elected as the President of the United States; for seven months anyway. I wonder why? Could it be because the White House and the Department of Justice were no longer fanning the flames of discontentment? Could it be that Saul Alinsky's book *Rules for Radicals* was no longer the playbook by our top leaders that pitted the rich against the poor, the left against the right, or black against white? I don't know exactly why things calmed down, I just know that they did. Law and order had been restored, and the men and women whose job it was to make sure that it stayed that way was the police.

ANARCHY

Now, I know a lot of you Millennials and Gen Zers hate the police, but I have news for you – the police are here to stay. They're never going to go away. No government in their right mind ever disbands the police, and rational citizens wouldn't want that either.

People who murder cops are, let's face it, rather stupid beasts. When one cop goes down there is another one to replace him or her. It's not like a war of attrition, or where the public gets sick of the violence and disbands the police. Doing such would be anarchy if that ever happened, and anarchy does not last long anywhere in the world.

For those places that have experience true anarchy, such as the country of Somalia from 1991 to 2006, you end up with faction leaders, aka "warlords," controlling things. Essentially the vacuum is replaced by a different type of authority. The soldiers of warlords tend to be brutal thugs acting as the "police." Despite a few bad apples from time to time in police departments across America we have it pretty darn good with our professional law enforcement agencies compared to most of the world. I know, because I've worked with many police agencies in Third World countries.

You've seen the symbol before. I'm talking about the anarchy symbol. It's a circle with the oversized sloppy letter "A" inside. It's the universal symbol for anarchy, and for some reason many Millennials love to graffiti it all over things, much like the hippies (the counterculture activists) used to do by putting the peace symbol on everything in the 1960s and early 1970s. The hippies didn't last very long, just like anarchists won't last any longer. Like the hippies, eventually people grow up.

Do you want to know one of my fantasies I harbor inside of me? Probably not, but I'm going to tell you anyway, because it's relevant to your reeducation.

It started back when the country of Somalia, that's East Africa in case you don't know your geography, had no central government. It's also right around the same time that the American anarchist movement had begun. Now, here's the fantasy. I always thought that it would be a good idea to take a Millennial, a young man who was always advocating anarchy, and have a Black Ops team snatch him from his bedroom, which would have obviously been in his parent's house because he was freeloading off of them, and whisk him away in the darkness.

Blindfolded they drive this young anarchist to a military base in a nondescript white van, and then toss him onto a C130 cargo plane that's idling its engines on the tarmac of the airfield. I was in a C130 once on a mission, and they're big and roomy inside. Within 24 hours the C130 lands in Mogadishu, Somalia. The rear cargo ramp of the plane is lowered as the engines are still humming, and then the ski masked Special Forces soldiers would point the way out of the aircraft and say, "You wanted anarchy. Well, here it is. You finally get your wish kid. Enjoy."

The big fat olive drab green C130 plane would then fly off into the sunset, back to *the land of the free and the home of the brave.*

Of course, nobody in his or her right mind would ever want anarchy (the absence of government). Governments, whether bad or good, maintain order. Without government (essentially the keeper and enforcer of rules) we'd eventually go back to the medieval feudal system like Somalia did in modern times. That's a system where the strongest rule, and where you had better have a good militia to protect your territory and keep serfs (common folk) in line.

The truth is that those wishing for anarchy only wish it for themselves. They don't want true anarchy or they wouldn't be able to have their McDonald's burgers, their NIKE shoes, or listen to their downloaded music. The reason we have the nice things that we enjoy is because there are governments that protect trade, who enforce traffic laws so that people and goods can move about freely in an orderly fashion, and who have police officers to ensure that order – *To Protect and To Serve.*

So, the next time you see that oversized letter "A" in a circle scribbled on a wall or someone's jacket, you'll know now that the person who drew it was an ignoramus.

THE DEATH PENALTY

If a criminal deliberately killed a member of your family, and the criminal was arrested and had a fair trial, what do you think would be a reasonable punishment? Well, it depends on your worldview – like everything does. It also depends on if the emotional pain of the loss is limited to those you don't even know, or it's your own pain. It's easy to be philosophical about crime and punishment if you're not the one touched by it.

Many liberals believe that prison is a satisfactory punishment for premeditated murder. Several years behind bars is sufficient if the murderer is "rehabilitated." After all, isn't that what prison is supposed to be all about? Most liberals are against the death penalty.

Conservatives believe that a vicious murderer should be locked up for the rest of his or her life without parole, and a good percentage of them believe in capital punishment. That is to say, legally authorized execution. Death.

To date there are 31 states with the death penalty, and 19 without the death penalty. The United States of America is the only Western country currently with the death penalty on the law books. The methods of execution in all 31 states that still have it do so by means of lethal injection, and some states allow their death row inmates with an execution warrant to choose their method of execution: electrocution, gas inhalation, firing squad, or hanging.

The worldview, literally, the United Nations Assembly, has called for a global moratorium on abolishing executions. The sixth resolution (A/RES/71/187) was passed on December 19, 2016 with 117 countries voting in favor, 40 against (including the United States), and five were absent. So, essentially, those vicious criminals that murder in 117 countries have no fear of their lives being taken by the government. The worse punishment they'll get is to be sent to prison. The punishment is a lot better than what they did to their victims.

So, why is there an aversion to capital punishment. Well, in the Western world capital punishment is a Judeo-Christian concept, and you can be sure that anything found in the Bible many liberals will insist on having the opposite. Marriage between a man and woman – homosexuality. No sex before marriage – living together. Animals as a food source – veganism. Spanking naughty children – take their phone away. Respect for sovereignty of nations – open borders. In God We Trust – atheism, communism, and neo-paganism. Capital punishment for the most grievous crimes – prison.

Norway signed the European Convention on Human Rights banning capital punishment. Then came along 32-year-old Anders Behring Breivik.

Breivik, an extreme right-wing militant who wanted to rid Europe of all Muslims and Marxists, had planted a bomb in the center of Oslo on July 22, 2011 that killed 8 people and injured 209. The explosion had severely damaged the Office of the Prime Minister and Ministry of Justice and Police. He then took a small boat over to the island of Utøya where he knew that a Labour Party (social-democrat) youth camp was being held. Armed with a legally purchased semi-automatic carbine he murdered 69 people. The average age of his victims was 20-years-old. 57 of those he killed he had shot in the head once or twice. He had literally hunted people down on the island.

Breivik was sentenced to 21 years in prison. Many Norwegians were outraged at the lenient sentence. In fact, many called for the reinstatement of the death penalty for horrific crimes. Nope! The government wasn't going to budge despite 1 in 4 Norwegians support of the death penalty. Well, at least 1 in 4 Norwegians have a grasp of what justice is.

If you don't think that the death penalty is a deterrent to crime, just ask anyone who has been executed in the United States. What? They're dead? See, they are no longer committing crimes, and thus no longer a threat to society. It works.

Capital punishment is not revenge, it's justice.

From the very beginning, in the first book of the Bible, it states, "Whoever sheds man's blood, by man his blood shall be shed, for in the image of God He made man." Genesis 9:6

In the New Testament, Chapter 13 of Romans, it's all about obeying the authority of God, and the authority of human government. When talking about capital punishment verse 4 states, "for he (the government) is God's minister to you for good. But, if you do evil, be afraid; for he does not bear the sword in vain; for he is God's minister, and avenger, to execute wrath on him, who practices evil."

This "life for life" truth is not based on men's own standards of morality. Murder is forbidden, because every human is "made in the image of God." Murdering others is murdering God's image. That's it. End of the argument.

Since God instituted the death penalty there must also be a spiritual significance to it. Well, there is. The Bible makes it clear that "all have sinned," and "the punishment for sin is death," both physically and eternally. Every human being is on death row, literally. However, that was what the cross was all about. God himself, Yeshua the Messiah, was executed in your place on a Roman cross, the sacrificial animal that symbolized the Mosaic law, and all you have to do is accept His sacrifice on your behalf. Do so, and you walk free. Don't, then the death penalty. That is the Gospel in a nutshell.

Obviously, not all conservatives are Jewish or Christian, but many conservatives do believe in the death penalty. Nobody is in favor of "cruel and unusual punishments," and this is why it is enshrined in the U.S. Constitution. Execution should not be vengeful, but swift and as painless as possible. Death is the sentence, not suffering.

The reason we have the law "no cruel and unusual punishments inflicted," as stated in the 8th Amendment is because of founding fathers such as Thomas Paine. He, and the American colonists were all too aware of what cruel and unusual punishment looked like under British rule. Founding father Thomas Paine wrote in *Rights of Man* (1791), "In England the punishment in certain cases is by hanging, drawing, and quartering; the heart of the sufferer is cut out and held up to the view of the populace. In France, under the former Government, the punishments were not less barbarous. Who does not remember the execution of Damien, torn to pieces by horses? The effect of those cruel spectacles exhibited to the populace is to destroy tenderness or excite revenge; and by the base and false idea of governing men by terror; instead of reason, they become precedents. It is over the lowest class of mankind that government by terror is intended to operate, and it is on them that it operates to the worst effect."

Once again, we can thank our founding fathers, and even those Americans on death row right now can give thanks, for giving us a system that is even considerate of our most horrid citizens. Thank God, the majority of our founding fathers believed in the God of the Bible.

And, speaking of death, we're going to talk more about it in the next cell block you're going to.

Well? What are you waiting for? As in, NOW! Get your miserable self over there! No talking in line either!

CELL BLOCK 6

CULTURE OF DEATH

ABORTION

Abortion is the removal of a fetus (a developing human being or human being no longer developing) from its mother's womb through medical procedures. In the case of a living fetus the life is terminated.

Sometimes abortions are performed to save the life of a mother, but the vast majority of abortions around the world are performed because the baby is considered an inconvenience or is simply not wanted. Approximately 56 million abortions are performed worldwide each year. That's the entire population of South Korea, and then some, every year. In America the number of reported legal induced abortions a year is 664,435 according to the Centers for Disease Control and Prevention (CDC) statistics for 2013. Most of these abortions were done by women in their twenties, meaning mostly healthy women. So, to put it into perspective the number of abortions done in the United States each year is equivalent of terminating the lives of the entire state of Vermont. As of July 1, 2016 the population of Vermont was 624,594. Think about it. 664,435 human babies killed in their mother's wombs. Of course, those are just abstract numbers to most. But, consider this number, and that is the number 1. "1" represents you. You're blessed to have come into this world alive. Your number is in the plus column, and not in the negative column.

You've heard of President Ronald Reagan. Most Republicans still adore him. He's right up there with George Washington and Abraham Lincoln. Well, anyway, he made a very profound statement about abortion, "I've noticed that everyone who is for abortion has already been born."

Since 1973 the "right" for women to get abortions has been protected by federal law based upon the United States Supreme Court decision Roe v. Wade (pronounced roe-vee-wade). Most liberals want the law to remain, while most conservatives would like to see it overturned.

The people who support abortions call themselves "pro-choice," which means they believe a woman has "the choice" to terminate human life in the womb or not. It's her decision. Many people, mostly my generation unfortunately, the latter half of the Baby Boomers, who ironically started the Sexual Revolution (1960s to 1980s), don't even believe a fetus is a human life until *fetal viability*. That's a fancy term that means that a fetus has the ability to survive outside the uterus after birth, be it natural or induced. To put it in practical terms a baby has a viability of 50%, survival chance, at approximately 24 weeks, which is known as the Second trimester. On average childbirth happens at around 40 weeks (9 months), which is the Third trimester.

So, does that mean that at 23 weeks, 6 days, and 23 hours the fetus is not human, and only at the stroke of midnight does it suddenly become human? It would seem logical that most pro-choicers would take that position, but they don't. The truth is that most liberals can't seem to answer, or won't answer, the question of when human life actually begins inside the womb, and so the lack of a specific point in time allows the more radical pro-choicers to support abortions even into the Third trimester. In other words, right up until just before the baby is ready to exit the birth canal. As long as the baby does not see the light of day, or suck in its first breath of air, then it is perfectly acceptable to terminate its life. Presidential candidate Hillary Clinton defended the practice of partial-birth abortion during her final presidential debate on October 19, 2016 even though the practice has been illegal in the United States according to the Partial-Birth Abortion Ban Act of 2003. Fortunately, Hillary Clinton, and those who take the same shocking position, are the minority on the left. Most pro-choicers can't even stomach the thought of partial-birth abortion. Yet, the majority will still not definitively state exactly when the cells forming inside of the womb, which they say are nothing more than a glob of "fetal tissue," actually becomes human life. They refuse to take a firm position, because that would open up the possibility of placing more restrictions on abortions. As long as the cells are not human life, then it is not murder, or so the reasoning goes. But, once you call a fetus a human being, then it would be protected under law like any other American citizen. Not leaving through the birth canal would not strip him or her of their Constitutional rights.

I'm now going to explain the conservative's position on abortion in a round-about way.

Astronomers, those who study outer space, have been searching for life outside of Earth ever since space exploration began. During the Apollo moon missions (1969 – 1972) no evidence of life, nor even the slightest hint of it ever existing on the moon, was found there.

We then sent unmanned space probes to the planet Mars, lots of them, but no signs of life there also. The same thing goes for Venus.

Our deep space probes have not found life either. Voyager 1, launched on

September 5, 1977, is the farthest probe to date, now approximately 12 billion miles from the Sun in interstellar space, and it has recorded no signs of life. However, a meteorite may be the answer to the age-old question according to NASA (National Aeronautics and Space Administration).

A NASA research team co-led by Johnson Space Center scientists Dr. David McKay, Dr. Everett Gibson, and Kathie Thomas-Keprta of Lockheed-Martin, did research on a 4.2 meteorite called ALH84001 that they believe fell to Earth, and that originated from Mars. A pretty good guess considering there was no UPS shipping label on it. According to these scientists this rock has several mineral features that indicates life, along with "possible" microscopic fossils of bacteria-like organisms. Dr. McKay said, "There is not any one finding that leads us to believe that this is evidence of past life on Mars. Rather, it is a combination of many things that we have found." In other words, they are stretching their findings to prove that life once existed on Mars. Mind you, this rock was found on Earth, a planet teaming with life, and not brought back from Mars from some space probe.

So, here's the point. Scientists get so jubilant at just the possibility of discovering life-sustaining water on other planets or far away moons, and they're even willing to pin their hopes of life having existed on other worlds because of a rock they found in 1984 in the Allan Hills ice field of Antarctica, but many pro-choice scientists and abortion doctors fail to define a fetus as a life. It's ironic that some scientists are spending countless time and money trying to find any type of life they possibly can outside of our planet, even if it is bacteria, while others define a developing human being, the most dominant life form on Earth, as nothing more than "tissue matter."

Now, I live in the State of California, and as I told you before, I was a cop there. California Penal Code Section 187 is the section for murder. Section (a) states, "Murder is the unlawful killing of a human being, or a fetus, with malice aforethought." So, in California a fetus is considered a person. You kill it, and you're going to prison for a long time. But, here's the catch, sections (b) subsections (1), (2), (3) says that killing that fetus through an abortion is perfectly legal.

Yeah, it's political, what did you think it was? Scientific?

Most conservatives, especially those who believe in the God of the Bible, believe that life begins at conception. Not only is it obvious that a new life has been created from a scientific perspective, but the Bible states emphatically that life, the soul, begins before physical life begins.

When God was talking to Jeremiah, who was a prophet during the Babylonian rule around 626 BC, He said to him,

Before I formed you in the womb I knew you, before you were born I set you apart; I appointed you as a prophet to the nations. Jeremiah 1:5

Those who believe in protecting babies in the womb call themselves "pro-life." The term says it all. The opposite stance would suggest "pro-death." If you really want to know the mind of most conservatives, it's quite simple. They believe abortion is, except in saving the life of the mother, flat out murder.

American society's accepted definition of murder is the *unlawful premeditated killing of one human being by another*. There's the key word "unlawful." Although abortion is the law of the land, because of Roe v. Wade as we discussed earlier, conservatives view this law no differently than when Nazi Germany made the murder of Jews legal in occupied Europe, and exterminated six million of them. Just because the law supports something doesn't always mean it's right.

Now, like I said before, not every Republican is pro-life. There are some who believe abortion is justified in the cases of rape or if the child is going to be born retarded or deformed.

I can sympathize with the rape victim, but in my opinion two wrongs don't make a right, and I'm not alone with this opinion. I've got a lot of support of the evangelical community, which you'd consider them to be the "extreme right."

In the case of retarded or deformed babies many doctors have been known to make mistakes diagnosing complications only for a perfectly healthy baby to be born. Even if a diagnosis is spot on the moral question is, "Does it give anyone the right to terminate a life?"

A good case in point is Nick Vujicic, an Australian, born in 1982. He was born with two small and deformed feet just underneath his hips, and no arms due to Tetra-amelia syndrome. However, despite his severe handicap he earned a Bachelor of Commerce degree with a double major in accountancy and financial planning, and went on to become a well-known motivational speaker. To top it off he formed the ministry Life Without Limbs that has helped the lives of others. Ask Nick if he wished he would have been aborted, and you'll get the answer that tens of millions will never be able to answer.

On the flip side there are many people with or without abnormalities who wished they had never been born, but the final question is, "What gives anyone the right to play God in the taking a human life, no matter what the stage of development inside the womb?"

Once again, a worldview based upon the belief of a righteous God prevents a great number of women from having an abortion or they become repentant after having one. According to the Bible, which millions of conservatives believe in, abortion is murder. Yet, according to the same Holy Bible there is no sin that cannot be forgiven by God except blasphemy against the Holy Spirit. Jesus said in Matthew 12:31

Therefore I say to you, every sin and blasphemy will be forgiven men (meaning mankind), but the blasphemy against the Spirit will not be forgiven men.

In other words, rejecting God, and His plan of salvation that came through the price that was paid on the cross, will not be forgiven. Theft will be forgiven, drunkenness will be forgiven, lying will be forgiven, and even an abortion will be forgiven if earnestly asked of God, but rejecting the Holy Spirit to come into you, *Behold, I stand at the door and knock. If anyone hears my voice and opens the door, I will come into him (her) and eat with him (her), and he (she) with Me, will not be forgiven.* Yeah, I know, it sounds harsh, and even very narrow, but I didn't say it. God said it through His Word, the Bible:

Enter through the narrow gate. For wide is the gate and broad is the way that leads to destruction, and many enter through it. But small is the gate and narrow the way that leads to life, and only a few find it. Matthew 7:14

So, yes, you're absolutely correct. Christians are very narrow-minded. No doubt about that. And, since much of American conservatism is based upon Judaism and Christianity it stands to reason that many conservatives are indeed very "narrow" when it comes to abortion.

For me personally abortion is not an abstract subject. My unwed mother at 14-years-old got pregnant with me, which was a big taboo back in the early 1960s in the South, even though the country was already a year into the Sexual Revolution by this time. My grandmother, on my mother's side, suggested, at first, that my mom get an abortion. My mother, who had no intention of marrying or staying with my father, refused to get an abortion, and the obvious result of doing nothing, and allowing nature to take its course, was me. Despite the initial advice of my grandmother, once I was born she doted over me for the rest of her life. I brought joy into her life, and she in mine.

In those days, around the time I was born, there was no simplistic chant, "It's a woman's right to choose!" My mother just knew in her heart of hearts that aborting her baby was morally reprehensible. I certainly wasn't given any say in the matter, for if I had I would have definitely protested, "Forget it grandma! I want to live! I don't care if mommy is too young. You had your chance at life, and I want the same. If it turns out mommy doesn't want me, then she can give me to someone that does, but this killing me thing – no way! Now, back off!"

Once my mother stood up to my grandmother I was safe and sound.

BACK ALLY ABORTIONS

"Back ally abortions" or "coat hanger abortions" are terms used today by pro-choice advocates in describing what will happen if the conservatives are successful in overturning Roe v. Wade thereby making most abortions illegal. So, why do many liberals use these two disturbing terms? Let's take a look.

With the advent of modern medicine it was acceptable to take the life of a fetus if the mother's life was in danger. That makes sense since both lives would perish if the procedure were not done, and we're only talking about a fetus that could not live on its own outside of the womb. For if he or she could survive outside of the womb a C-section could be done – duh!

Back alley abortions refer to a time in American history when most abortions were illegal. They were for unwanted pregnancies, and not for a mother's health. It was a common practice among prostitutes. Of course, they were never done in "back allies" as the term would imply, but the term is used for shock value. Our ancestors weren't that stupid to do abortions in filthy unsterile back allies with potentially tissue piercing metal coat hangers. The term also assumes that pimps or unscrupulous midwives with no medical training did this shady procedure. Of course, if one were to insert a straightened hanger rod into a woman's uterus there is danger of tearing, infection, internal bleeding, and death. It sounds so barbaric, doesn't it? The term "back ally abortions" is meant to sound that way.

Just supposing that there were once back alley abortions, the question then becomes, "When did they end?" Pro-choicers claim, "Right after Roe v. Wade." Therefore, they're terrified that the conservatives, who are now in power over-all, are going to overturn Roe v. Wade and millions of women are going to be forced to go into those dirty allies again. Is this something that they should fear? The answer is, yes. Is President Donald Trump leading the charge against abortion? Again, yes.

On January 23, 2017, only four days in office, and the day after the 44th anniversary of the Roe v. Wade Supreme Court ruling, President Trump signed an executive order that blocked foreign aid and federal funding, known as the Mexico City policy, for international nongovernmental organization that provide or promote abortions. I mentioned this to you before. White House Press Secretary Sean Spicer told reporters at his first briefing that day, "I think the president, it's no secret, has made it very clear that he's a pro-life president, and

I think the reinstatement of this policy is not just something that echoes that value, but respects tax payer funding as well, and ensures that we're standing up not just for life of the unborn, but also taxpayer funds that are being spent overseas to perform an action that is contrary to the values of this president."

President Donald Trump, the smart businessman that he is, doesn't want abortion to be used as a form of birth control. Not around the world, and especially not in the United States of America. First of all, it is immoral, and second of all it eliminates our country's greatest resource – human labor and ingenuity.

Right now, countries like Germany, France, Australia, and other Western countries are crying that their populations are dwindling, and that foreign immigrants are swelling the ranks to sustain the labor force. Well, maybe if their youth would stop having so many abortions the populations could replenish itself. A case in point is the country of Spain.

In February of 2017 Spain appointed Edelmira Barreira as the country's first Minister of Sex to encourage Spaniards to produce more babies, because they are faced with a population crisis. There were fewer births in 2016 than deaths among Spanish. The number of childless couples has tripled from 1.5 million in 1977 to 4.4 million in 2015. Some experts blame the lack of "baby making" on long working hours, and a culture that eats late at night, but nobody is pointing out the obvious – birth control and abortion. In 2015 Spain had 417,265 live births and 90,800 reported abortions. In ten years there has been 1,759,693 babies aborted. Now, add all of the other European nations having the same problem, and naturally there's going to be major cultural shifts in the near future throughout all of Europe. In 2014 Spain let in 305,500 immigrants, and those people are having babies, lots of babies. But, that's Europe's problem, let's get back to America.

When American mothers abort over half a million babies a year they are essentially eliminating over half a million future taxpayers a year. Gone forever from this possible pool of human resource are soldiers, doctors, nurses, school teachers, farmers, fork lift operators, and every career imaginable. Granted, some of them would have been criminals, blind, deformed, mentally challenged, but so what. Nobody can predict a person's destiny.

"Oh, but there are too many people on the Earth as it is," says many "green" pro-choicers. "It's better that there are less people than more," and so they see abortion as another way to protect the environment. This reasoning is greatly flawed. The Earth can support many more billions than we currently have on it. We have plenty of resources, and most of the land mass is uninhabited. Have you ever flown over the United States from coast to coast? There's a lot of space for potential new towns, cities, green houses, desert farming, and desalination plants to pump water where it is needed. The problem is not the number of people on the planet, but it's the tendency for populations to concentrate, corrupt governments, greed, wars, and other socially complex causes that prevent humanity from all working together.

If we Americans would stop butchering our unborn babies, have them, and raise them to both love and contribute to American exceptionalism we could "Make America Great Again" for the next generation as well.

WOMEN'S MARCH

HYPOCRITES! That's what most American feminists are. I'll give you the most blaring example, and you decide for yourself.

The day after President Donald Trump's inauguration there was the Women's March on Washington, but it was actually all across the country on January 21, 2017. The purpose of the march was to be an "all inclusive" march for every woman regardless of her race, ethnicity, religion, immigration status, sexual identity, gender expression, economic status, age or disability. The organizers wanted to send a clear message to the new president that "women's rights are human rights" according to their official website. Yeap, I read it myself. However, when pro-life women tried to register for the march, and yes there are pro-life feminists and anti-Trump conservatives, Women's March on Washington refused to include them. Apparently, one had to be a supporter of abortion to march against President Donald Trump.

As it turned out, just by looking at the signs and banners women were carrying on the day of the event, the Women's March was mostly about women wanting to keep Roe v. Wade. The unifying cry, and I am paraphrasing, "Let us keep killing babies in the womb! It's our human right." Apparently, this human right does not apply to the unborn human babies. Yes, I'll state it again, H-Y-P-O-C-R-I-T-E-S!

However, I must give Women's March some credit. After the march, the organization did make it clear on their website that they are not inclusive of all women. Under the drop menu + MY BODY, MY RIGHTS they wrote, "Access to reproductive health care is a basic right for over half the population to care for their bodies. Tell your member of Congress **we will not go back** to a time when the government made decisions about women's reproductive futures and limited our access to birth control, STD testing and lifesaving, preventive cancer screenings. Our partner **Planned Parenthood** has resources to help you brush up on the facts." Oh, and they are the ones who put certain words in this paragraph in bold print, not me.

What's interesting, if you dig a litter deeper on the Women's March website, is that it is much more than about "reproductive rights." The other causes they are supporting are, and I'll let the drop menu headlines speak for themselves: +PRO-TECTING IMMIGRANTS, + PROTECTING THE LGBTQIA COMMUNITY, + WE NEED HEALTHCARE, and + REDUCING GUN VIOLENCE.

Hmmmm, this sounds awfully familiar. On the BLACK LIVES MATTER website, under the headline *What We Believe* their sub headlines read GLO-BALISM, TRANSGENDER AFFIRMING, DIVERSITY, QUEER AFFIRM-ING, and, oh yes, some black causes are also included in there. The one that caught my attention was BLACK VILLAGES. It read, "We are committed to disrupting the Western-prescribed nuclear family structure requirement by sup-porting each other as extended families and 'villages' that collectively care for one another, and especially 'our' children to the degree that mothers, parents and children are comfortable."

Didn't we go over this before? Didn't Adolf Hitler want the same thing by creating the Hitler Youth? Isn't this what communists did in the former Soviet Union? Isn't this what Hillary Rodham Clinton hints at in her book *It Takes A Village*? There's that word again, "village." Whenever you hear that word again a red flag should pop up in your mind. It just so happens that many communist flags are red: the former Soviet Union's flag, today's mainland Chinese flag, the Vietnamese flag, et cetera. The plain red flag is often waved at socialist or communist rallies in America.

Well, if the Women's March on Washington was not enough, New York Gov-ernor Andrew Cuomo, on the same day, announced that he was requiring health insurance companies to cover medically necessary abortions and most forms of contraception for women FOR FREE.

So, let's get this straight. In the State of New York not only is the choice of taking the life of the unborn a supposed "human right," for the mother anyway, but state and federal governments should pay for it as well – with our tax dol-lars? Why are no other medical procedures absolutely free, like the treatment of cancer, coronary artery disease, or diabetes? Why does everything have to be free when it only comes to "reproduction rights?"

Of course, we have to back up a little bit and ask the question, "How are all of these women getting pregnant in the first place that would call for an abor-tion?" The majority of them are certainly not because of rape, and only a tiny percentage of pregnancies actually put a mother's life in jeopardy. Therefore, the vast majority of abortions must be a form of birth control. It has to be. At least Governor Cuomo got the chronological order correct. First give away the free contraceptives to prevent the births, and then if a woman gets pregnant it's time for a free abortion, if she chooses to get one. Of course, the sacrificing of babies after sex is nothing new in history.

Three thousand years ago the ancient Canaanites in the land of Canaan, which today is the land of Israel, sacrificed some of their babies, but they were much more honest as to why they were doing it than our society is. They did it for the Canaanite god Moloch.

Since having abortions in ancient times was too dangerous the women carried their babies to term. When the unwanted baby was born the priests set a bonfire under their god Moloch, who was made of metal, until his outstretched arms were red-hot. After a religious chant or two they'd place the live baby into the searing outstretched cradling arms and hands. The screams of the baby only lasted mere seconds, and then the deed was done. After the fire had gone out the priests would take the charred little body and place it in an urn. The urn was taken home and buried under the front doorstep of the home to assure prosperity for the mother and other members of the household. Some nearby cultures buried the urns inside the stone walls. This sounds exactly like some women's reason for having abortions today, does it not? "I'm too young to have a child," or "Having a baby is going to interfere with my education or career." After all, a child can hold one back from having fun and prosperity. I'll sacrifice him or her, and move on with my life.

In the Old Testament, in the book of Leviticus, God warned his people the Israelites "And you shall not let any of your seed (babies) pass through the fire to Moloch, neither shall you profane the name of your God: I am the Lord." Leviticus 18:21

Later in Jewish history we find that the moon goddess of the Phoenicians, Ashtoreth, was also another temptation to God's people. This goddess was connected to fertility, sexuality, and power. God warned his people about worshiping her as well.

They rejected His statutes (rules) and His covenant (contract), which He made with their fathers and His warnings, which He warned them. And they followed vanity and became vain, and went after the nations, which surrounded them, concerning which the Lord had commanded them not to do like them. They forsook all the commandments of the Lord their God and made for themselves molten images, even two calves, and made an Asherah (another name for Ashtoreth) and worshiped all the host of heaven (astrology) and served Baal (another Phoenician god associated with fertility along with the weather). Then they made their sons and daughters (babies) pass through the fire, and practiced divination and enchantments (witchcraft), and sold themselves to do evil in the sight of the Lord, provoking Him. 2 Kings 17:16

I find it interesting, and so should you, that some ancient cultures killed their unwanted babies by burning them with fire, and since 1934 many instillation abortions had been done by injecting a chemical solution into the amniotic sac to burn the fetus to death. Of course, burning babies inside the womb posed a lot of complications in this country, and so the most common method today is surgical abortion, either by vacuum aspiration, which is literally sucking the fetus out, or Dilation and Curettage (D&C), which is done by inserting a loop shaped surgical instrument to cut the baby into pieces and scrape the uterine wall. The body parts are then removed from the womb.

Not only did many people in the ancient Holy Land embrace the deity Ashtoreth, but she was also the same goddess of the Assyrians and Babylonians known as Ishtar. Pornography is nothing new in history, and her image has been found throughout the Middle East going back as early as 1300 B.C. She is always depicted completely naked cupping her breasts or having her arms held out to welcome the horny worshipper. The planet Venus is dedicated to this goddess.

Believe it or not you are exposed to the influence of Ishtar every spring in the United States. Did you ever wonder why Easter eggs and the bunny rabbit are symbols of Easter? They are certainly not Christian symbols, although they have seeped back into the day of remembrance of the resurrection of Jesus Christ. These pagan symbols go all the way back to Ishtar in Mesopotamia. The rabbit is a symbol of fertility, as in *breed like rabbits*, and the eggs represent renewal, as they do in the ancient cultures of Egypt, Armenia, India, Persia, China, and Europe. During the days of the Roman Empire the early Christians overlaid their holidays over some existing holidays in an attempt to eradicate the old pagan practices. Although Jesus the Christ was not really born on December 25th, the early Christians chose this day to celebrate the birth of the Messiah to turn the Roman Winter Solstice, which was proceeded by the Dies Natalis Solis Invicti, *birthday of the unconquered sun*, into a celebration of God coming to earth in the flesh; to become "one of us." On the other hand, Easter is a Christian holiday based upon the actual date of Jesus' crucifixion. The early Christians called this celebration Pascha, both in Greek and Latin, but in Old English it is eastre, which is derived from the ancient German word ostern. The ancient Germanic people worshiped the goddess Ostara, which was the celebration of spring.

Anyway, the Mesopotamian goddess Ishtar is also the Greek goddess Aphrodite, who in turn is the Roman goddess Venus, and what she stands for has not changed over time: sex, fertility, prosperity, and victory. That's right, she is also related to war. In both of these ancient cultures this goddess is depicted naked.

So, once again, it's all about one's worldview that determines one's position on abortion, and sex for that matter, for it is sex that produces babies.

Let me give you one more thing to think about that you'd never get in a public school. The Holy Bible, both the Old and New Testament, states that God loves children, and He is concerned about their welfare.

In the Old Testament God told his prophet Jonah (786-746 B.C.) that he was fed up with the sins of Nineveh, the capital of the Assyria (today's Iraq), and that He was going to wipe them out if they didn't repent. He wanted Jonah to relay that message to them, but Jonah couldn't stand these people, "for they were the enemies of his land, the land of Israel. He wished Nineveh to die in its sins, and not to turn to God and live."

The mission God gave to Jonah was like having someone go into ISIS held territory when they were at their greatest and telling them to change their murderous ways, or a God that they didn't even know was going to destroy them.

Even though Jonah went the opposite way, to avoid doing what God had ordered him to do, God eventually turned him around through a most unconventional way, and Jonah ended up preaching to the people of Nineveh, "Forty more days and Nineveh will be overthrown."

Right after completing his mission Jonah went out just east of the city, sat down under some shade from a plant, and waited to see what would happen to the city. He was hoping that the population would not repent, and that God's judgment would fall upon his enemies. He wanted a front row seat to see the destruction. However, God knew what Jonah was thinking, and he rebuked him by saying, "And should I not have concern for the great city of Nineveh, in which there are more than a hundred and twenty thousand people who cannot tell their right hand from their left, as well as many animals?"

The people God was talking about, the 120,000 people who "cannot tell their right hand from their left," were infants. To top it off, God let Jonah know that He was also concerned about the domestic animals as well. After all, they were His creatures too. The bigger picture was that God was concerned about all the people in the city, from the mightiest of them to the least of them, but He just needed to tug at Jonah's heartstrings by using the children and animals to draw out his compassion.

As the story goes, the people of Nineveh did repent of their sins, and God spared the city from destruction. Unfortunately, the book of Nahum prophesied that God would bring an end to the Assyrian empire; a future generation after Jonah, and in 612 B.C. history records just that. The Babylonians conquered

Assyria, and the capital of Nineveh fell. You should remember this, because it's also world history.

In the New Testament, around the year 30 A.D. something, Jesus' disciples were trying to prevent some children from seeing him, and when Jesus discovered what was happening He rebuked them saying, "Let the little children come to Me, and do not hinder them! For the kingdom of heaven belongs to such as these."

Jesus was so compassionate about children that he stated, "It would be better for him (or her) to have a millstone (a carved rock weighting approximately 1,500 pounds or 680 kilos) hung around his (or her) neck and be thrown into the sea than to cause one of these little ones to stumble (to lose their faith in God)." Luke 17:1

If the Bible is indeed the Word of God then how terrible it's going to be for a school teacher or an atheist that has turned a child's heart away from God. On the other hand, if the Bible is not really God's Word, then, oh well, it doesn't matter. Nothing is going to happen. I guess we'll all find out when we die, won't we.

For your reeducation, and you really must learn this one, because it's a test question, the Bible quote most often quoted by conservative Christians in condemning abortion is from Psalm 139:13. It reads, "For you formed my inward parts; You wove me in my mother's womb. I will give thanks to You, for I am fearfully and wonderfully made." This Psalm is attributed to King David, and it was written sometime between 1010-970 B.C. Beyond just giving thanks for his own life in the womb, it takes on even greater importance, because Yeshua, (Jesus) the Messiah (the Christ), was King David's descendant. The birth of King David eventually led to the birth of the greatest person in history, and in Cell Block 2 I gave you all the reasons why He was great: our calendar, laws, the concept of freedom, gift giving at Christmas, the beginning of women's rights, et cetera.

Most Bible believing Christians believe that life begins at conception, and that God places the soul of an individual into that first cell that is formed at the moment of conception. I say "most Christians," because there are some who call themselves "Christian" or "Catholic," but they cherry pick the scriptures they choose to accept, and they ignore the ones they don't like or don't want to follow. Therefore, some "Christians" are okay with abortion. I'm certainly not.

So that you are fully aware of the stance of the current Republican federal administration, and what you are going to be going up against if you slip back into your liberal way of thinking after your reeducation camp experience, here are two of the most significant events that took place within the first 100 days of the Trump administration concerning abortions.

The first significant event took place on January 23, 2017 when President Trump signed an executive order reinstating the so-called Mexico City policy, established by President Ronald Reagan in 1984, that blocks any federal funding for international family planning charities that promote or provide abortions. Since President Reagan all Republican presidents have reinstated this policy, while all Democratic presidents rescinded the policy. In other words, Republican presidents = pro-life and Democrat presidents = pro-choice. If Hillary Clinton had been elected POTUS our tax dollars would have paid for the abortions of foreigners.

Apparently, the culture of death has no bounds. On February 22, 2017 a Dutch ship, run by the Women on Waves, was detained by the Guatemala military and pulled into the port of Quetzal in San Jose. The vessel travels all over the world and offers free abortions where abortions are illegal, and the country of Guatemala, a predominantly Catholic country, is one of them. The medical crew aboard the vessel brings women who are up to 10 weeks pregnant from the shore to internationals waters so that they do not technically break any laws of a country. However, the president of Guatemala himself ordered the military to detain the ship, and the official statement by the army to justify their actions was for "defending human life and the laws of our country." But, according to spokeswoman Leticia Zevich, "We respect religious beliefs, but this [abortion] is a fundamental right in a democracy."

The second significant pro-life event that took place was held on January 27, 2017, and that was the 43rd Annual March for Life in Washington, D.C. Before the throngs of people started marching at this historic event Vice President Mike Pence kicked things off with a moving speech. In front of the Washington Monument he stated, "Life is winning in America, and today is a celebration in that progress. We've come to a historic moment in the cause of life, and we must approach it with compassion for every American. Life is winning in America, because of you." Then he finished with the words you'd never hear from the left, "Let this movement be known for love, not anger. For compassion, not confrontation." Other speakers included President Trumps' key adviser Kellyanne Conway, Cardinal Timothy Dolan, and Senator Jodi Ernst (Republican); a former lieutenant colonel in the Iowa Army National Guard, and the first female veteran to serve in the United States Senate. She's also a lifetime member of the National Rifle Association, and a member of the Mamrelund Lutheran Church in Stanton.

On September 6, 2017 President Donald Trump went a step further and even rolled back the Obama Care contraceptive mandate that forced all employers to provide health care insurance that covered contraceptives. You may not remember this, but in 2013 the Obama administration stated that religious-affiliated organizations opposing contraception would be able to opt out of the federal mandate. When I first heard it, I didn't believe a word of it. After all, it was coming from the same mouth that said, over and over, "If you like your health care plan, you can keep it," which was distinguished by Politifact as the "Lie of the Year." Just like I never believe the left when they plead, "We just want more thorough background checks for firearms."

Well, it did not take long for history to prove me right. Once the mandate went into effect the federal government changed their mind, *oh well, screw the Christians*, and demanded that all employers had to provide insurance that would cover contraceptives, and that included the Catholic organization Little Sisters of the Poor and Hobby Lobby who fought against it. In fact, over 200 entities brought lawsuits against the government because of the contraceptive rule, most of them faith-based. Fortunately, the Little Sisters and Hobby Lobby won their case in the U.S. Supreme Court on March 16, 2016. President Trump made sure companies and organizations did not have to provide this coverage if they had a "religious or moral objection." Of course, the American Civil Liberties Union filed a lawsuit and Planned Parenthood accused the White House of attacking women's rights.

Strange, I don't recall the "right to contraceptives" found anywhere in the U.S. Constitution. Who said this was a right? Oh, I know, it was the United Nations Human Rights Office of the High Commissioner that states it is discrimination if women are denied their "sexual and reproductive health rights." Yet, Uncle Sam is not preventing women, or men, from going to the drug store and buying contraceptives. The real issue is about money – tax payers forking over the money. On the Planned Parenthood website, under *How much do birth control pills cost?* It states, "They're totally free with most health insurance plans or if you qualify for some government programs."

There's no such thing as a free lunch. Somebody pays for it.

EUTHANASIA

This strange word, pronounced yooth-an-asia, is a Greek word that means "good death." Another way to put it would be "mercy killing." It's the deliberate killing of a person who is suffering from an incurable disease or believed to be in an irreversible coma.

There are, of course, two types of euthanasia. The first is voluntary euthanasia, such as a patient giving medical professionals consent to end his or her life, and the other is involuntary euthanasia; not giving consent, which in all countries to-day is considered murder. You've probably already guessed where we are going to go with this subject, and you're right. How one views mercy killing is based entirely upon one's worldview.

Most conservatives, especially those adhering to Judeo-Christian beliefs, find euthanasia morally and ethically wrong, even if performed by trained medical technicians. Not surprisingly these same conservatives are usually pro-life. Just as they defend the lives of the unborn they also argue for the sanctity of life even if someone is old, terminally ill, handicapped, or in a prolonged coma believing that only God Himself has the right to give and take a life.

Since this word comes from the Greek language naturally euthanasia is noth-ing new. You Millennials and Gen Zers always seem to think you are stumbling onto something new, that you're somehow original, and that we old farts are hanging onto our antiquated moral codes and traditions. But there's nothing new under the sun. Ancient Greek philosophers Socrates and Plato supported mercy killing. Hmmmm, how long ago was that? How about 470 B.C. to 347 B.C., but as Christianity spread throughout the world so did the condemnation of euthanasia.

It wasn't until the Gilded Age, between the 1870s to about 1900, in the United States that people started to float the old idea again of euthanasia. This was a time of the industrial age, rapid economic growth, urbanization, and the start of the modern hospital system.

The man credited for first suggesting that euthanasia be practiced in the United States was Robert "Bob" Ingersoll (1833-1899) who lived up to his nickname "The Great Agnostic." Agnostic is a nice sounding word for ignoramus. Al-though raised in a Christian home by a father who was a preacher, he eventually saw himself as an enemy of Christianity starting from a very early age. Quite an interesting man, Bob Ingersoll had been a Confederate colonel during the American Civil War who later went on to serve as the Illinois Attorney General. He was a staunch Republican, but he could never move up any higher on the po-litical ladder due to his agnostic views. He therefore gave many speeches about humanism (believing in man instead of a god), and attacked Christian doctrine.

Because Robert Ingersoll was a brilliant man, and considered "the nation's or-ator" ("motivational speaker" in today's vernacular), he influenced many in his time, and his views are repeated even today: secularism, separation of church and state, and, you got it - euthanasia. A fairly new book, released in 2005, edit-ed by Tim Page titled *What's God Got To Do With It?: Robert Ingersoll on Free Thought, Honest Talk & The Separation of Church & State*, is a collection of many of Robert Ingersoll's works, interviews, and letters. Yes siree, he was progressive even before there was such a thing as the progressive movement. I'm surprised you never heard of him. Well, that's one reason why you are in this reeducation camp, isn't it? To learn where some of your thoughts came from.

In 1894 Robert Ingersoll argued that if someone is suffering from a terminal illness they should have the right to end their own life by committing suicide. One of his contemporaries, Felix Adler, suggested that not only should a terminally ill patient be able to commit suicide, but it should be legal for a doctor to assist them in doing it. In the early 1900s some politicians tried to pass euthanasia legislation to make it legal, but they all failed to pass.

Although America was not ready for doctors to kill their patients at that time in our history, Nazi Germany had no qualms about it. In 1934, at a mass political rally, Rudolf Hess, the Deputy Führer, stated, "National Socialism is nothing but applied biology." Socialism became the definer of science.

According to the British Broadcasting Corporation, BBC, the first state-sponsored euthanasia in Germany was on July 24, 1939 of a severely disabled infant. On September 1, 1939 a euthanasia decree followed, which read:

Reich Leader Bouhler and Dr. Brandt are entrusted with the responsibility of extending the authority of physicians, to be designated by name, so that patients who, after a most critical diagnosis, on the basis of human judgment, are considered incurable, can be granted mercy death.

Adolf Hitler

This was the beginning of Aktion T4, the program for involuntary euthanasia.

The following year Nazi doctors were not only euthanizing patients who had been given "critical diagnosis," but they did the same to their mentally and physically disabled citizens as well. It is estimated that 70,000 adult Germans in this category were killed by the time the war had ended four years later. It seems that many of these "physicians" justified their actions because of the book The Right To Death, *Das Recht auf den Tod*, published in 1895 by Adolf Jost.

The Nazis didn't just stop with euthanasia, but then went onto wholesale genocide (the intentional murder of people based upon race, religion, ethnicity, or national origins), which today is known as The Holocaust. Six million Jews, 1.5 million of them children, were systematically murdered, along with thousands of political dissidents, religious leaders, homosexuals, and Gypsies.

If today's conservatives seem to be sounding the alarm in response to more and more Americans calling for euthanasia, it's not because they lack compassion for the terminally ill and their suffering, but it's because history has a way of repeating itself. That, and they believe it is just plain ol' wrong. Remember the Sixth Commandment, "Thou shalt not kill." This includes doctors.

SUICIDE

To many liberals it is perfectly okay to take your own life if you are termi-nally ill, for that is euthanasia, as we had just learned. However, it is not okay if you're not in physical pain. Mental anguish or personal problems does not qualify. Well, at least many liberals draw the line somewhere.

Putting a gun to the head and pulling the trigger is the most common method of suicide for males in America today, while taking poison is the most preferred method by females. I don't know why this is, but as a former cop I can agree with the statistic. I've seen it for myself. The third most frequent way that peo-ple take their own lives, if you're interested in knowing, is through suffocation: hanging, intentional drowning, running a hose from the exhaust pipe into the interior of a sealed car, that sort of thing. The greatest spike in suicide rates for males lately have been those aged 45 to 65, which is the time in life of the pro-verbial "mid-life crisis," whereas the increase in suicides among females lately has been between the ages of 10 to 14; a time when girls are developing into young women, which is sad. This shouldn't be.

For the past seventeen years the suicide rate in the United States has increased 24% according to the Centers for Disease Control and Prevention, National Center for Health Statistics.

All right, forget all these statistics! Let's just say that people taking their own lives is a problem in our society - a BIG problem. And, no, I'm not going to insinuate that more progressives commit suicide than conservatives. Neither side advocates suicide, provided you leave euthanasia out of the equation, at least not yet.

Nothing makes us feel as sad, or as helpless, then hearing that someone com-mitted suicide. I knew a couple of people who committed suicide, and I even discovered the body of one of them. He blew his brains out.

First of all, committing suicide is a selfish act. Those who are left behind are always left wondering, "Could I have done something, or said something, to have prevented him or her from doing it?"

Suicide is the ultimate act of weakness and surrender. We human beings have an incredible sense of survival and self-preservation instincts. For a person to come to the point where they feel that they can no longer cope with their prob-lems, or go on anymore with life, makes the survivors lose a certain amount of respect for them, or all of it.

Survivors may even feel anger or resentment towards the victim if they are left in a bad situation, like a wife whose husband happens to be the breadwinner of the family, and that security blanket is suddenly pulled out from underneath the family because of his suicide, not to mention the loss of future time together. Most couples expect to grow old together.

The one thing I will say about most Bible believing Christians, who are going through really hard times, is that they don't resort to suicide, because they know the Sixth Commandment, "Thou shalt not kill." This includes self-murder. The fear of God, and we are talking about a healthy fear, keeps them from doing it. Does this mean that if a God believing person does commit suicide that they are automatically going to Hell? I don't believe so, because suicide is not the unpardonable sin mentioned in the Bible. Yes, it is a lack of faith at that can-never-go-back moment, but it is not unpardonable.

THE MILITARY

When I joined the United States Army straight out of high school my drill sergeant told me that our purpose was to "kill people and destroy things." Death and destruction. I understood that, but many soft civilians don't seem to understand that.

A friend of mine named Roy, who is ten years younger than me, talked for many years that he wanted to join the United States Marine Corps, and I fully supported his decision. After all, I trained Marine units for 9 years. Then one day he finally stopped dreaming about it, and did something about it. He went to a recruiting office and signed up. HOOAH! Since he had a four-year degree, and was as highly knowledgeable when it came to computers, they sent him off to become an officer. He lasted all about a month, and then he was home again, back at his old job. Naturally, I asked him, "What happened?"

Roy replied, "All they talked about was killing. I didn't know it was going to be like that."

I was befuddled. Surely after studying everything about the Marines for three long years Roy must have known what the mission of the Marine Corps was. Even Hollywood movies always depict Marines shooting and bombing anything in front of them to smithereens.

Then it occurred to me. For two generations the United States has had a professional military. Nobody is obligated to join, and therefore very few do. Less than 0.5 percent of the American population serves in the armed forces today. That means 95% of the American population has no real idea of what the military is really like, other than what they see in films or on the news. A lot of Millennials and Gen Zers think they know what the military is like, because they've played countless hours of the video game Call of Duty. The only problem with getting all your information from screens is that you don't get the whole picture.

When I was in Boot Camp at Fort Jackson, South Carolina they did indeed teach us how to kill and blow things up. However, that was only part of the experience. The bulk of it was learning to be disciplined both physically and mentally. Learning how to care for the barracks and issued equipment. Learning to respect one's superiors as well as your own battle buddy. Above all it was learning the value of American history, and to honor the flag of the United States of America. Throughout any American military base there are always paintings and photographs of great battles fought by previous generations of American warriors that serve as a reminder of the tremendous cost of freedom. Soldiers, marines, sailors and airmen paid the price with their blood, sweat, and tears.

When I was serving, every sunrise the American flag would be hoisted up the flag pole, and the bugler played Reveille to wake military personnel. You've heard it before, but you should Google it, and play it, to experience it. Well, anyway, no matter where a soldier is on base, or what they are doing, everyone stops what they are doing, come to attention, and salute towards the direction of the music if the flag is not visible. Military personnel will even stop their vehicles if possible, get out, and pay the flag respect. At the end of the evening, when the flag is lowered, Taps is the bugle call. You might as well Google that one also and listen to it. It was first played at the beginning of the American Civil War by both the Union and Confederate forces, and in 1848 it became a custom to play it at military funerals. I want Taps played at my funeral to symbolize my military service, and to close the service. However, at the commencement of my funeral I'd like Amazing Grace to be played on the bagpipes to symbolize my law enforcement service, and my faith in Jesus Christ. Playing the bagpipes at police and firefighter funerals is a holdover from our British heritage. Plus, God and country, in that order.

Of course, whenever the national anthem is played, The Star-Spangled Banner, active military and veterans alike stop what they are doing, stand at attention, and salute or place their right hand over their hearts out of respect for the flag – the very symbol of our nation. Any American who decides to take a knee, walk away, or hang out in the locker room when the national anthem is played is disrespecting the flag, and thus disrespecting what it stands for.

In 2016 people started to notice that professional football player Colin Kaepernick, a quarterback for the San Francisco 49ers, kept sitting for the Star-Spangled Banner. He had done this for three games. During a post-game interview Kaepernick explained, "I am not going to stand up to show pride in a flag for a country that oppresses black people and people of color. To me, this is bigger than football and it would be selfish on my part to look the other way. There are bodies in the street and people getting paid leave, and getting away with murder," He was referring to police shootings, and the violent protests that followed.

During the 49ers August 2016 training camp Colin Kaepernick practiced his plays while wearing socks that had pig faces all over them, each wearing a police hat. The message was clear – POLICE ARE PIGS! Yet, a month earlier the Dallas Cowboys had wanted to wear a decal on their helmets to pay tribute to five police officers who had been protecting Black Lives Matter protestors only to be massacred by a police-targeting-racist sniper in their own city, but their request was denied by the NFL.

Then on September 1, 2016 Kaepernick started to kneel during the national anthem instead of sitting to show respect for U.S. veterans, while at the same time showing disrespect for the flag of their country. It was a compromise that a fellow football player told him to do. So, basically, NO to a pro-police "Arm in Arm" decal, NO to a small decal remembering the victims of 9/11 on the 15th anniversary, NO to Tim Teebow taking a knee to pray, NO to spiking the ball in the end zone as a sign of victory, but YES to taking a knee during the playing of the national anthem. And, it wasn't just a big YES to Kaepernick, but other football players started taking the knee, mostly African-American players. Of course, this turned into a national firestorm.

A year after Kaepernick took a knee for the first time, and football player after football player did the same, President Donald Trump, at a rally in Huntsville, Alabama, said that NFL owners should fire players who kneel during the national anthem, and encouraged fans to walk out. The owners did not fire any players, but many fans did walk out, and burn jerseys of protesting players, and stopped buying tickets and NFL products.

Was this form of protest a leftist, race motivated, movement something new? No, not at all. The left follows the same playbook over, and over, again. At the 1968 Olympic Games in Mexico City American gold medalist Tommie Smith and bronze medalist John Carlos made the Black Power raised fist while standing on the winner's podium when the The Star-Spangled Banner was playing. In response, the International Olympic Committee expelled the two athletes from the Games stating that their actions were "a deliberate and violent breach of the fundamental principles of the Olympic spirit."

Of course, NFL Commissioner Roger Goodell, and many of the team owners, didn't have the intestinal fortitude to follow the NFL game operations manual on the national anthem, which prior to 2017 used to state:

During the National Anthem, players on the field and bench area should stand at attention, face the flag, hold helmets in their left hand, and refrain from talking. The home team should ensure that the American flag is in good condition. It should be pointed out to players and coaches that we continue to be judged by the public in this area of respect for the flag and our country. Failure to be on the field by the start of the National Anthem may result in discipline, such as fines, suspensions, and/or forfeiture of draft choice(s) for violation of the above, including first offenses.

After the NFL saw that President Trump, and *We the People*, were winning the Twitter war on the kneeling issue NFL Commissioner Goodell sent a letter to all 32 teams on October 10, 2017 calling on the league to "move past this controversy," and "like many of our fans, we believe that everyone should stand during the singing of the Star-Spangled Banner."

Many of the left may not be willing to take a stand based on right and wrong, but they do understand money, or the lack thereof. So, when the NFL was losing millions of dollars, and the government threatened to yank their subsidies, they caved.

The moral of the story is, *sports teams should not push the majority of their fans away based on a false narrative.*

The California State Conference of the National Association for the Advancement of Colored People (NAACP) came up with a peachy-keen solution to end the NFL knee taking controversy, and that was to request Congress to remove The Star-Spangled Banner as the national anthem. That's right, ditch the song! According to the *The Sacramento Bee* on November 7, 2017 California NAACP President Alice Huffman stated, "I think this controversy about the knee will go away once the song is removed," because she believes the song written by Francis Scott Key is racist, and that it "disenfranchises part of the American population," despite the fact that prior to this statement not one NFL football player ever claimed The Star-Spangled Banner was "racist."

Apparently, there are those in our society so hell-bent on tearing down our culture that they will use any issue du jour as an excuse to achieve their goal. Of course, Ms. Huffman, like so many on the left, never suggested an alternative song to replace the national anthem. It's the same tactic that Senator Nancy Pelosi pulled on the American people when pushing through Obama Care, "We have to pass the bill so that you can find out what is in it." We have to remove The Star-Spangled Banner so you can find out what is in the new one.

My educated guess is that the lyrics of the replacement national anthem would be all about diversity, economic equality, sexual immorality, how aborting some

American citizens is a "woman's right" and good for the county, and no mention of God whatsoever. Does that sound about right?

The NAACP president also praised the man who started it all, "We owe a lot of it to Kaepernick."

Getting back to current reality, if the national anthem disrespecting NFL players, and even many high school football teams that imitated them, truly wanted to do something about police brutality, which was the original cause by Kaepernick, then they need to get involved with their city halls and state law makers, not disrespect the flag of the United States of America. It didn't work in 1968 with the fists held up high by a couple of athletes, it didn't work in 2017 by the NFL, and it's not going to work now.

Oh, and to be fair to Colin Kaepernick, he does profess to be a Christian, and has publicly spoken about his faith. His body is even covered with tattoos of Christian symbols and scriptures. On his right arm he even has the words To God The Glory. That's nice, because the famous 18th century composer Johann Sebastian Bach used to write the letters SDG at the bottom of the page of his music. Soli Deo Gloria, *Glory to God alone*. Yet, despite a fan poll in 2016 that voted him "the most disliked player in the NFL," and then filing a "collusion grievance" against the NFL on October 15, 2017 to make them reconsider his request to play for the league again, he has donated a lot of his own money to charity. He even wants you to donate your hard-earned money to some very good causes. Just visit his official website www.kaepernick7.com. On the homepage it states, *The mission of the Colin Kaepernick Foundation is to fight oppression of all kinds globally, through education and social activism.* Oh wait, those words "globally" and "activism" don't sound right. And, why is Kaepernick holding up the Black Power fist with others in the photo? Hmmm, one of the organizations he wants people to donate to is the United We Dream organization who are wanting to "stop the deportations of undocumented youth and their parents; and strengthen alliances and support DREAMers at the intersection of queer and immigrant rights." Dig a little bit deeper into their website and you can find out what QUIP is all about. Okay, maybe you shouldn't donate to that one, but you could donate to the Coalition for the Homeless. That sounds like a noble cause. Ahhh, hold on a sec! In ABOUT there is a posting on August 16, 2017 that has the headline *It's Time to Stand Up to Hatred and Bigotry*. What does that mean? Read on. The story starts off, "In the aftermath of the last presidential election, we all hoped that the ugly and divisive tactics of the campaign were merely political theatrics that would fade into memory once the new administration was sworn in and assumed the profound responsibility of defending the principles upon which our country is built. But," and they lost me with that language. Forget it. Let's go back to talking about the military.

According to the U.S. Army website (www.army.mil) *The U.S. Army's mission is to fight and win our Nation's wars by providing prompt, sustained land dominance across the full range of military operations and spectrum of conflict in support of combatant commanders.* The Marines' purpose statement is similar to the Army's, but with the addition of Humanitarian and Disaster Relief Missions (HADR). The U.S. Navy's mission statement reads, *The mission of the Navy is to maintain, train and equip combat-ready Naval forces capable of winning wars, deterring aggression and maintaining freedom of the seas,* because 90% of global commerce is conducted by sea, and 80% of the planet's population lives within close proximity of coastal waters. Finally, *The mission of United States Air Force is to fly, fight and win in air, space and cyberspace. Our rich history and our vision guide our Airmen as we pursue our mission with excellence and integrity to become leaders, innovators and warriors.* No, the term "airmen" is not sexist. Females in the USAF are also referred to as airmen. You know, as in mankind or as in "all men are created equal." Good for them for not playing the gender language game.

Anyway, all of the armed services have one thing in common, and that is to win wars and protected you and me at home.

WOMEN IN THE MILITARY

Neither the Greatest Generation, Baby Boomers, Millennials, nor the Gen Zers have any problem with women serving in the U.S. Armed Forces. Women have been serving in the military since the Revolutionary War, albeit in support roles: clothing repair, cooking and cleaning, and nursing. The question that arises today is whether American women should be in combat roles.

Well, let's first look at history. That's always a good place to start. If a group of people experienced something before us, should we not examine the results? Don't we want to avoid the same mistakes or likewise duplicate the triumphs?

In the Bible, the Book of Judges, there was a female prophetess, and judge, named Deborah (1235 B.C.). In her time the nation of Israel had been under the oppressive rule of Jabin, the king of Canaan, for twenty years. She called for Barak, no not Barak Obama, but Barak son of Abinoam, and reminded him that God had ordered him to take ten thousand troops and fight against Jabin's general Sisera. However, Barak refused to go to war unless Deborah went with him. She told him, "I will surely go with you; nevertheless, there will be no glory for you in the journey you are taking, for the Lord will sell Sisera into the hand of a woman." She went with the Israelite army, and they defeated the Canaanite army even though they were greatly outnumbered and had inferior weapons.

Fast forward 2,660 years to a teenage girl in France named Joan of Arc. In the year 1425, when she was 13-years-old, she claims to have had a vision from the archangel Michael, Saint Catherine, and Saint Margaret who told her to drive out the English occupiers. When she was 16-years-old King Charles VII allowed her to travel with the French army, and wear protective armor.

Although she never engaged in hand-to-hand combat, and only carried a religious banner into battle with her on horseback, Joan of Arc's presence was believed to have been divinely inspired based upon one French victory after another.

On May 23, 1430 Joan of Arc was captured in Compiegne, put on trial, and then executed by being burned alive at the stake. She was 19-years-old. Today she is revered as a national heroine of France.

Margaret Cochran Corbin is famous in American military history. During the Revolutionary War it was common for wives of soldiers to be "camp followers" in a support role. However, since Margaret Corbin was a nurse, and the 600 American defenders of Fort Washington in northern Manhattan anticipated heavy casualties against the British led Hessians, she was granted permission to bring pitchers of water to her husband, John Corbin, and the other soldiers of his artillery unit. That's how she got the nickname "Molly Pitcher." During the Battle of Fort Washington her husband was killed, and she immediately took over firing the cannon; a skilled she learned while watching her husband train troops. She was wounded and had to surrender. She survived the war, and was the first woman to receive a military pension. She is also the first, and only, Revolutionary soldier buried at West Point cemetery.

Harriet Tubman was also a remarkable woman. She was a negro who escaped slavery in 1849, and then afterwards set up an espionage ring for the Union during the American Civil War. She was also the first woman in our history to lead a military expedition. That expedition was a series of raids on several plantations in South Carolina, commanded by Colonel James Montgomery, that freed 750 slaves without a single Union soldier being killed.

During World War II 60,000 women served as nurses, 150,000 served in the Women's Army Corps (WAC), 84,000 served in the Women Accepted for Volunteer Emergency Service (WAVES), 11,000 in the United State Coast Guard's Semper Paratus Always Ready (SPAR), and the remainder in various units. The total amount of American women that participated in the war was 350,000. Although there were no combat roles for women at the time 16 were killed in action. Contrast that to a total of 291,541 American male service members who were killed in combat, and 670,846 wounded.

Fast forward to more recent times, and we come to the book *Ashley's War* by Tzemach Lemmon, which was a New York Times bestseller. It's the true story about First Lieutenant Ashley White who, in 2010, was "attached" to a newly created unit called Cultural Support Team (CST-2) of the U.S. Army Special Operations Command in Afghanistan. The unit was created for well-trained military woman to accompany their male colleagues during raids on suspected insurgent homes and hideouts. If during these raids any mothers, wives, sisters, or daughters of the insurgents were detained the CST-2 women would question them "woman-to-woman," which helped in obtaining intelligence. The American female soldiers were able to penetrate the cultural veil of Islamic culture, and thus many of these Islamic women opened up to them. Unfortunately, on October 22, 2011 First Lieutenant Ashley White was killed in action.

The first female soldiers to pass U.S. Army Ranger School, which is one of the most physically demanding courses in the American military, was Lieutenant Kristen Griest and Lieutenant Shaye Haver in Class 08-15 on August 21, 2015. The other 16 women washed out, while 381 men graduated from the same class. Promoted Captain Griest then went on to become the first woman in the U.S. Army infantry. On September 25, 2017, two years after the Ranger School graduates, the first woman in the U.S. Marines infantry school earned the coveted 0302 infantry officer Military Occupational Specialty (MOS), but she wished to remain unnamed. Thirty-two female officers had previously attempted the 13-week course since 2012, but had failed. Today women make up 7 percent of the U.S. Marine Corps. On August 11, 2017 the only woman to make it into U.S. Navy SEAL training dropped out, and the Navy would not disclose her name. She had attended the three-week SEAL Officer Assessment and Selection program, which is a precursor course to the half-year Basic Underwater Demolition/SEAL (BUD/S) training. The dropout rate for men in the SEAL training is approximately 75 percent. It's a rough program. I've done waterborne training with the U.S. Marines and various special operations groups, and I know I could have never passed BUD/S, even in my prime. I can only take so much cold water. It takes a certain mindset to get through that kind of training.

Here's how we got to where we are now. On December 3, 2015 Secretary of Defense Ashton B. Carter, under the Obama administration, lifted all restrictions for women serving in combat roles. All 220,000 military jobs in the military had become gender-integrated.

Although all combat jobs are open to women many liberals, especially the feminists, would have you believe that men and women will be "equally" represented in future combat missions. They believe that there is no difference between men and women when it comes to combat. However, the reality is that the percentage of woman who can perform effectively in combat will always remain low. Why is that?

Now, before I begin, I want you to keep in mind that I have trained many male and female soldiers for combat over many years. I have also served side-by-side with both men and women on real-world military missions; not combat missions, but military police and security forces missions. Under my command I have treated both sexes equally. In addition, I have done the same in law enforcement. That said, I will come back to my own personal observations and opinions after I fill your head with some facts.

Let's talk about up-close-and-personal combat. I'm not talking about dropping bombs from an airplane or pushing a button to launch a missile from a location that is miles away from the enemy, but shooting, stabbing, and bare-knuckle bludgeoning the enemy on the battlefield where the whites of their eyes can be seen; blood spurting, bones splintering, and pure brute strength.

When determining whether women are fit for combat we must first answer the age-old battle of the sexes question, "Who are more intelligent? Men or women?" This question has been answered in countless scientific research papers going back to the 1960s, and that is THERE IS NO GENERAL INTELLIGENCE DIFFERENCE BETWEEN MEN AND WOMEN. In American society we have both male doctors and female doctors, male chefs and female chefs, male politicians and female politicians, male professors and female professors, and the list goes on. Just about every profession imaginable can be satisfactorily filled by either gender. Therefore, intelligence alone should not preclude women from combat roles.

How about physical differences between men and women? Does strength make a difference in combat? There is no doubt that men, on average, are stronger than women. A study published on July 1, 2000 in the Journal of Applied Physiology titled *Skeletal muscle mass and distribution in 468 men and women aged 18-88yr* found that men have an average of 26 lbs. (12 kilograms) more skeletal muscle mass than women. Women have about 40% less upper-body strength than their male counterparts, and 33% less lower-body strength. Men have much stronger grips than women, and not just by a little, but a lot. 90% of the women in the study scored lower than 95% of the men.

Another study, *A comparative Study on Strength between American College Male and Female Students in Caucasian and Asian Populations*, conducted by researchers from the Department of Kinesiology at San Jose State University and the Beijing Sport University in China concluded that "females have 37-68% of muscle strength of males in general."

In general, men are faster runners than women. According to Live Science "the fastest woman in the world, Florence Griffith Joyner, ran the 100-meter dash in just 10.49 seconds in 1988, and that record remains unbroken. Yet her fastest time wouldn't have even qualified her for the men's 2016 Olympic competition, which requires competitors to finish the 100-meter sprint in 10.16 seconds or less."

When I was taking the physical agility test to become a police officer none of the women in my group could make it over the 6-foot wall on the obstacle course, and a few could not drag the 165-pound dummy the 32 feet that was required. However, a few women did succeed during the following testing cycle, but the other 80% washed out.

When I went back into the military I took the U.S. Army's Combat Lifesaver Course. We didn't just have to drag a 165-pound dummy, but we had to perform a Fireman's Carry, a Hawes Carry, and a Casualty's Dragon Harness drag of a fellow soldier with his "battle rattle" on; that's to say, a full combat load (helmet, ballistic vest, and weapons). Add that extra 25 to 30 pounds, and you're lifting or moving 200 pounds around. I've also personally taught many soldiers in casualty evacuation, and from my observations most of the women could not do what the men could. Oh sure, they were just as good at slapping a tourniquet on, or applying a bandage to stop the bleeding, but they could not remove the wounded soldier from the battlefield alone. They just didn't have the strength.

Now, some of you may be saying, "So, what's the big deal? She can do everything else. Why penalize her for one or two things she can't do?" Well, the "big deal" is this. Soldiers get injured in combat, and they go down. That's a fact. Evacuating them from the Kill Zone is just as much a part of the job description as the fighting is. Most people don't care, because they are not personally invested. Only a tiny, tiny, fraction of the population are warriors or ever have been a warrior. Playing warfare video games doesn't count. However, let me put it into a context that you can relate to. Let's say you are unconscious in a burning building. The only firefighter that can save you is unable to drag you out of there, and therefore you're going to burn to death. Would that matter to you? Of course, it would. You'd be crazy if it didn't. At that moment of need you wouldn't care if the firefighter was a man or woman, just so long as they can get your ass out of there to save your life. Most women don't have the strength to be a firefighter.

Now, I've just touched on just one aspect of combat to illustrate my point, and that was strength required for casualty evacuation. Yet, on the battlefield there are many more tasks a combat soldier may be required to perform, such as carrying large weapon systems, climbing with a full combat load, help pull a battle buddy over an obstacle, pushing heavy objects, and so forth. Whether a woman is applying for a position as a combat soldier, a police officer, firefighter, or even an Emergency Medical Technician on an ambulance crew, she must be able to pass the physical agility tests, and successfully perform all job tasks once she is on the job. If not, then she has no business being there.

The conclusion is that the "hardware" of men and women are different. However, there are a few exceptions, and those woman that can cut it ought to be allowed to be what they want to be. We have historical evidence to back it up, and this also happens to be my own personal opinion as well.

White House Chief of Staff John F. Kelly, who you may remember was the former United States Secretary of Homeland Security and a general in the United States Marine Corps, also concluded that few women will ever make it into combat roles, especially when it comes to the Special Forces, even though many politicians are trying to ramrod them in. "If we don't change standards," he said, "it will be very, very difficult to have any numbers, any real numbers, come into the infantry, or the Rangers or the SEALs, but that's their business." In other words, he is not in favor of lowering current military recruiting and training standards for women, and society is just going to have to accept this reality if they want an efficient fighting force. However, left-wing liberals, and especially the feminists, will never accept the physical differences between men and woman, and so they have come up with a solution to bring about their perceived "equality" needed in our military.

For you women in this reeducation camp, have you ever been in the U.S. Post Office and noticed the Selective Service poster on the wall, or the forms on the counter? All men are familiar with it, because by law all male U.S. citizens and male immigrants residing in the United States who are ages 18 through 25 must register for it. It's been around in its current form since 1980. The Selective Service System is essentially a government list of all young men that can be called upon, a draft, to serve in the United States Armed Forces in the time of a national emergency or war. Failure to register can result in penalties, such as the prevention of government jobs, denial of government security clearances, and blockage of citizenship for immigrants.

Well, you women ought to be concerned should the Democrats ever take the White House again, because many of them are calling for young women to be registered with the Selective Service System also, and if there is ever a draft that means that they may be forced to go to war also.

On June 15, 2016, in the fading glow of President Obama's presidency, the Senate approved a bill that would require women to register for the draft. The vote was 85-13, which means that it had bipartisan support. Yes, we have a lot of "RINOs," Republican In Name Only, in the Republican Party. Fortunately, it was fiercely opposed by Congress' most conservative lawmakers and conservative groups, and the bill was killed on April 27, 2017. Had Hillary Clinton been elected President of the United States you can be rest assured that young women would be right now registering, because she was in favor of compelling women to register for the Selective Service System. No wonder on September 27, 2017 former First Lady Michele Obama lamented, "Any woman who voted against Hillary Clinton voted against their own voice." It was because of the 2017 election results that you young women, for now, can't be drafted. What a shame! (sarcasm). Hey, but if you young ladies still want to be in the military, there's a recruiting office near you. Nobody is stopping you from joining.

Now, for my opinion as to why we should NEVER draft women, and especially for combat roles. You know I've already stated that I don't have a problem with women volunteering for the military, or even women in combat roles if they can meet all the physical requirements, but drafting women – Ahhhhhh, no.

For every generation in American history, until you Millennials came along, it was always women and children first. What does that mean?

Well, let me start off by asking you, "Have you ever seen the 1997 movie Titanic starring Leonardo DiCaprio and Kate Winslet?" It's a classic.

In this movie the luxury ocean liner Titanic collides with an iceberg and is sinking. The ship's crew in charge of loading the lifeboats shout out, "Women and children first! Women and children first!" A man, played by Billy Zane, tries to bribe his way onto a lifeboat, but to a crew member's disgust he is refused a seat, because he is a man, and they have not finished loading the women and children first.

That's the way I was raised, women and children first when it comes to any survival situation. I thought that it was the same for those younger than me until I went back into the military in 2006. Boy, was I in for a rude awakening. While in the California State Military Reserve's Basic Orientation Course (BOC) we had a mandatory group discussion. There were close to 70 soldiers in the room. The captain in charge of the exercise gave us a hypothetical situation that went like this:

"You have four people who need a heart transplant or they are going to die if they don't receive one. And, let's just say that the one heart you get fits perfectly in each individual that I am about to describe. You have a 12-year-old girl. Next, you have a 33-year-old mother of five, and all of her children are very young. Then you have a 21-year-old university student working on his degree in the field of medical science. Finally, you have a 68-year-old man who owns a large corporation employing thousands of people. There is no right or wrong

answer. I just want to know your justification for giving one person the heart over another."

I couldn't believe how easy making this decision was. I said to my group, "Well, it is obvious that either the 12-year-old girl or the woman with children should get the heart transplant. It's even easier to narrow it down, because the little girl has her whole life ahead of her. And so, I say the heart goes to the little girl."

A 23-year-old Private First Class, who had a boyish face and wavy-hard-to-comb blond hair blasted me, "What? That's ridiculous! How did you come to that conclusion?"

At first, I thought he was joking, and I was a bit taken back that he spoke to someone his senior like that, but then a young blond woman about his age chimed in, "Yeah, that doesn't make any sense."

I shot back, "You're kidding, right? Haven't you ever heard of women and children first? You know, the movie Titanic where all of the women and children were put into the life boat first to save them?"

They had seen it, but it had never registered with them.

When I looked at the clueless faces of the rest of the group, in order to get a better feel of the kind of people I was dealing with, it was painfully clear to me that they didn't know what I was talking about. The only one who came to my defense, although timidly, was a sergeant around the same age as me. When I tried to explain my position, they shut me down; kinda like how leftist university students try to block any conservative speakers today. The boyish man took control of the like-minded group and said, "No, we have to make a better choice than that. We have to decide what is best for society," and they all nodded in agreement.

My group, who had literally shunned me, chose the med school student to give the heart transplant to, because he was "going to heal a lot of people throughout his life, and may even be the one to cure cancer." That was their reasoning.

I felt like my guts had been twisted up into a ball that day. I knew that the poison of relativism was a direct assault on the Judeo-Christian American values of yesteryear. I knew at that moment that America was going to be in trouble down the road, and I was right. A few years later along came President Barak Obama, Hillary Clinton, Susan Rice, Eric Holder, Loretta Lynch, James Comey, and the whole lot of them.

Oh, by the way, nobody has been drafted since 1973, in case you were wondering.

GAYS IN THE MILITARY

For almost all of American history homosexuality was believed by the majority of citizens to be immoral, a "sin," as a result of 2,000 years of Western culture that is based upon Judeo-Christian values. As such, it was forbidden for homosexuals to serve in the United States Armed Forces up until just a few years ago. Prior to this, if it was discovered that a service member was a homosexual he or she would be discharged.

Although the Sexual Revolution that began in 1960 would eventually pave the way for acceptance of homosexuality by greater numbers of Americans, on February 28, 1993 homosexuality was still considered by the clear majority to be immoral. Therefore, on this date President Bill Clinton (Democrat) signed into law Department of Defense Directive 1304.26, which became known as "Don't ask, don't tell." It was the President's way of compromising with the left's pressure on the White House to prevent homosexuals from being kicked out of the military, while at the same time appeasing the military leadership on the right who officially stated that openly gay service members "would create an unacceptable risk to the high standards of morale, good order and discipline, and unit cohesion that are the essence of military capability." The policy of *Don't ask, don't tell* meant that military officials would not ask if service members were homosexual, and homosexual service members would keep their homosexuality secret. Everyone knew that they were just kicking the can further down the road for future politicians to deal with.

From 2001 to 2009 *Don't ask, don't tell* remained in effect, which also coincided with the leadership of President George W. Bush (Republican).

Once President Barak Obama (Democrat) took Office on January 20, 2009 the Democratic leadership in both the House and Senate immediately got to work on trying to end *Don't ask, don't tell* policy. Sixteen months later the U.S. House of Representatives voted, 234 to 194, on the Murphy amendment to the National Defense Authorization Act, and it passed. However, on September 21, 2010 Senator John McCain, a former U.S. Navy pilot who was shot down over North Vietnam and was a Prisoner of War, led a successful filibuster against the debate on the Act.

Two months later Secretary of Defense Robert Gates and Joint Chiefs Chairman Michael Mullen insisted on immediate repel of *Don't Ask, don't tell*, despite the heads of the Marine Corps, Army, and Air Force all advising against it. Five years later, as a private citizen, Robert Gates, was the president of the Boy Scouts of America, and under his leadership allowed gay adult troop leaders into the organization in 2015.

To make a short story even shorter, President Barak Obama (Democrat), the new Secretary of Defense Leon Panetta (Democrat), and Admiral Mullen provided the certification required by the Act of Congress that effectively repealed Don't ask, don't tell on September 20, 2011. 236 years of American military history came to an end. Of course, it was no surprise that shortly after lifting this policy that Christians came under attack throughout the military, even military chaplains. I don't have time to go through all the case studies, but a case in point is when Representative Doug Collins (Republican) of Georgia's 9th congressional district intervened on behalf of Chaplain Captain Joseph Lawnhorn who was issued a Letter of Concern (a permanent administrative censure that can adversely affect one's military career) by his commanding officer Colonel David Fivecoat who accused him of advocating Christianity during a mandatory suicide prevention training session for the 5th Ranger Training Battalion on November 20, 2014. What a horrible transgression! According to the Army Times the letter stated, "During this training, you were perceived to advocate Christianity and used Christian scripture and solutions." It went on to say, "You provided a two-sided handout that listed Army resources on one side and a biblical approach to handling depression on the other side. This made it impossible for those in attendance to receive the resource information without also receiving the biblical information."

Hello! This is what Christian military chaplains do! They encourage soldiers to turn to Jesus Christ, especially if someone is depressed or suicidal, but that didn't stop Colonel Fivecoat from ending his letter with, "During mandatory training briefings, it is imperative you are careful to avoid any perception you are advocating one system of belief over another." This statement is ironic considering a Christian military chaplain wears a Christian cross on his uniform. You can't miss it! The U.S. government pays these military chaplains to be chaplains. Even the U.S. Army's official website (as of the printing of this book) to recruit new Army chaplains has the headline YOU HEARD A HIGHER CALLING. NOW DISCOVER A MISSION. In case you didn't know, the U.S. military also have Muslim Imams, Buddhist Priests, Jewish Rabbis, in the Chaplain Corps to go for counseling or spiritual guidance, and atheists can even see an Army psychologist if they need to. An officer with a religious symbol on his or her uniform is a good indicator of their belief system, and one would expect them to give advice from that religious perspective. While I was serving in the military, if a Muslim Imam were to have told me in a mandatory suicide prevention meeting, "You need to turn to Allah for comfort," I would have politely kept my thoughts, *I don't think so*, to myself. The god of the Koran is not the God of the Bible. I'm strong enough to know what I believe in, and it certainly does not hurt to hear what others believe in. Likewise, soldiers listening to a Christian chaplain or a priest isn't going to hurt them.

Colonel David Fivecoat, now retired and on Linked in, had an impressive military record: service in Kosovo, Bosnia, three combat tours in Iraq, and a combat tour in Afghanistan makes him a true American hero worthy of respect. Yet, sadly, he is like so many teachers, politicians, and military leaders in our society today who ignore, or don't know, our country's Judeo-Christian history and foundation. He, of all people, should know what a huge part faith played in our military history, because he earned a military history degree from West Point. The men who the urged the creation of this very institution, an institution devoted to the arts and sciences of warfare, were George Washington (the Commander-in-Chief of the Continental Army, and our first president who saw God as guiding the creation of the United States), John Adams (the one who wrote, "Without religion this world would be something not fit to be mentioned in polite company, I mean Hell."), General Henry Knox (he owned a bookstore in Boston that sold a wide variety of Bibles and was an advocate of dealing with the Indian nations fairly), and Alexander Hamilton (who wrote about the connection between Christianity and political freedom), and who was the Secretary of the Treasury who authorized the purchase of the land in 1790 for the institution to be built at West Point; a military fort at the time. Then in 1802 President Thomas Jefferson signed into legislation the establishment of the United States Military Academy that would educate those attending to safeguard the democratic society as he knew it.

Anyway, in an interview with Fox & Friends Representative Collins said, "Chaplains are there for everyone, whether they have faith or no faith, and the chaplains need to be able to operate under their own faith background, and also operate within the military. And, right now they seem to be under attack for doing just that."

United States military chaplains have been in service for just over 100 years, which started during World War I. Former U.S. Army chief of chaplains, Douglas Carver, said, "Chaplains serve as a constant reminder to our troops that God is present with them, especially in a combat environment."

One man who has made it his mission to destroy Christian fundamentalists in the U.S. Armed Forces is Michael "Mikey" Weinstein through his non-profit organization The Military Religious Freedom Foundation. It the vehicle in which he brings law suits against the Pentagon and the Secretary of Defense. Although a Republican, he has an ax to grind with Christians, because when he was attending the United States Air Force Academy back in the 1970s he claims to have encountered anti-Semitism and "religious bigotry." Then when his own sons were in the Academy they too were exposed to Christian "proselytizing;" a fancy word for telling people about Jesus Christ. When you look at Weinstein's website the mission statement seems very pro-Constitution, very all-American, but read on and it's actually a hit list on Christianity.

Oh, you want an example? Okay, how about this. According to the American Center for Law and Justice on May 5, 2016 the MRFF threatened Brigadier General Helen G. Pratt, president of the Marine Corps University, with federal lawsuits for permitting a military chaplain to invite marines in training to a prayer service that was optional. In other words, a lawsuit for allowing a chaplain to do his job.

It was no wonder that a Washington Times Poll titled *U.S. Military Morale*, revealed that from when President Obama took Office in 2009 until 2015, there was a 35% drop in military morale, 70% said that the quality of life "will continue to decline," and only 63% said they would reenlist; it had been 72% before that.

So, where am I heading with all this? Since Judeo-Christian values are in direct opposition to homosexuality, not homosexuals, there will continue to be friction inside the military over this issue. Although Christians and chaplains were in the United States military for its entire history of over two and a half centuries, and homosexuals only allowed to serve openly for less than a decade, many in the military now do not want Christians to speak about their faith, and they certainly don't want chaplains counseling homosexual soldiers, airmen, and seamen away from homosexuality based on the Bible's definition of sexual immorality. It's now the left that wishes to impose *Don't ask, don't tell us about the God of the Declaration of Independence*.

Although the United States Armed Forces held out for much longer than civilian society when it came to Biblical morality, the Sexual Revolution eventually overcame them as well, and not just concerning homosexuality. For example, if a member of the military committed adultery, sexual intercourse between a married person and someone other than his or her spouse, they were sentenced to a year in confinement, received a dishonorable discharge, and faced the possibility of forfeiture of all retirement pay. Adultery is still a criminal offense today under the Uniform Code of Military Justice, but it's getting watered down, and the odds of facing such a severe punishment is unlikely.

The military recruits its personnel from an oversexed civilian population, and the problems associated with it are brought into the military culture. Despite sensitivity classes, warnings, and threats of punishment, the sad truth is that sexual assaults continue to increase every year in the military. It is a chronic problem, and the military leadership is at a loss on how to stop it. In 2016 there were 6,082 reported cases of sexual assault. Just four years earlier it was 3,604 cases. Even the government is throwing up their hands. Senator Kirsten Gillibrand stated, "The truth is that the scourge of sexual assault in the military remains status quo."

Of course, the very people that the left is trying to silence would say that it is all about cause and effect. The progressives took prayer and the Ten Commandments out of public schools, and then came unprecedented teen pregnancies, fatherless children, abortions, and school shootings. Then came the sexual degradation of the military that seeped in slowly, and we now have factions against factions, and many people in uniform that can't respect other people's bodies or their own.

An adulterer can still fire a weapon. A sexual predator can still shuffle military paperwork. A homosexual can still do his or her duties. Sexual drive does not inhibit someone from performing military tasks, and it certainly does not erase their patriotism. What sexual immorality does do is break down the very foundation of the U.S. military, and the cement that once held it all together – one nation under God.

Here's a Biblical truth that even most non-believers would agree with, and that is *Every kingdom divided against itself is brought to desolation, and every city or house divided against itself will not stand. Matthew 12:25*

TRANSGENDERS IN THE MILITARY

The Trump Administration did nothing to prevent homosexuals from serving in the military. When Donald Trump became POTUS nobody was discharged because of their sexual orientation. However, why did President Trump target the transgenders? Was their sin more grievous than homosexuals or bisexuals?

The answer is, "No." They are not wanted in the military by the Republican administration for another reason.

I have labeled the situation "three hots, and a cot."

When I was a street cop, especially around winter time, some homeless people would commit crimes just so they could be arrested and thrown in jail. They wouldn't do anything serious that would send them away to prison for years, but a misdemeanor offense that would land them in a county jail for a few months.

When I would ask them, "Why did you do it?" Some of them were quite honest with me and said, "Three hots, and a cot." In other words, they needed to get off of the cold streets and get three hot meals a day, and a bed to sleep in at night. Of course, they also received free medical care while incarcerated. I had one guy break the law just so he could get his teeth taken care of, and it worked.

The county footed the bill.

Well, this is what the military believes was happening with many transgenders coming into the military. It wasn't "three hots, and a cot" that they wanted, but sexual reassignment surgery at Uncle Sam's expense. After all, it is a "human right" for them to be what they want to be, and if they are a "federal employee" then their employer must accommodate them. That's why the *Presidential Memorandum for the Secretary of Defense and the Secretary of Homeland* of August 25, 2017 states:

(b) halt all use of DoD or DHS resources to fund sex reassignment surgical procedures for military personnel, except to the extent necessary to protect the health of an individual who already has begun a course of treatment to reassign his or her sex.

Sexual reassignment surgery is not just SNIP! SNIP! and it's done. It is a long drawn out process, and it's super expensive.

Expenses incurred a year before surgery includes hormone therapy at a cost of $40,000 to $50,000 and counseling that cost between $50 to $200 a session. Oh, and by the way, the hormone therapy is for life. Obviously, male bodies and female bodies have some differing hormones.

Reconstructive surgery on the genitals can cost between $15,000 to $25,000, and the chest up to $50,000. Since men and women's faces are different, facial surgery is also recommended to make the change look more natural.

After the surgery is complete there is a lifetime of doctor visits. Plus, it may include a lifetime of psychological counseling as well. According to the American Foundation for Suicide Prevention, in the January 2014 report *Suicide Attempts among Transgender and Gender Non-Conforming Adults*, 41 percent of people who identify as transgender will attempt suicide at some point in their lives, compared to 4.6 percent of the general population. And people who have had transgender surgery are 19 times more likely than average to die by suicide. So, for Uncle Sam sexual reassignment surgery is a risky investment.

Although the Pentagon does not know how many transgender people are serving in the Armed Forces, for there was never a need to know before, it is believed that it could be around 15,500. Now, obviously, not all of these transgenders go into the military with the intention to get free medical care, but enough of them have done it to make the Department of Defense slam on the breaks. The responsibility of the U.S. Armed forces is to defend this country, not pay for surgeries and treatments that go against natural processes.

Another transgender challenge the military is currently wrestling with is the use of bathrooms and locker rooms. In the civilian world they're trying to solve this issue by just having one-person INCLUSIVE bathrooms with a male-fe-male-transgender logo slapped onto the front of the door, but it's a little more complicated for military units where people have to actually live together in sometimes very tight quarters. Our infrastructure for the past two and a half centuries was only designed for two sexes.

However, since society and the military are wrestling with these new issues, I think it would be fiscally responsible if they start planning now for people's pets to a have accommodations for them in bathrooms, and dressing rooms as well. After all, bestiality (sex with animals) is a "right" some are pushing for.

It may sound ludicrous, if this is the first time you have heard this, but there are actual countries where sex with animals, also known as zoophilia, is legal. Oh yes, there exist actual underground sex tourism and animal brothels. Denmark, a country where Christianity once flourished, has a handful of animal brothels according to Ice News (a Nordic news agency). There are even now "erotic zoos."

Countries around the world have been dealing with this issue recently, because some claim zoophilia is animal abuse (zoophilia), while others are calling it just another form of affection. "It's love."

The Daily Mail printed an article titled *Bestiality brothels are 'spreading through Germany' warns campaigner as abusers turn to sex with animals as 'lifestyle choice.'*

Hmmm, where did I hear that term "lifestyle" before?

Anyway, the German zoophile organization ZETA "has announced it will mount a legal challenge should a ban on bestiality become law" in Germany. ZETA chairman Michael Kiok stated, "Mere concepts of morality have no business being law."

Mr. Kiok has a good point. So, who said sexual relationship with animals is wrong? As long as an animal is not hurt, and is "loved," why should it matter? If people do not adhere to Judeo-Christian values any more, then *What difference does it make?*

Anyone who has sexual relations with an animal must be put to death.
Exodus 22:19

There are many more scriptures dealing with the subject, but you get the point. Zoophilia is just one more sexual immorality on the list. What has been will be again, what has been done will be done again, for *There is nothing new under the sun. Ecclesiastes 1:9*

When the State of California was wresting over Proposition 8, a proposed law to keep marriage between one man and one woman, the Los Angeles Times on October 27, 2008 had the headline *A gay-marriage Pandora's box?*

Well, Pandora's box has been indeed opened.

For many progressives the box needed to be opened. For many God-fearing, conservative, Republicans they're now saying, "See, we told you so." This was just one more reason why the 2016 elections turned out the way they did.

Okay, you're outta here! Go report to Cell Block 7. Now!

CELL BLOCK 7

"WHAT IS TRUTH?"

"I can say what I want to."

Have you ever heard someone say that before? It's usually followed by, "It's a free country, you know."

Be it business, relationships, or conversing with strangers it is always best to avoid bickering with people. There is such a thing as "healthy conflict" and "unhealthy conflict." The definition of "conflict," of course, is *a serious disagreement or argument.*

If you have an opposing view to that of another person you are speaking with, and that person is willing to engage in civilized dialog with you, then that is a healthy conflict. When both sides are respecting the other's point of view, and common ground can usually be found, and if not then you can *agree to disagree.* However, if one side or the other tries to shut the other one down, and friendly discourse stops, then the conflict becomes a controversy. The strife will divide people, and it can be agonizing or volatile if you are unable to walk away from the situation.

There's no better way to get into a heated discussion, or even an outright argument, then to talk about religion or politics, that's why the host at some social gatherings, or even at a family gathering, will make the request, "Please don't talk politics," because they know that the subject in mixed company can spoil the event.

We are at a point in our history where many on the left do not want Americans, specifically those on the political right, to have *freedom of speech* that is enshrined in the U.S. Constitution. And, when I say "left" I'm talking mostly about you Millennials and Gen Zers. But, thank God, the left is no longer in power, and I can say what I want. So, here goes...

FAKE NEWS

I took a journalism course when I was in high school, and I learned the basics. Always start with a headline that grabs people's attention, yet instantly informs them as what the story is about. In the lead paragraph give the most important facts first, because some people only read the first paragraph, and then they skip to the next story. Always have the Five W's and H: who, what, when, where, why, and how. Finally, just report all the facts, and nothing but the facts. Most of all don't give your own opinion. That's what true journalism is all about.

Our founding fathers had it right when they wrote the First Amendment of the U.S. Constitution. Like a newspaper they had a catchy headline that not only grabbed people's attention, but it said what the document was all about in just a few words, *We The People*. They didn't write *We The Right* or *We The Left*. The first three words include EVERY citizen. Then they wrote the most important facts first in the "lead," in the First Amendment, *Congress shall make no law respecting an establishment of religion, prohibiting the free exercise thereof; or abridging the freedom of speech, or of the press..."*

The most important freedom is religion, then speech, and then the press. I think this needs repeating. The most important freedom is RELIGION, SPEECH, and then PRESS. We've talked about the government not establishing a religion, i.e. "the Church of the United States," or prohibiting the free exercise of religion. If a coach at a public school wants to take a knee on a football field to pray before or after a game he is not to be prohibited from doing so. If NFL football players want to take a knee in disrespect of the National Anthem then the government cannot prohibit it. If a Muslim wants to pray in the break room of a government building on his or her break they're free to do so. If an atheist does not want to utter the words "one nation under God" in the Pledge of Allegiance in a class-room, then they don't have to.

We just got done talking about the freedom of speech less than a minute ago, and so now I'm going to reeducate you about the press – *journalism*.

When I read a news story from any news source I just want the facts, and nothing but the facts. I don't want the journalist's bias to influence the story. If I wanted his or her opinion, I'd go to the opinion section of their publication. When it comes to news I just want news.

When a journalist is reporting about government activity, or putting a politician under the microscope, I want them to discover the truth. I want them to present all the facts, which allows me to make up my own mind as to what all the information means.

When it comes to the President of the United States, regardless of party affiliation, I want journalists to ask the tough questions, and be the watchdog of freedom. I want every government official held accountable for what they say and do, and only the press has the power to do that. That power is in the form of informing *We the People*. That is what the press is supposed to be all about, not trying to push their own agenda. Unfortunately, most journalism in the United States has become *yellow journalism*. That was an old term my high school teacher used when I was in the journalism class. It means journalism that is based on sensationalism, exaggeration, or stories that are not well researched. Back in the old days the tabloids, stories about UFOs and a bunch of other weird stuff, were printed on cheap paper, and soon after it was sold the paper would start turning yellow. Since much mainstream media has decided to push the left's agenda, rather than just give the facts, they have essentially jettisoned their journalism ethics and have become yellow journalism. Today we call it "fake news."

SOCIAL MEDIA IS A PETRI DISH FOR FAKE NEWS

Social media is a tool. It's another form of communication. Just like a gun the user determines its use. It can be a tool for good or a tool for evil. Social Media can promote a conservative message, or it can push a liberal agenda. The tool is not in question, the intent is.

One of the biggest problems with social media is that most people, and I am including both the right and left when I make this statement, do nothing more with their social media than parrot others when it comes to political or social issues. You know, Polly the Parrot that just repeats everything it hears. "Ahhhh, Polly wants a cracker. Ahhhhm Polly wants a cracker." They see a social media quip or quote that someone shared with them that they believe reflects their own views, and they share it with their friends to influence them. The problem with doing this is THEY'RE NOT YOUR OWN THOUGHTS! They're somebody else's. Now, I'm not saying you shouldn't share a good social media quip or quote with your friends, but if you do, at least write a sentence or two in the comment box as to why you agree with the quip or quote. If it's just your feelings, then state it. "I feel strongly about this subject, and here's why…" Or, back up the quip or quote with some facts, or more facts. Let me give you an example.

My Millennial nephew Seth posted on Facebook a meme from Americans Against The Republican Party. The headline read THIS BOOK, and it had a photo of the Holy Bible, HAS ABSOLUTELY NOTHING TO DO WITH THIS DOCUMENT, and the second photo was of the U.S. Constitution. The sub headline read KEEP THE BIBLE IN YOUR CHURCH AND OUT OF MY GOVERNMENT…

Well, I decided to share this social media text and graphic with my friends, not because I agreed with the message, but because I disagreed with the message.

To effectively educate my friends on my views I didn't write, "This is crap!" or some other vulgarity like I've seen many Millennials do when they disagree with a message, but I wrote my views in an educating impactful way. Here is what I wrote in the comment box under the meme:

This is what my nephew posted on his Facebook page. And, here are my comments, because, unfortunately, many young people do not really know American history. HERE WAS MY COMMENT: Like I keep telling you Seth, please learn American history. Here's some of what George Washington said in his Farewell Address after his term as President. Do you know who he is? He's on the One Dollar bill in your pocket. The same money that says boldly and proudly IN GOD WE TRUST.

"Of all the dispositions and habits which lead to political prosperity, religion and morality are indispensable supports. In vain would that man claim the tribute of patriotism, who should labor to subvert these great pillars of human happiness, these firmest props of the duties of men and citizens. The mere politician, equally with the pious man, ought to respect and to cherish them. A volume could not trace all their connections with private and public felicity. Let it simply be asked: Where is the security for property, for reputation, for life, if the sense of religious obligation deserts the oaths, which are the instruments of investigation in courts of justice? And let us with caution indulge the supposition that morality can be maintained without religion. Whatever may be conceded to the influence of refined education on minds of peculiar structure, reason and experience both forbid us to expect that national morality can prevail in exclusion of religious principle."

George Washington, 1st President of the United States of America, and I can give you hundreds of other examples that our government was founded on the Bible.

It was not democracy that made us a great nation, for even many communist nations have claimed they were "democratic," but it was our national morality, and sense of fairness, based upon the Bible as George Washington so eloquently stated. We saw what happened in the Obama administration when the Bible was deemed no longer relevant. So, no. I decided to tell my Facebook followers that the Bible was not going to only stay IN MY CHURCH, but that I wanted it to continue to be the book that the President of the United States puts his hand upon when he is inaugurated, when our judges consider their rulings, when school children pledge their allegiance, and so forth.

HATERS

Several months before the 2016 presidential election I was having a conversation with of my relatives, no not my nephew Seth, and I simply stated my position, "I prefer marriage between one man and one woman, which has been the norm for the human race for six thousand years."

Well, that comment set her off like a firecracker, and she immediately called me a "hater!"

I was shocked, to say the least, for I didn't hate anyone. Just because I supported traditional Judeo-Christian values did not make me a "hater." I was called that because she also knew that I was a conservative, born-again, Christian.

When I was a police officer in Southern California I had always treated homosexuals equally under the law in my jurisdiction, and mind you, this was in the mid-1990s when homosexual acts were a misdemeanor punishable by law. There was no such thing as gay marriage anywhere in the United States at that time in history. Hater my ass!

We'll hit on the LGBTQ topic again.

A couple of months before the 2016 Presidential Election I posted on Facebook that I was going to vote for Donald Trump. To my complete surprise my cousin, who had never called me any names before, called me a "hater."

"What? Me, a hater?" I said out loud at being accused of this a second time. "Unbelievable!"

If I had commented that I was going to vote for Hillary Clinton I'm sure I wouldn't have been labeled a "hater."

I think you get the point. The word "hater" is abused by the radical left all of the time. It's probably abused as much as the name "Hitler." For example, after the election the Mormon Tabernacle Choir was invited to sing at Donald Trump's inauguration. Nothing unusual in that since the Mormon Tabernacle Choir had performed for United States presidents of both parties in six previous presidential inaugurals. Trump's was to be the seventh. Then came the twist. CNN reported that Jan Chamberlin, a member of the choir, resigned because, as she put it, "I only know I could never 'throw roses to Hitler.' And I certainly could never sing for him."

Whoa! Hold on a moment! How could she compare him to Hitler? Donald Trump had never been a politician in his life, and he had not even been sworn in as the President of the United States of America when she said these inflammatory words. Yet, Ms. Chamberlin was convinced that she'd be "endorsing tyranny and fascism by singing for this man."

Since we are on the subject about Adolf Hitler, let's go rabbit trailing for a few minutes to discuss this historical man we also mentioned in Cell Block 2. Now, I'm not going to make the same mistake that many of my generation make about you Millennials, and that is the assumption that you know your history and geography. I've learned, quite painfully, by talking with many of your peers that at least half of you don't. Okay, I'm guessing on the "half" part, but I do I know for a fact that too many Millennials and Gen Zers don't know history or geography like they ought to. To prove my point, I'm going to stop writing this book and go ask my Generation Z 13-year-old niece Manique if she knows who Adolf Hitler was, and then ask the same question to my 15-year-old nephew Gary. They both are in high school. Hold on a couple of minutes. I'll be right back.

Long pause.

Okay, I'm back. I started with Manique by asking her, "Tell me everything you know about Adolf Hitler.

Her response was, "Adolf Hitler? Oh, isn't he the one who killed a bunch of Jews."

I responded, "Yes, he did, about six million of them. What else can you tell me about him?"

She scratched her head, tried to recall something more, but she couldn't. I then went to go look for Gary.

Her brother did much better. Gary answered, "He was the dictator of Germany during World War II."

I asked him, "How did he become dictator of Germany?"

He had no idea.

"Oh, and he killed Jews," he quickly added.

I asked the pertinent question, "Why did he kill Jews?"

He really didn't know why, and he gave me the generic answer, "Because he didn't like them."

Well, I thought to myself, *he has three more years left in high school. Hopefully he'll learn about this monster, and this significant time in history, before he graduates.*

I gave my niece and nephew a pass on who Adolf Hitler was because of their relative young age, but sadly I've asked the same question to university students and their answers were generally no better, and this is actually quite dangerous.

Philosopher George Santayana put it best when he said, "Those who cannot remember the past are condemned to repeat it." Yes, most young people have heard of Adolf Hitler, but they couldn't tell you the important details about this extreme socialist. This is exactly why you have uneducated people like a

Mormon Tabernacle Choir singer comparing President Donald Trump to Adolf Hitler. This also is why Rachel Maddow, host of the nightly MSNBC news show "The Rachel Maddow Show" since 2008, a lesbian according to Wikipedia, stated in a Rolling Stone magazine interview in July 2016, "Over the past year I've been reading a lot about what it was like when Hitler first became chancellor. I am gravitating towards moments in history for subliminal reference in terms of cultures that have unexpectedly veered into dark places, because I think that's possibly where we are." She was referring to President Donald Trump.

It's not just leftist news commentators that are slinging the "Hitler" word around as a comparison between our leader, but academia as well. Yale University history professor Timothy Snyder also compared Donald Trump's rise to power with Adolf Hitler's rise to power in the 1930s during an interview on MSNBC's "Morning Joe" on May 17, 2017 promoting his book *On Tyranny: Twenty Lessons from the Twentieth Century.* You can see this interview by Googling it. So shocking were Professor Snyder's comments that Willie Geist, the host of the news program, asked him for clarification, and yeap, Professor Snyder meant what he said.

Before you start making comparisons like a popular singer, television host, and professor did, we must ask ourselves, "Is comparing President Donald Trump to Adolf Hitler justified? After all, Herr Hitler was considered one of the biggest 'haters' in human history." Well, let's see. Let's make some actual factual comparisons.

Adolf Hitler wrote the book Mein Kampf (My Fight) from his prison cell in 1925. The book basically blames all of the political problems in Germany on the Jews (anti-Semitism), the Social Democrats, and the communists. He viewed Marxism as a "Jewish doctrine," even calling it "Jewish Marxism," designed to destroy Germany. When Hitler had gained control of the German government, establishing the Third Reich that would "last a thousand years," he passed the Enabling Act of 1933 that prohibited opposing parties. The party leaders were exiled, imprisoned, or killed. Then the Nazi Party divided the German people, and then later those living in occupied Europe, into two major categories. First was the National Comrades, *Volksgenossen*, which were the so-called good citizens of the state, and second category was the Community Aliens, *Gemeinschaftsfremde*, the people viewed upon as ruining the purity of German society. The Community Aliens, labeled as "enemies of the state," were further divided into three more categories. The first category was the political enemies: communists, liberals, and Christians. That's right, Christians, because they answered to God first rather than the state. Second were those who had gone wayward: criminals, homosexuals, or those just not quite patriotic enough under the swastika symbol. The people who fell into these two enemies of the state categories were sent to reeducation camps with the goal of changing then into good Nazis and rejoining the rest of society once they shaped up. The third category of enemies was racial, and in the minds of "the master race" there were two that were not: the Jews and the Romani; also known as the gypsies. For these people there was only one solution, and that was The Final Solution, *Endlösung*, - extermination. We refer to it today as "The Holocaust." It was the murder of 6 million to 11 million people by approximately 200,000 participants. To wrap your head around the number of people that were exterminated it would be the equivalent of murdering every single person in the country of Greece. And, we're not even talking about the millions of deaths Adolf Hitler ordered his military to do through warfare against other Europeans, nor the approximately 300,000 Americans fighting Nazi Germany who lost their lives; your fellow countrymen. That would be like everyone in Cincinnati, Ohio getting killed. That's 600,000 parents who lost a child, brothers and sisters who lost a sibling, wives and children without their fathers for the rest of their lives, friends who... You get the message. Adolf Hitler was the embodiment of evil, if your worldview even believes that there is evil in this world.

Donald Trump wrote his first book in 1987 called *TRUMP: The Art of the Deal*, which was on The New York Times Best Seller list. His book is not only an autobiography, but it also contains his 11-step formula for business success, which many people have looked to for inspiration in achieving their own business or personal success. I read the book, and I liked it.

Over the years he went on to write several other books. Half of them were about how to become successful, and the other half of them are about America returning to her traditional values, and the capitalistic system that made us a global economic superpower.

In 2017 Donald Trump was the 544th richest person in the world with an estimated net worth of $3.5 billion. He was indeed an authority when it came to financial success in business. During the 2016 Presidential Election he ran on the campaign promises of protecting religious freedom, respecting the United States Constitution as the law of the land, growing the economy, securing our borders, and restoring a strong national defense. When he had come to power the Democratic Party had not been outlawed, and opposition party leaders had not been exiled, imprisoned, or murdered. Those holding different views than those of the President's, such as atheists, homosexuals, Muslims, or even Trump haters, were not rounded up and disposed of. Although progressivism had been stopped dead in its tracks at the federal level, American democracy continued. Everybody's Constitutional rights stayed intact.

I think it's safe to say that there is no legitimate comparison between Adolf Hitler and President Donald Trump. Evil is not the same thing as having differed political opinions. Being on the right is not equivalent to being a Nazi, not even close. So, now that you have been reeducated, and not the way Adolf Hitler would have done it, don't ever use that monster's name side by side with an American politician. In the future you may have to, but not at this time in history. If you do it, you will sound like an uneducated ass-clown.

Now, back to the topic of haters. Just because someone disagrees with you, and your worldview, does not make him or her a hater. In fact, just get rid of the word "hater" from your vocabulary. You shouldn't hate anyone. You can hate people's actions, but you should not hate the person, even if they seem "out of touch." Many who get their worldview from the Bible believe what is written in 1 John 3:15, and that is, "Whosoever hates his brother is a murderer, and you know that no murderer has eternal life abiding in him."

MONEY

I've heard Fox News talk show host Sean Hannity say many times on the radio, and on his T.V. show *Hannity*, "I never got a job from a poor person." I echo his sentiment. Only people with money, or corporations, have hired me to work for them. I can also tell you that I've even been stiffed by people who said they had money, and it appeared as if they had the money to pay me for a job I did for them, only to have been cheated of my hard-earned money. When I was hired to protect actor Brad Pitt I knew that I'd be paid. When the Walt Disney Company hired me I had no doubt in my mind that every week they'd transfer money into my bank account.

Are you part of the 1/3 of Millennials living with your parents? For you Gen Zers, it's understandable that you'd be living with Mommy or Daddy, because you are much younger. However, the Millennials? That's not good. Wouldn't you rather get out and be on your own?

Now, I didn't just make up this "one third" number. It comes from the U.S. Census Bureau in their report *The Changing Economics and Demographics of Young Adulthood: 1975-2016*. Well, for many of you I can't blame you for being down in the dumps. During the entire Obama administration (2009-2016) the economy sucked for the middle class. The GNP, *Gross National Product*, never went above 2.6%, and even dropped down to 1.9% by the time he left office. These dismal numbers certainly torpedoed my once thriving business as well. The only thing that saved me from going under is that I also did business in Europe, and Germany was my cash cow.

Eight years under Democratic rule was a long time not to see what economic prosperity looked like, i.e. good ol' American capitalism. That's why even for those of you who are not living with your parents you're stressing over finances according to a report from Bank of America Merrill Lynch in May of 2017. "More than twice as many Millennials as Baby Boomers said that stress negatively impacts their work. And 68% of 20- and 30-somethings say stress takes a toll on their health versus 56% of Generation X and 51% of those in their 50s and 60s."

It sounds a little depressing, but cheer up! The moment Donald Trump took office businesses, both large and small, knew that things were going to improve. According to the U.S. Department of Commerce Bureau of Economic Analysis the Gross Domestic Product (GDP) at the end of the 1st quarter of 2017 was 1.2 percent. That was the economy that President Trump inherited from President Obama. However, by the end of the 2nd quarter, September 28, 2017, only nine months in office, the GDP was up to 3.1 percent, that despite major hurricanes devastating many parts of the country and Puerto Rico. At the same time the S&P closed at its sixth consecutive record on October 6, 2017, which was "its longest streak of highs since 1997," according to The Wall Street Journal. In other words, the economy keeps growing at a slow and steady pace, because of the leadership in the White House.

Part of what is fueling the upswing in the economy is that common sense is prevailing. On May 19, 2017 President Trump announce that he was granting a permit for construction of the 1,179-mile Keystone XL pipeline from Canada to Louisiana, putting thousands back to work, and beginning "the first of many infrastructure projects."

Although the project was originally approved for construction by the Bush administration, it was President Obama on May 1, 2015 who refused to have it built due to his concern on its effects on climate change. "America is now a global leader when it comes to taking serious action to fight climate change," he said from the White House. "And, frankly, approving this project would have undercut that global leadership."

"Global leadership!" Since when did we give up our sovereignty and place it under global leadership? That's not the America I grew up in. Well, thank God that all changed, and the eight previous years were being erased. On September 19, 2017, when President Trump addressed the United Nations General Assembly, he told the world, "In America the people govern, the people rule, and the people are sovereign. I was elected not to take power, but to give the power to the American people where it belongs." Finally, a president who understood the concept of *We the People*. However, although the President made it clear that it was "America first," he also stated that it did not mean "America alone," and that sovereign nations need to work together.

The President also declared the end of the "War on Coal," giving utility companies the option to use coal for energy if they so choose. The Obama era climate change regulations were crippling. Again, we can count our blessings that Hillary Clinton did not become the President of the United States, because when she was running in the Democratic primary she said, "We're going to put a lot of coal miners and coal companies out of business." Because of that remark West Virginia, "coal country," turned on her. The oil companies knew that if she won the presidential election they'd be next in the crosshairs.

Now that there is no heavy progressive hand upon the energy sector, the country can not only be fuel self-sufficient, but we can now sell our fuel products to the rest of the world. This is good business.

What a difference a year makes. On December 13, 2017 President Donald Trump and the GOP gave a "giant tax cut for Christmas" to American families and companies. The Republican House and Senate Republican leaders got together to pass a massive tax cut the first in 30 years. However, the Democrat leadership was totally against the plan. That's right, not one single Democratic vote. House minority leader Nancy Pelosi (Democrat) declared that it would be "the end of the world," (kinda dramatic, wouldn't you agree) and Bernie Sanders (Democrat) said, "The Trump-Republican tax plan is one of the worst pieces of legislation in the modern history of our country." Nonetheless, Democrats will also benefit from it by getting to keep more of their hard-earned cash and make it possible to leave their children more of their wealth thanks to the eradication of the estate tax, referred to by the Republicans as the "death tax."

Prior to the tax bill being signed into law in 2018 several big American corporations were so optimistic about the future that they promised to give their employees bonuses and invest in the United States. On that list was AT&T, Boeing, Comcast, Wells Fargo, Fifth Third Bankcorp. AT&T CEO Randal Stephenson said, concerning the tax legislation, that is was "a monumental step to bring taxes paid by U.S. businesses in line with the rest of the industrialized world," and that is because prior to this legislation the United States of America had the highest top marginal corporate tax rate among advanced and large emerging economies at 39.1 percent.

I was a young, newly married, adult when President Ronald Reagan was President of the United States, and when he signed into law the Tax Reform Act of 1986. This law reduced the top marginal individual income tax rate from 50% to 28%. It reduced the corporate income tax rate from 46% to 34%, and it reduced the total number of income brackets from 14 to 2. The result was a time of prosperity and a tremendous optimism about the future. However, it did not take long before both Republicans and Democrats alike got greedy and started taxing the American people again, something governments can hardly ever resist doing, starting with President George H. Bush (Republican). He raised the top marginal tax rate for individuals from 28% to 31%, and it's the reason he was a "one term president." Then President Clinton (Democrat) raised the top rate to a whopping 39.6% . President George W. Bush (Republican) brought it down to 35%, and I remember getting that extra cash in the form of an IRS check in the mail. I went out and spent it to put it back into the economy. A lot of Americans did. I also remember the Democrats blasting President Bush for reducing the tax. Then came along President Barak Obama, and he raised it back up to 39.6%, after all, he needed the additional revenue to help fund Planned Parenthood and fix "climate change."

The new top rate was reduced from 39.6% to 37%; not exactly the significant reduction that President Reagan gave us, but enough to heal an anemic Democratic economy of 8 long years. And, to think, the Democrats threw a hissy fit over a 2.6% top rate reduction for you.

Finally, you Millennials and Gen Zers will be able to compare a conservative, Republican, economy to a liberal, Democratic, economy for the first time in your lives. Come Election Day you can decide for yourself which system, which direction, based on your own experience, is best for your wallet or purse.

ACTIVISM

Gender neutral bathrooms. Black Lives Matter. Climate change. Save the whatever… There are a lot of causes that Millennials and Gen Zers "support," and the more zealous of them are activists. An "activist" is a person who works hard, really hard, to bring about political or social change. Of course, most of your peers don't give a single dollar to any cause, but they do pay good lip service to them, and on occasion they'll show their "outrage" on their social media account.

So, what do conservatives do when it comes to supporting the causes they believe in? Rarely do they take to the streets, and almost never do they try to destroy property or beat up those who have differing views. Instead, they put their money where their mouth is. They give to worthwhile causes that change things for the better, or make people's lives better, and they get a tax deduction for doing so.

You might be asking, while snarling, "What are worthwhile conservative causes?" Well, for starters, any organization that feeds people, clothes people, or provides shelter for people.

Now, if you want to try to understand how conservatives truly think, instead of supporting some agenda that wants to overthrow the government or turn our culture upside down, you need to give to a worthy cause. I said "WORTHY." You don't need to go big or give big. There are people in your own city or community that could use some of your money, skills, or your time. I'm sure there is a soup kitchen, an orphanage, an old folks home, or the American Red Cross you can volunteer for. You could even find a true homeless person and hand them a gift card to a local restaurant. By doing this you are helping to make society better. Yes, I know, it is not as exciting as telling corporations or the cops to "F--- off!" or try to push failed socialism for the umpteenth time, but the conservative way just feels better deep down inside. Building something up is always more satisfying than destroying something or tearing it down.

And, speaking of "destroying" and "tearing down," we're going to take a look at violent activism later on.

CELL BLOCK 8

PHOEBIAS

HOMOPHOBIA

The left has come up with a lot of terms that were never in the English language. Of course, "phobia" was always a term in the English language, which is a Greek word we borrowed meaning *fear*, but tack on a politically correct term in front of it and voila, you have a new word for social and political purposes. Repeat it enough times, like communist propaganda suggests, and many people come to not only accept the term, but believe it.

A lot of Millennials and Gen Zers are using the word *phobia* to promote their chosen agendas, when in fact there is already a word in the English language to describe their intent, and that word is "deculturate." The definition of deculturate is *to deprive of culture or cultural attainments*. The problem is that most of you have never heard this word before, and so you need a whole slew of words to express this one idea.

One such made up word that had never been used in American history, until its first known use in 1969 according to Merriam-Webster, was the word "homophobia," which means *an irrational fear, aversion to, or discrimination against homosexuality or homosexuals.* So, why don't we start here first, with the word "homophobia." Let's determine if it's a legitimate fear that we should all have, or a good term that we should keep on using to describe those less enlightened.

Whenever you come to a fork in the road of life, and you must make a decision as to which way to go, you must always ask yourself, "Where will this road eventually lead me?" This is the exact same question any society must ask itself before taking the first step. So, let's take one of today's current topics, and a controversial one at that, homosexuality, which is s*ex between people of the same sex; men with men, and women with women.*

For the sake of argument let's ask the question, "If today every single person on earth became homosexual where would the road lead us? Where would it lead mankind?"

What is your answer?

The answer is obvious. The human race would cease to exist within 100 years, assuming a newborn today lives to be 100-years-old; leaving test tube babies out of the equation. Without procreation a species is unable to continue. It takes a man and a woman to produce a baby. This is biology 101. So, obviously having sexual contact between like gender is not a matter of biology, it is a social issue.

"Oh, but some people are born that way!" you protest.

"Are they?" I must ask you. For this is certainly the argument of many today. I've heard it a million times from my goddaughters, "Some people are just born gay."

Then let's start with that presumption, that some babies are indeed "born gay." That would mean that some babies are also born with a predisposition towards necrophilia, they just don't know it until they reach puberty. Necrophilia is the attraction or sexual contact with corpses – dead people. I'm sure there are some people out there right now saying to themselves, "I always wondered why I got turned on at funerals."

What about those babies born with a predisposition towards incest? Who says that it is wrong for a grandchild to have sexual relations with their grandmother, or a father with his daughter? "They were born that way" should also apply equally.

What about being born a pedophile? At what age does that child realize they are sexually attracted to children? "They were born that way," and they just grew up with that desire.

Wait, how about this! Some babies are simply born with a predisposition towards bestiality, which, as you well know, is sexual relations between a human and an animal.

When I was a cop I arrested a man for having intercourse with a neighbor's poodle. He was caught right in the act by the dog's owner looking out from her two-story window into her backyard, and he confessed to me that he had done it; not to mention the dog was walking in a tortured way as circumstantial evidence. It was a misdemeanor at the time, and this was during the mid-1990s. Of course, since some people are "born" to have sex with animals then it also stands to reason that it will be with a particular animal. Since it is an unchangeable code within the DNA some people have no choice but to be partial to horses, while in other people their code informs them that they are to desire sheep, while others it will be dogs, like the guy I arrested.

I think you get my point. If some people are "born" to have a predisposition to homosexuality, then that means that the other sexual preferences must also be a condition at birth as well, and thus unchangeable.

So, how does that explain those homosexuals who decided to become heterosexuals? It happens quite a bit you know. Are they going against their own DNA? What about one of my principals I did some bodyguard work for? You might have heard about her – actress Angelina Jolie. In a television interview with Barbara Walters she talked about her Foxfire (1996) co-star Jenny Shimizu stating that she was "surprised when I suddenly found myself having these feelings I always had for men, but for a woman."

Wait a second! Is it "feelings" or "born-that-way" DNA?

Oh, no, I get it. One can have sexual feelings, excuse me, DNA code from birth, for both sexes. That's where the bisexual stuff comes in, doesn't it? After all, Angelina Jolie married actor Billy Bob Thorten, divorced him in 2003, and then married Brad Pitt in 2014; another one of my principals.

Now, before you jump my case, accusing me of clinging to a Victorian era morality because of my disagreement of a client's sexual history, keep this in mind before you rush to judgment, that I was willing to take a bullet for her; Angelina Jolie, that is. I didn't protect her with a Smith & Wesson model 645 .45 caliber semi-automatic pistol for nothing. The same was true for Mr. Pitt. I did not like the fact either that he was rumored to have hopped into the sack with a few of his female co-stars or divorced his former wife Jennifer Aniston, but I was ready to shield him with my own body if someone tried to attack him. What these two actors didn't know, at the time I was employed by Sunset Protective Services, was that each night that I was on duty protecting the property and their souls, from 6 p.m. to 6 a.m. for two straight weeks, I stretched out my hand towards their Malibu home after everyone had gone to bed and I prayed for them. Not only did I pray that they would repent, and stop living together in sin as an unmarried couple, but I prayed they would come to know the Lord Jesus Christ as their personal Savior.

Then there's asexual, which is the lack of sexual attraction to others.

I've also heard many transgender people, people who had a gender identity or assigned sex (meaning that they were turned over by the doctor at birth, who looked at the genital, and in their medical opinion stated either, "It's a boy" or "It's a girl"), but it is actually the opposite. Some call it a "third gender." In other words, don't judge a book by its cover.

If the XY sex-determination system, that is to say "the sex chromosomes," determines one's physical sex, XY for males and XX for females, then it's scientifically safe to say that chromosomes don't lie about somebody's gender. This fact can only mean that transgender people must have something else going on inside of them, because it's certainly not physical. Putting on a dress or slipping on a pair of pants does not change one's sex, nor does simply making a statement contrary to one's chromosomes. It's a social issue. This social issue parallels how many people since the 1880s, and all the way up until recent years, were saying that alcoholism is a "disease." Sadly, some still believe this lie today, because it takes the responsibility off the shoulders of the abusers. The Bible claims that drunkenness is a sin, and for one's own good not to do it. Yet failing to heed the Bible's warning, and ignoring scientific evidence supporting the Bible later on in history, put the responsibility of the "cure" in the hands of rehab centers, pharmaceutical companies, and it created a new pop-psychology market. Fortunately, when it comes to alcoholism today, the pendulum is swinging back to "alcoholism is a choice." Hmmmm, it seems that the Bible is right once again. I also know that alcoholism is a choice from my own observations, because the pastor of my church was a drunk for ten years of his life. He openly admits it, and everyone who knew him testifies as to just how awful he was. Yet, one day, thanks to the healing power of Jesus Christ, he decided to stop, and has not had a drink since. Now he is an unbelievably loving husband, father, grandfather, and teacher. He's my shepherd, and for a former cop to be under a former drunk's teachings is no small matter. I have arrested hundreds of drunks during my career, and I have seen countless relationships torn apart by it. Unfortunately, I have also seen a few people die from alcohol poisoning.

Nobody today is calling certain sex acts, or sexual identity, a disease like they once did for alcoholism. It's quite the opposite. What is plainly called sin, the sin of homosexuality, in the Bible is now considered by many as perfectly "normal." Yet, for something that is normal there are certainly a lot of new terms our society is coming up with to explain it all: genderqueer, bigender, pangender, trigender, gender fluid, cross-dresser, queer, and so forth.

We can go on for hours disputing about whether one is born with a particular sexual preference or a person is just hard wired that way because DNA makes it so, but the best way to approach I can take is to give you the conservative point of view.

First, there are homosexuals inside the Republican Party. On July 21, 2016 Peter Thiel, the co-founder of PayPal, a great company by the way, was the first openly gay speaker to declare his sexuality at a GOP convention. "I am proud to be gay," he declared. "I am proud to be a Republican. But most of all, I am proud to be an American."

Nobody ran him off the stage or tar and feathered him. He was treated with respect like all the rest of the speakers at the convention.

Now, I'm not going to lie to you, a lot of Republicans were uncomfortable having him speak. If you want to know the truth, a good majority of Republicans are not thrilled about homosexuality.

"And why is that?" you are asking.

If you can bear with me, and not get all bent out of shape calling me a "homophobe" in your mind before I am finished, then I will educate you as to why homosexuals are accepted equally under the law, but not their homosexuality. After all, this is a reeducation camp. You're here to learn.

Remember, a lot of people in the top positions of our government are Christians, and as such their belief in God shapes their worldview. Doesn't yours?

Why are you acting all confused? Don't you see the connection? It's the same connection that exists between communism and Christianity. Karl Marx hated Christianity and wanted it abolished, and many communist leaders did just that, and they still do today. Likewise, many homosexuals would love to silence conservative Judeo-Christian Republicans. It's something many groups on the left have in common. Don't tell me it ain't so when in fact Lady Gaga, the talented singing genius that she is, lumped God and gays together in her 2011 song *Born This Way*, which many LBGTQs adopted as their anthem. The lyrics do not reflect an accurate Biblical context, but Lady Gaga obviously supports the theory that the homosexual community is "born this way:"

I'm beautiful in my way
'Cause God makes no mistakes
I'm on the right track, baby I was born this way

Some of you are saying, "That's just your interpretation of the song. The right is always jumping to concussions. They're just haters and homophobes!"

Oh yeah, then why does the official *Born This Way* music video start out with the pink triangle? Do you think I'm stupid? This pink triangle goes back to the Nazi concentration camps in 1942 when they had it sewn onto prison uniforms to identify homosexual prisoners, and since then it has become a gay pride and gay rights symbol. Just as Christians took the Roman cross, an instrument of execution, as their symbol of faith, so too the homosexuals took the triangle, also a symbol of execution. Likewise, as homosexuals have imitated God's institution of marriage between a man and a woman, they have also imitated the taking of a once evil symbol. Taking this homosexual symbol one step further, is the pink triangle with a green circle around it, which means "a safe-space free from homophobia." The meaning of this green circle originates from the concept of the heavily fortified zone in the middle of Baghdad after the 2003 American-led invasion of Iraq known as the "Green Zone." Only "friendlies" were allowed in the Green Zone, and all enemies were kept outside of it.

Do you remember when you first came into this camp, back when you were in

Cell Block 1, we talked about American universities creating safe-spaces right after the election of President Donald Trump. It's a place where conservative views are not welcome; a place that stifles *freedom of speech.*

So, now let's take a look at 20 people within our current government, and begin to understand why the LGBTQ, and other leftist groups, want them outside of the green circle; a circle that they would like eventually to circle the entire country. Oh, quit your bellyaching, certainly you can learn about just twenty people, even if you don't like them, because, like it or not, they have a tremendous impact on your life as your national leaders in the here and now. Plus, you should know these people in detail anyway just to stay current with current affairs or do your Sun Tzu thing after you're released from this camp. Let's start with the top dog. POTUS, President of the United States. You should go to Wikipedia right now and type in the song *Hail to the Chief*, and then press play as you read this next paragraph. It will set the mood.

1. **President Donald Trump** considers himself a Presbyterian, which has its roots in England and Scotland, and this denomination of Christianity has been in the United States since the 17th century. He speaks openly about his faith, and gave a reveling interview to the Christian Broadcast Network (CBN). On January 18, 2017 his wife, **First Lady Melania Trump**, gave a speech at the Orlando-Melbourne Airport, and started off by reciting The Lord's Prayer in its entirety. First Lady Trump was born in communist Yugoslavia. Since the Communist Party in her home of Slovenia was atheist she was secretly baptized in her mother's village by Franc Čampa, the parish priest of St. Lawrence's Church in Raka, when she was five months old. When the First Lady gave her speech at the airport many on the left became unglued. The shouts of "separation of church and state!" were predicable, but the vile comments were over the top like, "Melania read the 'our father' like a whore in confession after a night escorting." Then a lot of people attacked her for her Eastern European accent. That's right, the left who wants open borders, and who welcomes every foreign immigrant into the country whether they're terrorists or not, made fun of her for her accent. What uneducated, hypocritical, idiots! Melania Trump's education included learning French, Italian, German and English. The average American, if they did not grow up speaking a second language at home, speaks zero foreign languages at conversational level. Now, I was no big fan of First Lady Michelle Obama, but if someone would have called her a "whore" I would have been outraged. That's not just a conservative Republican thing to be offended by filthy comments against our leaders; it's just being civilized.

2. **Vice President Mike Pense** was raised a Roman Catholic, and as a young adult was a Democrat. While attending college he accepted Jesus Christ as his Lord and Savior, thus being "born-again," made him an "evangelical Christian" if you were to label him. His worldview changed as a result, and politically he shifted to the right. When President Donald Trump had his very first cabinet meeting at the White House he asked Vice President Pense to open it up with a word of prayer. That is how this administration began, a sincere prayer to Jesus Christ.

3. **Secretary of State Rex Tillerson** was a Boy Scout earning the rank of Eagle Scout. The Boy Scouts of America was formed in 1910, and the Scout Oath is "On my honor, I will do my best, to do my duty, to God and country, and to obey the Scout Law, to help other people at all times, to keep myself physically strong, mentally awake, and morally straight." As an adult Rex Tillerson served as president of the Boy Scouts of America from 2010 to 2012. He and his wife are affiliated with the National Association of Congregational Christian Churches.

4. The second highest position in our government when it comes to representing the United States of America to the nations of the world is **United States Ambassador to the United Nations Nikki Haley**, who was the former Governor of South Carolina. This is the woman that on September 8, 2017 the communist North Korean government called a "political prostitute" for warning them to stop threatening to nuke us. However, she is not intimidated by anyone, and America is fortunate she is in the position that she is in. Anyway, Nikki Haley was born to Sikh parents who emigrated from Punjab, India. Ambassador Haley converted to Christianity and attends a United Methodist Church with her husband and two children when at home. As the Ambassador to the U.N. she, by the orders of President Trump, is unashamedly pro-Israel, and stated to the world that the days of "Israel-bashing" by the United Nations is over. We'll talk more about Israel before you are released from this camp. It's kind of the linchpin to future world events.

5. Should tragedy befall President Trump or Vice President Pense the next in line to rule the country is **Speaker of the United States House of Representatives Paul Ryan**. For his early education Speaker Ryan attended St. Mary's Catholic School in Janesville, Wisconsin. In January of 2017 Speaker Ryan announced that the Republican effort to overturn Obama Care would include defunding Planned Parenthood. At a news conference he said, "Planned Par-

enthood legislation would be in our reconciliation bill." Planned Parenthood, with the motto, *Care. No matter what*, which is a bit ominous, received 554.6 million dollars in government funding (government health services reimbursements and grants for the year ending June 30, 2016), which was paid by your taxes. According to their own 2015–2016 Annual Report their 650 Planned Parenthood health centers served 2.4 million patients with, "557,672 unintended pregnancies averted by Planned Parenthood's contraceptive services." 3% of their medical services were "Abortion Services." There were "328,348 Abortion Services" according to their own count. In simple English, that's 557,672 lives prevented from forming, and 328,348 lives certainly ended. So, in 2016, if we just looked at the abortions alone, that was equivalent to just over the entire population of Corpus Christi, Texas and slightly under the entire population of the nation of Iceland.

6. United States Secretary of Housing and Urban Development Ben Carson is a remarkable man; an African American man that the liberal left does not seem to respect very much, because of his conservative views. Well, actually, they don't like him because he never uses the "race card," nor did he ever adopt the victim mentality like so many of today's black leaders do. His mother, a strong woman, made sure that he and his older brother spent more time concentrating on their education, and less time on frivolous pursuits. However, as a teenager Ben Carson had a nasty temper, and one day he tried to stab a boy in the guy, but fortunately the boy's belt buckle prevented the blade from going in. Realizing that he had deep seeded issues Ben Carson started reading all the verses about anger from the Book of Proverbs, which is the book of wisdom in the Old Testament. Trusting in God worked, and Ben Carson went on to be one of the most famous neurosurgeons in the world, and wrote six bestselling Christian books. On February 7, 2013 Ben Carson was the keynote speaker at the National Prayer Breakfast, with President Barack Obama sitting only 10 feet away from him as he spoke. Ben Carson blasted the President for some of his failed policies. Because of that speech Ben Carson became a conservative sensation, which landed him in politics. He ran for the office of the President of the United States, but lost out to Donald Trump. Once he was out of the race he soon afterwards endorsed Donald Trump. In my opinion Ben Carson's autobiography *Gifted Hands* should be read by every young person of school age, especially those kids that live in impoverished neighborhoods.

7. United States Attorney General Jeff Sessions, the highest law enforcement officer in the nation, is a Sunday school teacher at the Ashland Place United

Methodist Church where he and his wife are members. He has also served on the church's administrative board. According to Human Rights Campaign, the largest LGBTQ advocacy group in the United States, Attorney General Sessions has earned a "zero rating," which indicates his stance on the LGBTQ issues. He believes marriage is between a man and a woman, he is against the legalization of marijuana, and he stated, "that the sanctity of life begins at conception." As the top law enforcement officer of the land he got tired of all of the Christian bashing, that had been so prevalent in the Obama years, that on October 11, 2017 he announced, "We're putting this country back on a lawful path, a constitutional path, a path that respects religious faith." By now you should be picking up on how one's worldview determines how leaders govern. This is why I'm bringing it up, and this is why you're in this camp. Now, moving on.

8. United States Secretary of the Interior Ryan Zinke was a former U.S. Navy SEAL. That has nothing to do with Christianity, but I just thought it was cool to mention. He was an officer leaving the service with the rank of commander. Oh, by the way, Secretary Zinke is Lutheran, which is a major branch of Protestant Christianity. Martin Luther (1483-1546) was a priest in the Roman Catholic Church who basically told the church, and later Pope Leo X, that some of their teachings had gone way off course from Christ's original teachings, and that they needed to stick with Biblical doctrine. That didn't go over very well, and Nailing his Ninety-five Theses in 1517 to the local church door didn't go over very big either. To make a long story short the Protestant "protest" Movement came about, and Europe was divided along religious lines. After almost 400 plus years of dispute, ugly persecution, and lots of wars, the two sides have basically *agreed to disagree*. Both Protestants and Catholics, the Bible believing ones anyway, are pretty much in line when it comes to social issues.

9. United States Secretary of Health and Human Services Tom Price is a white male, conservative, rich (estimated to be worth $13.6 million according to Politico in 2014), and Presbyterian; the same domination as President Donald Trump. Their symbol is the burning bush that Moses stood before, and the Latin inscription underneath it states ARDENS SED VIRENS, *burning but flourishing*. Anyway, Secretary Price was not always a politician you know. Nope, he went to med school then ran an orthopedic clinic in Atlanta, Georgia for 20 years, and then after that returned to Emory University where he did his residency to be an assistant professor. He was a member of the Association of American Physicians and Surgeons (AAPS), which is a conservative non-profit association dedicated to fighting socialized medicine. On their website they ask the question, "To serve the state? Or to serve our patients?" Therefore, when Tom Price was the U.S. Representative for Georgia's 6th congressional district he opposed taxpayer monies to be allocated for abortions. Not only did he use the power of his vote to fight abortion, but he participated in the 2011 March for Life. So, as a conservative Christian where do you think he stands on other issues? I'll tell you. He opposes gun control, and strongly believes that the Second Amendment applies to all law-abiding citizens. He believes that marriage should be defined as one man and one woman, and he voted against H.R. 2965, which ended President Bill Clinton's *Don't ask, don't tell* policy for the United States military.

"Ah, ha! I've got you now!" You're saying. "He's a fraud! He was caught using private charters and military aircraft for travel, and because of that President Trump forced him out! Gotcha!"

You're right. Because he did wrong he resigned as head of HHS on September 29, 2017. He admitted that he did wrong. Wasn't that refreshing, especially after the Obama era, that a politician in Washington would admit to wrongdoing, and step down. That was the honorable thing to do. He didn't lie to the American people or Congress like President Bill Clinton (Democrat) did during his impeachment process as a result of the the Monica Lewinsky scandal – "I did not have sexual relations with that woman, Miss Lewinsky." Tom Price faced the music, unlike Secretary of State Hillary Clinton (Democrat) did during the Benghazi scandal cover up – "What difference, at this point, what difference does it make." Four Americans she was responsible for lost their lives. Tom Price took his punishment like a man, whereas U.S. Attorney General Loretta Lynch met with President Bill Clinton aboard her Justice Department jet on the tarmac, while his wife was under investigation by the FBI for conducting government business on a private server and destroying those hard drives with hammers, stating that the conversations were about "travels, golf and grandchildren." Need I go on? There are more, but I'll spare you. So, nobody said Christians are perfect. But, I wanted to leave Tom Price on this list of heroes to give you a comparison between integrity and the lack of integrity. Plus, when somebody screws up big time the President of the United does what is right also. He didn't just get rid of Tom Price, but also White House Communications Director Anthony Scaramucci for basically having a potty mouth, Former White House Chief of Staff Reince Priebus for failure to stop leeks to the media, and former National Security Advisor Michael Flynn for lying to Vice President Pence.

10. **United States Secretary of Energy Rick Perry** grew up in the United Methodist Church. Like so many American male leaders he was a Boy Scout

and earned the rank of Eagle Scout. He attended Texas A&M University, and then after graduation was commissioned as an officer in the United States Air Force. After flight school he was a C-130 pilot. Missions included relief efforts in Mali, Mauritania, Chad, and Guatemala. After the service he went into business with his father cotton farming. He then went into politics being elected to the Texas House of Representatives as a Democrat from District 64. He even supported Al Gore in the 1988 Democratic primaries. Then on September 29, 1989 he did a switcheroo. Yes indeed, Rick Perry publicly announced that he was a Republican, and then went on to become the Agriculture Commissioner, then Lieutenant Governor, and eventually the Governor of Texas in 2000. In 2010 he and his family started to attend a non-denominational evangelical church in Travis County. Throughout his governorship he was very open about his faith in Jesus Christ, and those on the left in Texas were very critical of it. Back in 2011 Governor Perry had the audacity to proclaim August 6th as a Day of Prayer and Fasting, and even invited other governors to join him. Who would do such a "separation of church and state" thing like that? Well, do you ever celebrate Thanksgiving Day? The final Thursday of November is officially observed, starting in 1863, because of a presidential proclamation by Abraham Lincoln. Anyway, Governor Rick Perry ran in the 2016 GOP primaries, but he lost to Donald Trump. Well, despite the mainstream media always trying to make Rick Perry look like a buffoon, President Trump knew that he had made Texas one of the most prosperous states in the Union and he tapped into his skills to govern and appointed him as the Secretary of Energy, which was confirmed by Congress. Like clockwork you can predict where he stands on social issues. He's not quiet about them either. He wrote a book in 2008 titled *On My Honor* where he compares homosexuality to alcoholism stating that he was, "no expert on the 'nature versus nurture' debate, but that gays should simply choose abstinence." In other words, he said it was a sin just like alcoholism is a sin. And, where did he get this idea from? Yes, the Bible. Both are named as sin in the Bible.

Or do you not know that the unrighteous will not inherit the kingdom of God? Do not be deceived; neither fornicators, nor idolaters, nor adulterers, nor effeminate, nor homosexuals, nor thieves, nor the greedy, nor drunkards, nor verbal abusers, nor swindlers, will inherit the kingdom of God.   1 Corinthians 6:9

What? What an outrage! God does not want thieves in Heaven! What a kleptophobe (the fear of theft) He is!

Of course, this scripture is talking about people practicing these sins. Should they turn away from these sins, and ask Jesus Christ into their hearts, then the former things they had done will not prevent them from entering Heaven. Again, it's all about one's WORLDVIEW.

Moving right along, Secretary Rick Perry loves to pack heat. In Texas he has a Conceal Carry Weapons (CCW) permit. The NRA loves him. He is tough on crime and supports the death penalty. He's against all abortions, except to save a mother's life. Finally, he saw to it when he was governor that security was beefed up along the Texas-Mexican border to deal with the surge in illegal immigration.

11. **United States Secretary of Education Betsy DeVos** is the wife of Dick DeVos, the former CEO of Amway, whose father was the co-founder of Amway. In 2016 the DeVos family was listed by Forbes as the 88th richest family in America. Well, good for them. This makes some people infuriated, as if being rich is somehow wrong, but I never hear anyone complain about how rich singer Beyoncé is, or actress Meryl Streep, or rapper EMINEM. I guess idols are okay, but people who make things or provide services for others isn't. Secretary De-Vos grew up attending the Christian Reformed Church in North America, and went to high school at Holland Christian High School, which is a private school. She is an elder at the Mars Hill Bible Church in Grand Rapids, Michigan. Her brother, Erik Prince is a former U.S. Navy SEAL who is the founder of Black-water USA; a private security group that provided trained personnel for the support of military security missions in Afghanistan and Iraq, and the company even supported law enforcement in the aftermath of Hurricane Katrina. She got her start in politics in 1982 with the Michigan Republican Party working her way up to local precinct delegate, then the Republican National Committee, and then... ahhh, I see that you're getting bored. All right, I'll skip her political history, as interesting as it is, and move on by saying that Secretary DeVos' interest in education goes back to her own experiences with private education, and for many years she has been a firm believer in allowing parents to pick their children's own education, be it public schools or private schools. She supports "school choice," which is implemented by a voucher system. Of course, a lot of teachers and teacher unions, many who are on the left, do not like her position, because they don't want any funds taken away from public schools, and they certainly don't like what faith-based schools are teaching, namely God, creation, abstinence, et cetera. Yes, most private schools are producing outstanding students, many of who are better educated than their public school counterparts, but that doesn't matter. It's all about $$$, and to indoctrinate the children with the false narrative of "the separation of church and state."

12. **White House Chief of Staff John Kelly** was the second cabinet member confirmed by the U.S. Senate just hours after Donald Trump took the oath of office. It wasn't for the job of White House Chief of Staff, that had originally belonged to Reince Priebus (a member of the Greek Orthodox Church, and who had met his wife in church when they were teenagers), but for the position of United States Secretary of Department of Homeland Security. Eighty-eight senators approved Secretary Kelly, 11 opposed him, and one senator didn't vote. Those numbers should tell you something, and that is that he's highly trusted by both the Republicans and the Democrats. After six months on the job President Trump was tired of all the information leaks flowing from the White House, blamed on the deep state, and he needed someone who could enforce a chain of command, and so he pushed Priebus was out, and gave the position to Kelly who was sworn in on July 31, 2017. Now, there is not much on the Internet about Kelly's religious beliefs, other than he was born into an Irish Catholic family, but this great man is worthy of mention. After all, he had been in charge of the security of our country, and is now runs the White House for the most powerful man in the world. This man is a true warrior. Before taking the top job with DHS, *Department of Homeland Security*, he retired as a four-star general in 2016 with his last post heading the U.S. Southern Command – that's all of South America. HOOAH! Before that he led the Multi-National Force in West Iraq under the Obama administration, and he was later the senior military aide to Defense Secretaries Robert Gates and Leon Panetta; two secretaries, not just one. The rest of his military career is no less impressive, and besides seeing the horrors of war himself he knows the cost of serving this wonderful country of ours. His 29-year-old son, First Lieutenant Robert Kelly, was killed in action by a land mine while leading a platoon of Marines on patrol in Sangin, Afghanistan. It was his third combat tour. His other son, John Jr. is a Marine Corps major. When Secretary John Kelly took office he stated to his subordinates, "my only plea is that together we focus our loyalty on the Constitution that we all have sworn to preserve and protect the nation we love." Notice, the focus was not a political party, or even to the President himself, it was to the United States Constitution, as it should be.

13. **Director of the CIA Mike Pompeo** is, yes, a Christian. As soon as he was confirmed as the Director of the Central Intelligence Agency he spoke at a church event in Wichita, Kansas, as reported by CNS News, stating that radical Muslims want "to wipe Christians from the face of the Earth," and that Christians need to pray, fight, and understand that "Jesus Christ our Savior is truly the

only solution for our world." Director Pompeo is a former U.S. Army captain who patrolled the Iron Curtain during the Cold War. He became a businessman, and then was elected to the U.S. House of Representatives where he served for six years. He's as conservative as a conservative can be having been a member of the Tea Party movement. He is also a lifetime member of the National Rifle Association. What? Don't you want our country's top spy to love guns? I certainly do. Aren't all spooks into guns? He opposes closing Guantánamo Bay detention camp. Aren't you glad you're in this camp instead of there? And, he was against President Obama closing the CIA's secret prisons, aka *Black Sites*, around the world. Most of all, he wants to see Muslim leaders step up and condemn acts of terrorism done in the name of Islam.

14. **Director of National Intelligence Dan Coats'** wife Marsha Coats summed it all up when she wrote, "As a conservative, pro-life, evangelical, female Republican, I understand the conflict many in our party feel about supporting Donald Trump. Trump was not my first or even my second choice. He is not a humble man, but he is the choice of Republican voters all over the country, and many Democrats too. The people have not only spoken, they have roared! We are a democracy still." When Director Coats was a senator he helped write the policy *Don't Ask, Don't Tell*. In 2010 he made it clear that he believes marriage is a union between a man and a woman saying, "I don't think we have to interfere with someone who chooses an alternative lifestyle, but I just don't think it falls under the category of marriage." He opposes abortion, and on his own Senate website vowed to "defend the sanctity of life from the moment of conception," and "I will also continue to oppose the use of taxpayer funding for abortions, the promotion of human cloning or government funding of embryo-destroying stem cell research." Of course, he is former military. Director Coats served in the United States Army from 1966 to 1968, earned a Doctor of Law degree from the Indiana University Robert H. McKinney School of Law, but surprising enough has worked to impose stricter gun control measures not in line with the NRA. See, not every conservative is stamped from the same cookie cutter, but I'm not going to skewer him just because I disagree with him on some issues, and neither has most conservatives.

15. **Director of the Office of Management and Budget Mick Mulvaney** is a Roman Catholic, and on May 25, 2017 he set the record straight when responding to the criticism that came after the rollout of President Trump's first budget proposal, "Republicans care about poor people," because for decades the Democrats claimed that they were the party for the poor, and the Republicans were

the party for the rich. Director Mulvaney continued the list, "Republicans care about kids. Republicans care about the elderly. Just like many Democrats care about national defense. And the rhetoric, this demagoguery, just doesn't help the debate at all."

16. **Administrator of the Environmental Protection Agency Scott Pruitt** is a Baptist, and according to the Oklahoma Office of Attorney General, for which he served as the Attorney General from 2011 to 2017, he serves as a deacon at the First Baptist Church of Broken Arrow. He earned his Juris Doctor in 1993 from the University of Tulsa, and then went into private practice as an attorney specializing in constitutional law, contracts, labor law, insurance law, litigation and appeals. As Attorney General of Oklahoma he supported religious freedom and opposed abortion, same-sex marriage, the Affordable Care Act (known as Obama Care), and "against the EPA's activist agenda." That's right, for years Scott Pruitt rejected the "scientific consensus" on climate change. He, and many conservatives, didn't buy into "the sky is falling" rhetoric that liberals were screaming almost daily. But, don't worry. We are going to walk you through the climate change controversy very shortly as part of your reeducation process. But, before we do that, let me add that Scott Pruitt, is a pit bull that was put into the EPA's top position by President Trump to curtail the agency's power grabs. They were infamous for declaring mud puddles on people's property as "navigable waters" or "wetlands," and then they would bankrupt landowners who didn't comply with their demands. Things were getting so bad under Obama's leadership that on May 14, 2014 Ernest Istook wrote an opinion piece in the Washington Times about the EPA with the headline *Watch where you spit! EPA may declare it a wetland*. That's because the EPA was going to expand their power by adding "temporary and seasonal flows of water" to be under their control in order to "clarify" the 1972 Clean Water Act. So, if a person ended up with a seasonal puddle on their property after a rain it belonged to the EPA – FOREVER!

17. **Administrator of the Small Business Administration Linda McMahon** grew up in a conservative Baptist family, and in her later years she converted to Roman Catholicism. Linda McMahon married her high school sweetheart Vincent McMahon, professional wrestling promoter, when she was 17-years-old and he was 20-years-old. Together they created the Word Wrestling Federation empire, and that is what she did, become a magnate, from 1980 to 2009. In 2008 she and her husband donated over $8 million, giving grants to the Sacred Heart University, the Fishburne Military School, and East Carolina University. She

also supported other organizations such as the USO to support American troops, and the Make-A-Wish Foundation. Isn't nice that there are rich people that not only provide jobs for many people, but they can give back even more to society with some of their profits. The same year that she left professional wrestling Linda McMahon ran as a Republican for a seat in the United States Senate in Connecticut, but she lost in 2010. She ran again in 2012 for the second Senate seat, but lost that race also. All that talent could have gone to waste had it not been for President Donald Trump who saw her potential, and he nominated her for the Administrator of the Small Business Administration. After all, she had experienced success as a small, medium, and NASDAQ traded company. The Senate Committee on Small Business and Entrepreneurship voted 18 to 1 to confirm her, and then the full Senate voted 81 to 19, and the rest is history. It's nice to have a billionaire who wants to help others grow their businesses in the good ol' USA.

18. **Counselor to the President Kellyanne Conway** was raised in a Catholic family, but it was a broken home. Her parents divorced when she was three. She graduated from St. Joseph High School, a four-year co-education Catholic school, and then received her Bachelor of Arts degree magna cum laude in political science from Trinity College, a Roman Catholic university, in Washington, D.C. Her claim to fame is that she was the first woman to run a presidential campaign, and win. Originally, she co-chaired a pro-Ted Cruz political action committee during the Republican presidential primaries, but when he withdrew from the race Donald Trump appointed her as a senior advisor for his campaign, and then later to the position of campaign manager. Good move on her part, for when he won the election she was appointed as Counselor to the President. Both before the election, and after, she has appeared on the Christian Broadcast Network. On October 28, 2016 journalist Jenna Browder started off the interview by asking Kellyanne Conway about her faith, to which she replied, "My faith journey started the day I was born, the day I was conceived, because I was born into a very religious family where God, and faith, and country, and family were always most important to us."

19. The single most important thing President Donald Trump did to keep the country from losing conservative values in the highest court of the land was to appoint **Neil Gorsuch** to be the **Associate Justice of the Supreme Court of the United States**. After Senate confirmation he filled the vacuum left by Associate Justice Antonin Scalia, a self-described originalist when it came to the interpretation of the United States Constitution, who died on February 13, 2016 when

President Obama was in power. His mother, Anne Gorsuch Burford, had been appointed by President Ronald Reagan to be the first female Administrator of the U.S. Environmental Protection Agency. Neil Gorsuch started his education attending Christ the King Catholic school, and later graduated from Georgetown Preparatory School, a Jesuit boarding school for boys 9th grade to 12th just outside of Washington, D.C. He received his Bachelor of Arts degree in Political Science from Columbia University, and graduated from Harvard Law School with a Juris Doctor. One of his classmates there was Barak Obama, but Gorsuch was a committed conservative whereas the future president of the United States was a liberal "on a campus full of ardent liberals." He then received a Doctor of (legal) Philosophy degree from University College, Oxford where he met his wife Louise. Although raised Roman Catholic Associate Justice Gorsuch and his wife attend an Episcopal church. Of course, he is a staunch conservative. In an article he wrote for the National Review titled *Liberals' N' Lawsuits* Associate Justice Gorsuch outlining the dangers of the liberals using the courts to affect social changes. He wrote, "…American liberals have become addicted to the courtroom, relying on judges and lawyers rather than elected leaders and the ballot box, as the primary means of effecting their social agenda on everything from gay marriage to assisted suicide to the use of vouchers for private-school education."

There are nine Justices on the U.S. Supreme Court. Anthony Kennedy was appointed by President Reagan, Clarence Thomas was appointed by President George H. Bush, Ruth Bader Ginsburg and Stephen Breyer were appointed by President Clinton, John Roberts and Samuel Alito were appointed by President George W. Bush, Sonia Sotomayor and Elena Kagan were appointed by President Obama, and Neil Gorsuch was appointed by President Trump. That makes the score 5 appointed by Republican presidents, and 4 appointed by Democrat presidents. President Obama tried to get in his guy, Appeals Court Judge Merrick Garland, appointed to the position, but the Republicans played hardball. The Senate refused to hold a hearing or vote on his nomination knowing that President Obama was on his way out. So, because of this, many liberals say that the seat given to Associate Justice Gorsuch was "stolen." Forget the fact that Senator Joe Biden (Democrat) in 1992 didn't want Republican President George H. Bush to nominate anyone until the presidential election was over. I guess it always sounds better when your side is the one saying it.

20. **Jay Sekulow, Member of President Trump's Legal Team**, came on most people's radar because of his many appearances on main stream media defending the legal position of President Trump, his son Donald Trump Junior, and

other key inner circle figures on the subject of "Russian collusion." What makes Jay Sekulow unique is that he is a self-described Messianic Jew. "What's that?" you ask. It is a Jew who believes that Yeshua, Jesus in Greek, is the Messiah, or in Greek Christos (the anointed), as foretold in the Hebrew Scriptures. In other words, a Messianic Jew is a Jew who believes Jesus Christ is the same God of the New Testament as the Old Testament. They are one and the same. Instead of "Messianic Jew" some Jews prefer to use the term "complete Jew" instead. Anyway, Jay Sekulow looked into Christianity while attending the Atlanta Baptist College, and converted after making contact with the non-profit organization Jews for Jesus founded in 1973. He then earned his Ph.D. from Regent University, a university founded by evangelical Pat Roberson, who also founded the Christian Broadcasting Network, which Jay Sekulow is a frequent legal commentator on the television show 700 Club. Evangelicals know him well, and don't forget, 80% of the evangelicals voted for Donald Trump.

Honorable mention for **Ralph Drollinger, Bible Teacher**, who teaches weekly Bible studies in the U.S. House and Senate, and who started Bible studies in 40 state capitals. He currently leads about a dozen high-ranking officials of President Trump's Cabinet in studying the Holy scriptures for guidance. That's right, some of those who attend are Vice President Mike Pence, Energy Secretary Rick Perry, Education Secretary Betsy DeVos, Agriculture Secretary Sunny Perdue, and CIA Director Mike Pompeo. Former Health Secretary Tom Price used to attend, and so it's no wonder why he confessed his indiscretion and resigned, *for though the righteous falls seven times, they rise again, but the wicked stumble when calamity strikes. Proverbs 24:16* President Trump gets a hard copy of the Bible study each week.

Of course, there are many more solid Christians in the Trump administration, as well as those serving at the state and local levels. By no means am I suggesting that those mentioned in the top 20 are perfect just because they are Christians, for they are not. Case in point, Tom Price. They'd all be the first to tell you that if you sat down and talked to each one of them. They're just forgiven.
"Say what?"
I love that expression, *Christians are not perfect, just forgiven*. Well, besides being forgiven of their sins, their worldviews do indeed influence how they govern us, *We the People.*
So, now that you know that God does indeed influence American politics today I'm going to share the Christian worldview with you when it comes to sex. That's right S-E-X. It's a hot topic. After all, we Christians believe God created

sex, but He also put some restrictions on it, just like he has done with many things: eating, drinking, personal hygiene, and so on.

For the majority of Bible believing Christians the question of LGBT is actually an uncomplicated issue, and it can all be summed up in one word – sin. Sin, of course, is doing something wrong, or a "crime" if you will, against God's written law, which means lawbreakers are subject to punishment for any violations. Being in God's image we humans also have created laws, and we generally punish those who break them.

Before we continue you must know something important. The general consensus among Bible believing Christians is, and we say this expression all the time to non-believers, and even to ourselves to be reminded of it, "Love the sinner, but hate the sin." True Christians don't hate anyone, let alone homosexuals. They are to hate the sin.

Let love be without hypocrisy. Abhor what is evil; cling to what is good. Romans 12:9

But I say to you, love your enemies, bless them that curse you, do good to them that hate you, and pray for them which spitefully use you, and persecute you. Matthew 5:44

Wow! Those last words of Jesus certainly go against human nature. "Love your enemies." Is He kidding? I'd rather take revenge on my enemies. I want to get even with those who have wronged me or disagree with me. That's what my flesh wants to do. But, that's what He said, "Love your enemies."

Even when the LGBT community adopted the rainbow flag, which was a finger poked into the eye of Jews and Christians, the faith-based community did not lash out. Oh yes, conservative Christians take great offense to the rainbow flag, for the rainbow is a Biblical symbol. After God destroyed the earth for mankind's wickedness he told Noah, "I have set my rainbow in the clouds, and it will be the sign of the covenant between me and the earth." The bow is an instrument of war, but is a symbol of truce without the arrow. Take a close look at our nation's Great Seal of the United States. It's on the back of the One Dollar bill. The American bald eagle firmly grips a bundle of thirteen arrows of war in his left talons. In his right talons is an olive branch, which is a symbol that comes from the Bible verse Genesis 8:11. What? Didn't Congress know when they adopted the Great Seal in 1782 that it was unconstitutional? How dare they use a Biblical symbol! "Separation of church and state!" Oh, and by the way, the very first time that the Great Seal of the United States appears on a Congressional document is for the purpose of defining Commander in Chief George Washington's powers ending in the date "the Sixteenth day of September and in the year of our Lord one thousand four hundred and Eighty two." Whose Lord? "our Lord," the Lord of "The United States in Congress Assembled." So, can we finally drop the charades once and for all that the God of the Bible is "unconstitutional." Clearly from history He is constitutional, and the founding documents and testimonies prove it. What's truly unconstitutional are those deceivers in the government and public schools pushing *separation of God and state*. Anyway, back to the gay rainbow. Bible believing Jews and Christians were infuriated at President Obama lighting up the White House at night with the rainbow flag colors on June 26, 2015 in wake of the "landmark Supreme Court ruling that allows same-sex couples nationwide to marry" (CNN story *White House shines rainbow colors to hail same-sex marriage ruling*). The Bible believers didn't take to the streets to riot. Nope, a year later they went to the voting booths and voted for conservative Republicans instead; most notably the one at the top of the list you just read.

Oh, and one more thing about the rainbow flag. It's interesting that the current version of the flag, since 1979, has six stripes upon it. For the number six is the number of man. On the sixth day of creation God created mankind. It's also a significant number in Revelation 13:18. I'm not implying anything; I just thought it was interesting to point out. Based upon the wording of the scriptures, some Christians believe that the Antichrist who is to come will possibly be homosexual.

Back to the subject of Christian tolerance. You don't see Christians tossing homosexuals off of tall buildings to their deaths, or administering other forms of cruel executions, as you do in other parts of the world that do not have Judeo-Christian cultural roots. We just don't do that in the United States. In the New Testament homosexuality is not a capital offense, and therefore capital punishment is not administered for those caught in the act, nor is anyone requesting it.

When I was a police officer back in the 1990s, in sunny Southern California, homosexual acts, even among consenting adults, was an arrestable offense. However, it was only a misdemeanor.

However, in the Old Testament, the old law, if two people were caught in homosexual acts it was punishable by death:

Do not have sexual relations with a man as one does with a woman; that is detestable. Leviticus 18:22

If a man has sexual relations with a man as one does with a woman, both of them have done what is detestable. They are to be put to death; their blood will be on their own heads. Leviticus 20:13

You might be saying to yourself, "So, the New Testament changed things. God must be okay now with homosexuality."

Good try, but no. God did not change His mind about the issue. Certain laws in the Old Testament were for the Jews only, like the old dietary laws or circumcision of boys at eight days old, while other laws applied to all mankind - forever. If a law was for all mankind it was reemphasized in the New Testament, and marriage between a man and a woman, as well as the sin of homosexuality, were clarified even further in the New Covenant. Here are a few scriptures on those clarifications.

But since sexual immorality is occurring, each man should have sexual relations with his own wife, and each woman with her own husband.
1 Corinthians 7:2

It is interesting that the very first human institution God established was marriage, and it is between one man and one woman. Yes, some characters in the Bible had multiple wives, but God did not condone it. When some Pharisees (priests) asked Jesus if divorce was okay he told them, *"But at the beginning of creation God 'made them male and female. For this reason a man will leave his father and mother and be united to his wife, and the two will become one flesh.' So they are no longer two, but one flesh. Therefore, what God has joined together, let no one separate." Mark 10:6-9*

When it comes to homosexuality any student of the Bible knows very well Romans 1:26-27 *Because of this, God gave them over to shameful lusts. Even their women exchanged natural sexual relations for unnatural ones. In the same way the men also abandoned natural relations with women and were inflamed with lust for one another. Men committed shameful acts with other men, and received in themselves the due penalty of their error.*

Notice how the Bible labels homosexuality as both "unnatural" and "lust," and not love. No wonder the LGBT community has declared a culture war on Bible believing Christians. There's just no getting around what the scriptures say about the subject, and true Christians are not going to back down from it. Yes, you have some apostate churches that have gay ministers, but the Bible did warn us that this would happen as human history comes to an end. *For the time will come when they will not endure sound doctrine; but wanting to have their ears tickled, they will accumulate for themselves teachers in accordance to their own desires, 2 Timothy 4:3*

You might be saying, "Well, this passage in Romans you just brought up only addresses the "LGB" part of the acronym, but not the "TQ" part."

Remember that there is nothing new under the sun, and the Old Testament addresses the transvestite lifestyle clearly. *A woman shall not wear man's clothing, nor shall a man put on a woman's clothing; for whoever does these things is an abomination to the Lord your God.* This verse is found in Deuteronomy 22:5

I'm not the one who said this. God said it. If you have a problem with it, take it up with Him. I'm just the messenger.

Some of you are now saying, "Master Sergeant Wagner, you forgot about us IA people."

You're right, I did. Do you want me to say it? Okay, I will. For you LGBTQIA people the Bible addresses you all, and we can sum it up in just two words: SEXUAL IMMORALITY. For you that don't know, because this is a mixed camp, the "IA" in LGBTIA stands for "intersex and asexual." This LBGT acronym is constantly expanding. By the end of your stay in this camp I wouldn't be surprised if it is LGBTQRSTUVWXYZ.

This brings us to the next subject, and it's not a phobia, but it's intertwined with homophobia. But, fear not, it's time to shine the light on wayward heterosexuals as well. We're going to call it (read the next subhead)

SEX, DRUGS, AND ROCK N ROLL

American culture is obsessed with sex today. You can't get away from it. It's peppered in the movies, in advertisements, embedded in the lyrics of popular songs, and even used as the worst swear word one can say to another person, "F- - k you!" However, it wasn't always like this.

The views on sexuality in America had remained unchanged for 353 years of our history; from the first colony founded by the Pilgrims in 1607 right on up to 1960. Naturally, the views on sex were consistent with the teachings of the Bible. Premarital sex was a sin; a wrong. As such, young women were taught not to have sexual relations with a man unless he first married her. A man who attempted to do otherwise did not "respect" her. Once a couple was legally married it was to be for life, until death do us part, because divorce was a sin. Divorce was practically nonexistent for the majority of U.S. history. Bound together for life there was also to be no sexual relations outside of marriage. That too was a sin, the sin of adultery. Families were stable, and thus American culture was stable.

An unmarried couple living together was simply not something people did in the past. Polygamy, marriage to more than one woman, was also a sin. It was not only socially unacceptable, but illegal. The state of Utah had not been allowed to enter the Union until they abandoned the Mormon practice of polygamy on September 25, 1890. Prostitution, pornography, and homosexuality were all illegal as well. Prior to 1962, the year prayer was taken out of public schools, sodomy was a felony in every state punishable by imprisonment or death.

In 1960 Hugh Hefner, the founder of the soft porn publication *Playboy* magazine first published in 1953, opened the first Playboy Club in Chicago. This event marked the beginning of the Sexual Revolution, not just in the United States, but throughout the Western world. It was called a "revolution," because it was a revolt against the Judeo-Christian belief system that had guided Western civilization for over 2,000 years, which was traditional heterosexual, monogamous, relationships in the context of marriage. This one man was credited to giving the country the shove in the direction of sexual immorality that it had been edging toward. At first it was confined to a small, loud, minority that supported public nudity, premarital sex, legalization of abortion, an acceptance of homosexuality. However, the movement was not short-lived like it had been in the Roaring 20s, but it eventually found acceptance over the decades with the general population.

With these so-called "modern values" on such a large scale came the obvious consequences. Prior to World War II the sexually transmitted diseases (STDs) that promiscuous people had to worry about was syphilis and gonorrhea. During, and after, the Sexual Revolution Hepatitis B and C, chlamydia, genital herpes, genital warts, and HIV/AIDS became part of the list, not to mention gonorrhea became antibiotic-resistant. In fact, according to the University of Maryland Medical Center in 2015, there are more than 20 types of STDs today, and 13 million men and women are affected each year. Free sex has its price.

Just before getting married in 1986 my finance and I had to take a blood test. Everyone did. It was the law. The government made sure that engaged couples knew exactly what they were getting into from a health standpoint. If a potential spouse was infected with a venereal disease or rubella the government informed the uninfected mate about it, and some states even refused to issue a marriage license if the results were positive. Of course, the laws were all written back when most people abstained from sexual intercourse until they were married. All fifty states required a blood test. However, with the changing times one by one the required premarital blood test by the states was disregarded to reflect the country's moral decay, and as such the country now faces an epidemic of sexually transmitted diseases.

I remember in the early 1980s when GRIDS, *Gay-Related Immune Deficiency*, first appeared on everybody's radar. Many government officials were demanding that the infected people, which was limited to a small group in the male homosexual community at the time, be quarantined to keep the disease from spreading and becoming an epidemic. That was the standard procedure back then for any highly contagious diseases. However, the political pushback was fierce, and the quarantine never happened, but the epidemic did. The disease was even renamed AIDS, *Acquired Immune Deficiency Syndrome.*

When I was working as a jailer, from 1988 to 1991, political correctness concerning AIDS was so out of control that officers were prohibited from telling each other if they knew that a prisoner had AIDS. Not only was this a great health risk to officers, but to the inmate population as well. Yet, we used our common sense, and we just used code words to indicate that a prisoner had AIDS. We knew that certain prisoners had it because of the medications they were required to take while in custody, or the medical personal told us outright. Political correctness was more important than people's health.

Tragically, since the beginning of the epidemic, which could have been prevented, until 2016 approximately 675,000 people have died from HIV/AIDS in the United States according to the Centers for Disease Control and Prevention. Do you know what the number is worldwide? It's 35 million. That's right, 35 million people died from HIV/AIDS, and 1.0 million are dying from it each year. At this moment 36.7 million people are living with HIV/AIDS according the United Nations World Health Organization.

Moses, the prophets, Jesus, and the apostles all warned against sexual immorality. Not only does the Bible speak of it destroying individuals, but entire societies. If we would have followed their advice, as non-progressive as it is, we certainly wouldn't be facing all these new strains of STDs. So, how did we get to this point?

When Hugh Hefner died on September 27, 2017 in his Los Angeles home at the age of 91, his 26-year-old son Cooper released a statement about his death the same day. It stated, "My father lived an exceptional and impactful life as a media and cultural pioneer and a leading voice behind some of the most significant social and cultural movements of our time advocating free speech, civil rights, and sexual freedom."

Unfortunately, Cooper is correct in stating that his father impacted American culture, as we had discussed, but not in the glowing light his son made him out to be in his press release. Playboy magazine, which is essentially virtual fornication or infidelity, however you want to look at it, led to the pornography industry: publications, videos, and Internet porn. According to Focus on the

Family, a great resource for building strong families, "an estimated 28,258 people every second, mostly men (72 percent), but also women (28 percent), view pornography. Every 39 minutes a new pornographic video is being created in the United States."

So, let me ask you a question. Do you think Hugh Hefner was politically on the right or on the left?

How did you know?

In an interview with talk show host Larry King Mr. Hefner stated, "I was raised in a very conservative, Midwestern, Methodist family." However, in another interview years later he referred to this time as "a home with a lot of repression," and thus he became progressive rather early in his life. As would be expected he donated money to the Democratic Party. According to the New York Times on August 14, 2000, "In the last decade, Mr. Hefner, the founder and editor in chief of Playboy Enterprises, and Ms. Hefner, the company's chief executive, have given about $95,000 to Democratic candidates and committees, with a large portion of their donations going to female candidates and to liberals – and at least $8,000 going to the Clinton and Gore campaigns." He supported President Barak Obama, same-sex marriage, and abortion rights. He was angry with the "religious right" that had "put Reagan in the White House," and was furious at the Republicans for labeling Playboy as "pornography." In his own mind he was the great liberator of women. He stated, "The major beneficiaries of the Sexual Revolution, that Playboy played such a part in, were women. For so many centuries, women were just the property of their fathers and their husbands – they were held hostage and perceived as cattle for almost 2,000 years."

It's no coincidence that Mr. Hefner chose "2,000 years," which coincides with the history of Christianity. He certainly could have gone back further than that if he had wanted to, but he didn't. So, let me get this straight, he liberated women by photographing them nude so that men could lust after them in the pages of Playboy. Yeah, right. Now his ashes sit in an urn interred in a crypt he bought for $75,000 in 1992 beside Marilyn Monroe's remains, because, as he said to the Los Angeles Times in 2009, "Spending eternity next to Marilyn is an opportunity too sweet to pass up."

Is there a connection between promoting pornography and the political left? And, if so, why? You've been in the camp long enough to see the pattern.

Let me ask you another question. Who benefited most from the Sexual Revolution, men or women?

In the past, which I eluded to earlier, if men wanted to have sex outside of marriage they either had to find a prostitute to pay for the service, which they knew to be a sin and have possible health risks associated with it, or find a "loose woman" desperate for a man's affections or she was sex crazed herself. The Sexual Revolution convinced many women to no longer withhold sex from a man as a condition for marriage. For many men this was a dream come true or a temptation too hard to resist. The result of this dissolving societal barrier was to be expected. The old adage was never truer for many men, *why buy the cow if you can get the milk for free?* When many men realized that they could have sexual relations with the "good girls" without having to marry them they took full advantage of the changing culture.

What started out as exploitation of a confusing cultural situation eventually became the norm. It just didn't happen overnight, but it took several years to make it habit. People became like undisciplined children in a candy shop. Sugar under very controlled guidelines is not harmful, yet too much of it is unhealthy and even deadly.

So, here we are six decades later and divorce is as common as marriage. Abortions are as common as births, and people are no longer shocked to hear about school teachers, priests, or prison guards having sex with vulnerable people under their care. The problem is that this "revolution" has just got started.

Now, I'm in no way implying that only the left engages in sexual sins. In this case Republicans and liberals are in bed together, pun intended. However, due to the fact that many conservatives respect the country's Judeo-Christian heritage the push for moral purity comes mostly from the right. It's usually right-leaning Christian-affiliated sexual abstinence groups that convince their young women to wear purity rings, also known as chastity rings. An oath is given to abstain from sex until marriage, and a ring is worn as the symbol of that oath. It's right-leaning organizations that are predominantly pro-life, even if a baby was conceived out of wedlock. It's mostly conservatives that voted against same sex-marriage in state elections only for liberal judges to strike down election results declaring them "unconstitutional." I'm pretty sure our founding fathers, the brains behind the U.S. Constitution, would be opposed to same sex marriages as well if they were here today. Thomas Jefferson wrote a Virginia law in 1779 recommending castration for men caught in the act of sodomy instead of the death penalty. Hmmm, maybe this is another reason why so many on the left want to also tear down Thomas Jefferson statues.

Okay, you already know that many God-fearing conservatives are also sexually conservative. So much so that even a Christian baker will refuse to bake a wedding cake for a gay couple. Any other type of cake, fine, but not when it comes to God's first institution. I'm talking about Jack Phillips, owner of Masterpiece Cakeshop, in Colorado, and the lawsuit brought against him by homosexual couple Charlie Craig and David Mullins in 2012, that went all the way up to the U.S. Supreme Court on October 2, 2017; the same day as the worse active shooter massacre in U.S. history in Las Vegas. The big question is, "Why? Why is the God of the Bible against sex outside of marriage? What's the big deal?"

The Bible describes the union of a man and a woman as becoming "one." It's not just physical, but also mental and spiritual. The Bible describes this union as a "mystery" that we won't fully understand on this side of eternity. That is why several warnings in the Bible are given to men to avoid sexual relations with a prostitute, because the two souls fuse together, and one should not fuse their soul with an ungodly woman who the Bible claims has "one foot in Hell." Another reason to keep sex within marriage is for health reasons, which we talked about. Then add genuine love into the mix, and any infidelity is devastating to the spouse that has remained faithful. We are emotional creatures, and jealousy has even sent some people into a murderous rage when they caught their significant other cheating on them.

If you play with fire, you're going to get burned. That's common sense, isn't it? Well, not for the television and film industry. For decades Hollywood has been known for its indulgence in sexual immorality, and trying to convince others that they should do the same. Knowing that story telling is a very powerful medium, producers, directors, writers, and actors constantly produced material that made it appear as if fornication, adultery, and even violence were "normal." Of course, their excuse was "art imitating life." However, television shows and movies are like guns. Cameras, sound systems, props, and editing programs are merely tools. Depending on who is making the show or film depends on whether these tools are used for good or evil.

For years conservatives, especially those of the evangelical Christian community, sounded the alarm that all of this gratuitous sex and violence on the big screen was harmful. The rise in STDs, sexual assaults, and shootings was evidence enough, yet Hollywood told us that we were a bunch of prudes, and that there was no correlation between the two. Even when conservatives, initiated by the House of Representatives, impeached President Bill Clinton on December 19, 1998 stemming from a sexual harassment lawsuit filed by Paula Jones, many on the left stated that it was merely a witch hunt for political purposes. The Democrats claimed that Paula Jones lied about the harassment, as did Monica Lewinsky, a former intern, about being seduced by the President in the Oval Office. "I did not have sexual relations with that woman, Miss Lewinsky," the President claimed under oath.

Not only did Hillary Clinton, the self-proclaimed guardian of women's rights, know about Paula Jones and Monica Lewinsky, and discredited both publicly, but she also said that the accusations leveled by Juanita Broaddrick and Kathleen Willey against her husband was nothing but a "vast right-wing conspiracy." Thank God she was not elected President of the United States!

Then something very interesting happened in October of 2017. Several women went public that prominent Hollywood film producer Harvey Weinstein had sexually harassed, assaulted, and even raped a few of them. As the months passed a total of 80 women came forward against him, and several police investigations were launched. Although the Hollywood elite claimed to be "shocked" and "dismayed" that one of their own would do such things, many within the industry had known about his behavior for years and kept silent. In 2012 actress Meryl Streep jokingly called Harvey Weinstein "God." And, to think, I even appeared in a 2008 Harvey Weinstein distributed movie titled *Where in the World Is Osama bin Laden?* Well, I didn't know anything about Harvey Weinstein at the time of the filming, and I only worked with actor Morgan Spurlock and his film crew. He was a good family man at the time, and his parents had raised him as a Methodist. Unfortunately, he divorced three years later, and remarried in 2016.

According to Morgan Spurlock's ex-wife Alexandra Jaimeson it sounds like she was a victim of modern society's flippant attitude towards sex, and perhaps even the victim of "the Hollywood scene," because on her website www.alexandrajamieson.com under ABOUT ME she posted:

You see, my husband at the time was a very famous man with whom I co-starred and co-created Super Size Me, an Oscar nominated, Sundance award-winning documentary.

We had the beautiful New York City apartment. We traveled the world. And we were friends with some of the most recognizable people in Hollywood.

I was living a pretty glamorous life and spent my time the way I wanted: writing, raising my son, and building my reputation as a devout vegan and nutrition expert in the wellness industry.

Life looked d--n good on the outside. On the inside, sh-t was hitting the fan.

My marriage was rapidly coming undone. And what initially felt like a rough patch of discontent and disconnection turned out to be much worse; he was having an affair. Pain, anger, sadness, insecurity, and desperation swelled in my body.

F---k, this hurts.

I don't know if her accusation about her ex-husband is true or not, but she expressed the agonizing consequences of sexual immorality. Sin is never a "victimless" crime.

Morgan Spurlock is currently the host and producer of the CNN show *Morgan Spurlock Inside Man.*

Just after the Harvey Weinstein sexual allegations surfaced Hollywood exploded like a volcano, and fingers were then pointed at actor Kevin Spacey, actor Ben Affleck, actor Jeffrey Tambor, actor Ed Westick, actor Andy Dick, director James Toback, Head of Pixar and Walt Disney Animation John Lasseter, Nickelodeon's Chris Savino, Head of Amazon Studios Roy Price, Co-chief executive of Primary Wave Entertainment David Guillod, editor at DC Comics Eddie Berganza, Warner Bros. TV Group Executive Producer Andrew Kreisberg, Warner Bros. producer and director Brett Ratner, comedian Louis C.K. (who once even "joked" during his monologue on Saturday Night Live in 2015 how good pedophilia must be), and celebrity chef John Besh. Then came the finger pointing at the media starting with CBS television host Charlie Rose, Matt Lauer of NBC, Director of CBS's Diversity Showcase Rick Najera, The New York Times reporter Glenn Thrush, ABC News journalist Mark Halperin, NPR editor Michael Oreskes, E! news correspondent Ken Baker, editorial director for Vox Media Lockhart Steele, Publisher of Artforum Knight Landesman, and president and publisher of The New Republic Hamilton Fish. Even politicians were caught in the web of 2017 accusations, like: former President George H.W. Bush (Republican), Senator Al Franken (Democrat), Alabama Senator candidate Roy Moore (Republican), and Kentucky Speaker of the House Jeff Hoover (Republican).

Now, I don't know if the men listed here are innocent or guilty of their accusations. I'd bet that some are. Yet, I can tell you one thing, had we, as a society, stuck to our Judeo-Christian heritage we'd have seen a lot less of this sexual abuse. We'd have seen a lot less of it in the U.S. Armed Forces, a lot less in our universities, and a lot less in our corporations. People can poke fun all they want at God's laws, but they were designed to keep people from harming themselves and others. Remember this, God's laws are just as sure as the physical laws of the universe. Over and over again we keep witnessing this, and our history books tell us the same. Harvey Weinstein brought this truth to light for not just the Hollywood elite, and their millions of adoring fans, but to our entire nation.

They sow the wind and reap the whirlwind. Hosea 8:7

ISLAMOPHOBIA

Throughout your stay here in the camp you've learned about Karl Marx and communism. Now, imagine if during the Cold War, the time when we were fighting the ideology of the Soviet Union, Americans started accusing the government as "commuphobes;" those who have a fear of communism. Yes, I made up the word commuphobe, because it doesn't exist, nor did it ever. It wasn't until recently that this whole "phobia" ending attached to every word resurfaced; mainly as a result of political correctness run amok during the Obama administration era. Oh sure, there were a lot of Americans back during the Cold War that were enamored by communism, Bernie Sanders and actress Jane Fonda being two of them, but everybody else knew communism was a clear and present danger to our American way of life. That's why at 18-years-old I joined the United States Army, and I was issued a magazine fed, gas operated, M-16A1 rifle that had the effective range of 500 meters. The plastic shaped human silhouette targets we shot at on the rifle range at Fort Jackson, South Carolina were painted like Soviet soldiers: sporting an AK-47 rifle, with a communist five-pointed gold star in a red circle on the helmet and belt buckle. There was no doubt in our minds about who the enemy was at the time. Now, did we hate all the communists? No. We hated their system, and their system was a danger to us. Heck, many on my wife's side of the family were communists. They had to be just by living there, but they gave up their communist beliefs when they left the Soviet Union, and I love them today. They're all great people.

Wait! I want to add something about actress Jane Fonda here. She's the one who On November 21, 1970 gave a speech to over 2,000 students at Michigan State University, and she said the following, "If you understood what communism was, you would hope, you would pray on your knees, that we would someday become communist."

Well, first of all, if you were caught on your knees praying in a communist country in 1970 you'd be tossed in prison or worse. Two years later she visited North Vietnam, the enemy we were literally fighting with bullets and bombs, and posed next to an anti-aircraft position wearing a communist helmet surrounded by jubilant North Vietnamese troops.

Liberals tend to ignore history, and that is why I am reminding you of it. So, here's a part of history that you'll never hear about it unless you dig a little deeper past the leftist version of history. Throughout most of the Vietnam War protesters, from 1964 to 1973, demanded that American troops get out of Southeast Asia. They lamented the casualties that we were inflicting on the communists, and yes, sadly, also the military personnel we lost on our side protecting South Vietnam. What liberal historians fell to tell you is that more people were killed in the first three years of "communist peace" than had been killed in all 13 years of the war fighting the communists. Once American troops pulled out of the country it was a bloodbath in Vietnam, Cambodia, and Laos. The communist were brutal.

Fast forward to right now, and communism is no longer a threat, from the outside anyway, but radical Islam is.

Now, before you accuse me, your Master Sergeant of this camp that you're staying in, of being an Islamophobe (the "dislike or prejudice against Islam or Muslims, especially as a political force," according to the dictionary definition), know this, as a devout Christian I love Muslims, all Muslims. I also have, believe it or not, Muslim friends. Alright, they may not consider me a real friend, the fundamentalist ones anyway, because in the Quran, Surah 5:51 to be exact, it states, *O you who believe, take not the Jews and the Christians for friends. They are friends of each other. And whoever among you takes them for friends he is indeed one of them. Surely Allah guides not the unjust people.*

To top it off I have visited Muslim countries and territories: Egypt, Jordan, and Samaria (what the Palestinians call *ad-Diffah l-Garbiyyah* – the West Bank), and over there I met a lot of good people, and a lot of bad people, just like everywhere else in the world. One of my fondest memories over there was having tea in the home of my Palestinian cab driver, Abraham, and his lovely family in East Jerusalem. He didn't have to invite my wife and me into his home, but he did, and they showed us their legendary Middle East hospitality.

To put myself through college I drove a delivery truck all around Orange County, the "OC," delivering Arabic pita bread to all the ethnic Arabic food shops in the area; a time before pita bread and pita chips became popular nationwide. It was in those very food shops, dealing with the shopkeepers, where I learned the various Islamic cultures and how to negotiate with them, for it was my job to try to sell them the bakery's surplus stock.

Over the years I have also worked with, and have trained, Muslims here and abroad. Muslims are people, and people are people. I treated them no differently than anyone else. As long as a person is not unethical, immoral, or engaging in criminal or terrorist activity then I'm good with them.

Now, here is where I, and most conservative Republicans, draw the line. We accept Muslims to live and thrive in the United States, but to do so only under the United States Constitution, just like everybody else. For those who became naturalized citizens of this country they raised their right hand and swore the oath, *"I hereby declare, on oath, that I absolutely and entirely renounce and abjure all allegiance and fidelity to any foreign prince, potentate, state, or sovereignty, of whom or which I have heretofore been a subject or citizen; that I will support and defend the Constitution and laws of the United States of America against all enemies, foreign and domestic; that I will bear true faith and allegiance to the same; that I will bear arms on behalf of the United States when required by law; that I will perform noncombatant service in the Armed*

Forces of the United States when required by law; that I will perform work of national importance under civil direction when required by law; and that I take this obligation freely, without any mental reservation or purpose of evasion; so help me God."

Wow! For you that were born here, you probably didn't realize the heavy obligation that a naturalized citizen has to this country. I did, because my wife, from the former Soviet Union as I told you before, had to give this very same oath, and I stood in the audience as proud as could be witnessing it. As corrupt and oppressive that her former country was, she loved many aspects of it, and its culture. But, on that very day she took the oath she embraced the American way of life, and became 100% American. There was no looking back. Sadly, she knows American history and the U.S. Constitution better than most of her American born friends and coworkers. Happily, she became a conservative Republic, by her own choice and not me pushing her into it, and over the years she has persuaded her family to do the same.

Fortunately, most Muslims that come to America embrace our traditions and values. They took the oath, and they keep it. They have no intention of breaking that oath. On the other hand, there's a small minority of Muslims that come to this country, and they have no intention of defending "the Constitution and the laws of the United States against all enemies foreign and domestic." In fact, some of them do quite the opposite; they become the enemy on our own soil. Instead of being willing to *bear arms on behalf of the United States when required by law* they take up arms, or strap on a bomb belt, and use them against their fellow citizens in the name of Allah. "Allah oo akbar! *Allah is greatest!* is the war cry when carrying out their jihad (Islamic holy war); or as we call it – terrorism: the LAX shooting 2002, Arkansas recruiting office shooting 2009, Fort Hood shooting 2009, Times Square bombing 2010, Boston Marathon bombings 2013, Vaughan Foods beheading 2014, San Bernardino attack 2015, Orlando nightclub shooting 2016, New York City attempted bombing 2017, just to name a few. Then there is another small group of American Muslims, and we will call them "radical Islamists" for lack of a better term, that will never carry out an attack personally, but they support those organizations that aid and abet those that do, either financially or through comfort. These are the "passive supporters."

Now, in case you don't know your world history very well, or not at all, Islam and the Christian East and West have been at each other's throats since Muhammad's last wishes were carried out after his death on June 8, 632 A.D. by his successor, Abu Bakr, and that was to conquer the Sasanid Empire (ancient Christian Armenia and Zoroastrian Persia) and the Christian Byzantine Empire (what is today Turkey, Israel, Egypt with most of North Africa all the way up to southern Spain, Albania, Bosnia and Herzegovina, Bulgaria, Greece, Macedonia, Montenegro, Serbia, Slovenia, and parts of Italy). After all, did not the Quran clearly state in Surah 9:33 *He it is Who sent His Messenger with guidance and the Religion of Truth, that He may cause it to prevail over all religions, though the polytheists are averse.*

Over who? Over "all religions." And, to be in line with today's belief by many radical Islamists, you can also throw in all the atheists and prognostics in there as well with the polytheists. After all, an infidel, *an unbeliever*, is an unbeliever in Allah. Oh, and by the way, the crescent moon expansion and wars did not end with just the two empires mentioned thirteen hundred years ago. Oh, no. The wars and skirmishes still rage to this very day: violence between the Muslims and the Buddhists in Myanmar, the Uighur Muslims and communists in China, the Muslims and Hindus in Kashmir, Muslims and the Russians in Chechnya, Muslims and Armenian Christians in Nagorno-Karabakh, Muslims and Jews in the West Bank and Gaza, Muslims and Coptic Christians in Egypt, Muslims and Christians in war torn Syria, Muslims and Christians in Southern Sudan, Muslims and tribal religions in Mali, Muslims and the Philippine government in Mindanao. And, these are just the "hot" conflicts we're talking about. We'll get to the radical Islamic terrorism happening, and about to happen, worldwide in a moment.

Now, do I personally have an issue with those who believe in Islam, which means *submission* in Arabic? No, not at all. People have the right to choose what they want to believe in. It only becomes a problem to me when we are talking about instituting some of the commands of the Quran and Islamic law, *sharia law*, on American soil. Oh, and by the way, if you think you have a problem now with "separation of church and state" in the United States, you should know that Islamic law, as followed by Muslim countries, does not distinguish between the religion and matters of the state. They are one and the same. So, with that in mind, let's take a look-see at what an America would look like with sharia law in her midst. After all, some European countries have allowed sharia courts to flourish, and most are conducted inside of mosques. The United Kingdom is reported as having over 80 such courts spread throughout their land despite the 2003 judgment of the European Court of Human Rights in Strasbourg that stated that is was "difficult to declare one's respect for democracy and human rights while at the same time supporting a regime based on sharia, which clearly diverges from Convention values."

Notice that they stated "difficult," and not impossible. It was a rather weak statement for a very good reason. They are scared to death of the almost 20 million Muslims (19,720,000 to be exact as of 2016) living in Western Europe.

I left out the 14 million living in Russia. Well, when I say "they," it's obviously not everyone who is scared. Some on the left want "open borders," just like many on the left here do, and they'd love for many millions more to immigrate there in Europe. Oh well, it's their money and cultures.

Back to America, and sharia law.

Sharia law is religious law, and the religion is Islam, thus the law of Allah. Some laws are compatible with the U.S. Constitution and American laws, while others are not.

Let's take a look at a few of our rights to determine if sharia law would safeguard these current rights we enjoy or take them away. By "our rights" I mean every American citizen, be it Christian, Muslim, atheist, Mormon, Buddhist, Hindu, Native American tribal religions, et cetera.

The First Amendment of the United States Constitution states:

Congress shall make no law respecting an establishment of religion, or prohibiting the free exercise thereof; or abridging the freedom of speech, or of the press; the right of the people peaceably to assemble, and to petition the Government for a redress of grievances.

Let's parse the first sentence, shall we. "Congress will not make any laws **respecting an establishment of religion**." Of course, taken in the context in which this document was written in 1787, our founding fathers did not want there to be a State church – the Church of the United States. They had personally experienced what life was like under British rule prior to their independence, which meant that all ministers under the Church of England gave an oath to support the King.

A lot of Millennials and Gen Zers don't know this, mainly because it is not taught in the public schools anymore, but religion was one of the main causes for the Revolution. The political fighting between the different Christian denominations caused great division among the colonists. The faithful to the Church of England sided with the crown, the Quakers were pacifists, many Anglicans believed the Church of England to be almost diabolical, and that it was their Christian duty to resist tyranny. Presbyterian minister James Caldwell felt it his duty to serve as a chaplain during the war on the side of the Americans, and for this he paid the ultimate price. Heck, even one of the Revolutionary battle flags, the Gostelowe Standard, had the words RESISTANCE TO TYRANTS IS OBEDIENCE TO GOD.

It's quite obvious from mountains of historical records that our founding fathers were not turning away from God when they penned these words, but making sure that one particular Christian denomination did not rule over the others.

The second half of the first sentence reads, "or prohibiting the free exercise thereof."

It does not state "or prohibiting the free exercise thereof only outside of the classroom," or "only on private property." No, it clearly states that the government will not prohibit the free exercise of religion of any denomination.

Keep in mind that in 1787 there was no Buddhist population in the United States at the time. Chinese immigration did not begin until 1849, some 62 years after the First Amendment was written. There was no Muslim population in the United States either. The first wave of Muslim immigrants was from the 1880s to 1914 when several thousand Muslims came from the former Ottoman Empire and the Mughal Empire. Yes, obviously, there were a handful of Muslims in the United States priory to Revolutionary War, but our founding fathers did not consider Islam, nor the Native American religions, when they wrote the First Amendment. But, fortunately, their wisdom in the wording of the First Amendment applied to all indigenous peoples, and the immigrants who would come to this country. This is why the U.S. Constitution has stood the test of time.

Now that we have established the meaning of the First Amendment, what does sharia law say about "freedom of religion?"

If a person converts to Islam, or is born and raised a Muslim, then he or she will have full rights of citizenship in an Islamic state.

So, what happens to those people who do not convert to Islam? Are they not given "full rights?" Well, in many Islamic countries non-Muslims are second class citizens. Would an America under sharia law change that? Would we be different and allow Muslims and non-Muslims alike full rights? After all, sharia law, just by its nature is religious law.

Let's go to the next law. *Leaving Islam is a sin and a religious crime. Once any man or woman is officially classified as Muslim, because of birth or religious conversion, he or she will be subject to the death penalty.*

Whoa! Wait a moment! Someone can be put to death if they were "born a Muslim" or if he or she were once a Muslim and then had a change of heart?

You see, nobody is "born a Christian." There is no such thing. According to the Bible one becomes a Christian when they come to an age of understanding, repent of their sins, and ask Jesus Christ, God, into their heart making Him their Lord and Savior. It's where we get the term "born again" from.

So, if we allowed sharia law to reign in America, or even within small enclaves of America, like some European countries are experimenting with now, does that mean that we'd allow the death penalty for the sin of Muslims leaving Islam? Many liberals don't even support the death penalty for mass murders.

Or, would we do away with the death penalty, and just let 'em do some prison time for leaving the faith? If we as a nation want to go down this road, then we had better start talking about it now. Isn't wisdom trying to understand where a road ends?

There's more to the law. *He or she will be subject to the death penalty if he or she becomes an apostate (denying or questioning Islam) in order to become an atheist, agnostic or to convert to another religion.*

The good news for these people is that sharia law demands that an individual be offered one chance to return to Islam before the sentence is carried out.

All you atheists who want to do away with Christmas Day as a holiday or do away with IN GOD WE TRUST on our currency are going to have a lot more issues you can sink your teeth into when sharia law takes root. Your new opponents are going to definitely keep you on your toes. You'll just have to hope that a U.S. Supreme Court of Sharia Law will interpret the law of blasphemy against Allah or the Prophet Mohammed liberally confining the punishment of blasphemy to a fine, imprisonment, flogging, or amputation like is done in various Muslim nations, and not death.

I'm kinda of getting the picture here that sharia law in America will not be exactly tolerant of all religions or *freedom of speech*, as found in the First Amendment:

or abridging (to cut away) the freedom of speech, or of the press.

Do we even need to go on with the other 27 Amendments? For those of you who like drinking alcohol, you should read the 18th and 21st Amendments, because I think those two would be reinstated. Don't worry. Sparkling apple cider is a good substitute.

The bottom line is that sharia law is not compatible with American law at all. In fact, it's not compatible with any country's law outside of the Muslim world. Now, that's not to say that sharia law is somehow invalid, or that those who want to be under its control should be ridiculed. A lot of people in Muslim countries are content with sharia law. According to the Pew Research Center, that conducted thousands of face-to-face surveys to see if Muslims supported sharia law, the result was that 74% of the population in Egypt supported it. 89% of the Palestinians. 71% of the Jordanians. 91% of the Iraqis. 56% of the Tunisians. 29% of the Lebanese. 99% of the Afghans. 84% of the Pakistanis. 86% of the Malaysians. 82% of the Bangladeshis. 77% of those in Thailand. 72% in Indonesia. However, the numbers are quite a bit lower for those in Central Asia and Southeast Europe. Those are people who have been greatly influenced by the Russians and other Europeans.

That was a really brief evaluation of sharia law, and now let's look at the very foundation of Islam, and that is the Quran; the holy book of the Muslims.

The Quran was believed to have been written over a 23-year period; from December 609 to the death of Muhammad in 632. That was 482 years after the final book in the New Testament was written and widely distributed. Muhammad himself knew of the Biblical scriptures.

I've read the Quran. Have you?

It amazes me how many non-Muslims that cry out "Islamophobe!" have never read the Quran in their entire life, nor the Bible for that matter. It's hard to have an intelligent discussion with most Millennials and Gen Zers when trying to compare our country's Judeo-Christian foundation to that of Muslim culture if they know niether.

What? Are we going to wait until the United States is 10% Muslim, like France, before we start having serious discussions about how it can change our own culture?

When I was in charge of a Security Forces unit, tasked daily to protect our military base in Southern California from a terrorist attack, I'd occasionally ask my soldiers, "How many of you have read the Quran? Let me see a show of hands." Out of 25 soldiers I'd get one or two hands that shot up.

When I was working security for The Walt Disney Company, who were very much concerned about a possible terrorist attack on one of their resorts, the instructor in our Security & Emergency Services Training Academy asked the question, "Who can tell me about Islam?" I was the only one in the class who knew anything about the religion.

The reason I asked my soldiers the question about having read the Quran, and why Mickey Mouse asked my class essentially the same question, was to see if anyone was "Know Your Enemy" savvy. Sun Tzu and *The Art of War* always pops up in the tactical world.

Now, obviously, not all Muslims are the "enemy of the state" But, many of our enemies happen to be Quran believing Muslims. Now, if there ever comes a day when Eskimos start doing terrorist attacks worldwide then I'm going to learn everything I can about Eskimos to help me figure out their mindset. That would not make me an Eskimophobe, just prudent.

Remember the story I told you about my experience in the U.S. Army. The Russians were the enemy at the time, and it seems like we are heading back that way again, and at the rifle range we shot live rounds at plastic human silhouette targets painted like Soviet soldiers. We were also told about the evils of communism from our drill sergeants, which only reinforced what I had been taught in high school by my history and economics teachers. Plus, on my own, I had read The Communist Manifesto. I was just a lowly private when I enlisted, but above me there were a lot of high ranking officers who studied communist doctrine, along with the enemy's military strategy and tactics. Why? To know how the enemy thinks. When you know how the enemy thinks, you can make an educated guess as to how to defend against their assaults at every level.

The Quran is divided into 114 chapters, each one called a "surah," which literally means high degree.

Let's look at Surah 3, which is "chapter" 3, and it is known as the book of Al-Imran. Within a chapter there are verses. Verse 11 states:

Say to those who disbelieve: You shall be vanquished, and driven together to hell; and evil is the resting place. Surah 3:11

Okay, this is a spiritual text. If one does not believe in Allah then they will be defeated and driven into hell. If someone wants to believe this, then fine. Have at it. However, further along in the chapter we come across this verse:

And whoever seeks a religion other than Islam, it will not be accepted from him, and in the Hereafter he will be one of the losers. Surah 3:84

Alright, on the face of it this does not seem to conflict with the U.S. Constitution. Freedom of religion allows citizens to believe that Islam is the true religion, and everyone else are "losers." No criticism there. The problem is that this verse, enforced through sharia law, means that the death penalty could be applied for any Muslim who decides to become an atheist, Christian, Wicca, or whatever. We know this to be true in a historical context, and by what we see in many of today's Islamic nations.

What about this next verse?

We will cast terror into the hearts of those who disbelieve. Surah 3:151

Most Muslims have not "cast terror into my heart," but some did on September 11, 2001 when radical Islamic terrorists seized a few passenger planes and flew two of them into the World Trade Center towers like missiles, one into the side of the Pentagon, and a fourth one nosedived into the ground in Shanksville, Pennsylvania killing a total of 2,996 innocent people. These guys were from the terrorist group known as Al-Qaeda (Arabic for *The Foundation*), and they took this verse from the Quran literally. Even today when I am sitting on a passenger plane I can't help but wonder if some radical Islamic terrorist is aboard and wants to take the plane down. There's a reason we have to go through a rigorous security screening process in every airport around the globe.

"Okay, but maybe they just misinterpreted the verse," you may be questioning.

Yes, that's a fair position to take. That's why we call them "radical." Here's another one:

So let those fight in the way of Allah who sell this world's life for the Hereafter. And whoever fights in the way of Allah, be he slain or be he victorious, We shall grant him a mighty reward. Surah 4:74

Now we're getting into the concepts of "jihad" (holy war), and "shahid" (a fighter who lays down his life for the true religion). Of course, the moderates say, "jihad" is an internal struggle to do what is right." Of course, they are correct. Others say that "jihad" is an outward struggle against the oppressors of Allah, and they're correct also. It could be interpreted both ways. In Western eyes, a Muslim who keeps the "struggle" internal is a "moderate," but those who pick up the sword of Allah to fight against the "infidels," the unbelievers, are labeled "radical" or "extremists." Okay, to be fair, many Muslims also label those carrying out physical jihad as radical or extremists, and they don't want any part of it.

Some of these so-called "radicals" or "extremists" have murdered Westerners for offending Allah or the Prophet Muhammed. On November 2, 2004 Dutch filmmaker Theo van Gogh was murdered by a Dutch-Moroccan Muslim for producing the film *Submission*, which criticized the treatment of women in Islam. The killer shot van Gogh eight times in the street. Then when van Gogh pleaded for his life to be spared the killer, Mohammed Bouyeri, executed him with several more rounds. He then attempted to decapitate the victim, right there on the street in front of everyone, and then stabbed a note to the corpse with a knife. The note was a threat to Western countries, and to the Jews.

Have you ever heard that expression Je suis Charlie Hebdo, *I am Charlie Hebdo*. Now it has become a common expression after many terrorist attacks since then; the "I am" part of it anyway, and then fill in the blank with the name of latest incident. Here's the history behind it. Charlie Hebdo is a French satirical weekly magazine published in Paris. They had printed some cartoons about the Prophet Muhammed, and for this "blasphemy" 12 people paid with their lives, and 11 more were wounded.

On January 7, 2015 two armed "radical" Islamic terrorists entered the Charlie Hebdo building and massacred several employees of the magazine while shouting, "Allah oo Akbar!" *Allah is greatest!*

A police officer engaged the two terrorists when they exited the building, but he got wounded and collapsed on the sidewalk. One of the gunmen ran towards the police officer, who had raised one hand to surrender to the terrorist, but the terrorist shot him in the head at close range.

As the two terrorists were leaving the scene one of them yelled out, "We have avenged the Prophet Muhammad. We have killed Charlie Hebdo!"

Let me reemphasis this, the slaughter was over some cartoons. However, such revenge killings are just done "over there" in faraway places. Four months later in Garland, Texas two radical Islamic terrorists were planning to slaughter as many Americans as they could at an event that displayed controversial cartoons of the Prophet Mohammed in support of Charlie Hebdo. Fortunately, security was tight around the event, and a security guard shot and killed both advancing attackers before they could get into the building to do their murderous deed. The two terrorists were both wearing body armor and armed with assault rifles. One of the terrorists, Elton Simpson, tweeted before the attack, "May Allah accept us as mujahideen." Of course, a "mujahideen" is a term for one engaged in jihad (holy war).

That's right – "war." Why does that surprise you? In February of 1998 Osama bin Laden, the head of Al-Qaeda, declared war on "North Americans," that's you, and their allies in the name of the World Islamic Front for Jihad Against Jews and Crusaders.

In 2014 Islamic State, also known as ISIS, established the caliph (one leader controlling all Muslim nations), and demanded that all devout Muslims give their allegiance to him. That man was Abu Bakr al-Baghdadi. Their goal was pretty straight forward, and that was to "conquer the world," and that "all religions who agree with democracy have to die."

Yes, we made the list. The United States was named as a "Crusader-Zionist enemy." You may have forgotten the tens of thousands of people that ISIS murdered in Syria and Iraq, Christians and Muslims alike who did not believe the way they did, but you might happen to remember the Manchester suicide bombing of the Ariana Grande concert on May 22, 2017. Oh yes, ISIS took responsibility for that one. Twenty-two people were killed, and 250 injured. Ten of those people killed were under 20-years-old. They were Gen Zers. The others were mostly Millennials. So, let me ask you this, "Why don't we see the political left in America protesting against American Muslims like we do against the American Christians?" Have you ever noticed that? Question number two, "Why do so many on the left welcome Sharia law in America, just as they have in many parts of Europe, but want to see removed or silenced anything related to the Bible?"

Many Muslims living in America believe that women are half the value of men. Many American Muslims are against homosexuality, and most American Muslim bakeries in the country would never bake a wedding cake for a homosexual couple. Secretly, some Muslims living here even believe that the United States is "The Great Satan," and Israel is "The Little Satan," and that democracy is anti-Islam, for in other countries many Muslims openly say these things without the authorities batting an eye. And, yet, not a peep from the left in the United States about these things.

In bring up these provocative questions I'm certainly not saying that the left should now target American Muslims in this country like they have the Christian community, because they shouldn't. I'm just merely pointing out the hypocrisy of the progressive left, and suggesting that perhaps the God of the Bible is indeed the Word of God, because it certainly offends a whole lot of people like no other religion in the world does. Mention Allah, Buddha, meditation, aliens from outer space or any number topics in a mixed group here in the States and things remain civil. However, mention how we ought to follow the Ten Commandments, have our children go back to The New England Primer to learn how to read, or pray in the name of Jesus Christ, and you have fireworks even though these things were all a part of our history! Oh, and you want to see real fireworks, just casually mention to people at school or work, "I believe that in order to heal our society we ought to return to the morality taught in the Bible: no sex before marriage, marriage between one man and one woman, no lusting, yada yada yada," and see what kind of explosions you'll get. This pinpoint directed hostility towards Christians only proves to me that there is indeed spiritual warfare going on under the physical surface. Around six hundred years before Muhammed came onto the world scene Jesus said, *If the world hates you, keep in mind that it hated me first. If you belonged to the world, it would love you as its own. As it is, you do not belong to the world, but I have chosen you out of the world. That is why the world hates you. Remember what I told you, 'A servant is not greater than his master.' If they persecuted me, they will persecute you also. If they obeyed my teaching, they will obey yours also. John 15:18-20*

Not only is the progressive left vehemently opposed to Christianity, but many Muslims are opposed to them worldwide as well. The left hates anything having to do with the Bible, because progressivism is deeply rooted in communism, and although Muslims do believe that Jesus was a prophet, and a Muslim prophet at that to be revered, they do not believe that Jesus was, and is, God in the flesh. Here are some verses of the Quran to support their beliefs:

And they say, Be Jews or Christians, you will be on the right course. Say, No, we follow the religion of Abraham, the upright one, and he was not one of the polytheists.

We believe in Allah and in that which has been revealed to us, and in that which was revealed to Abraham, and Ishmael and Isaac and Jacob and the tribes, and in that which was given Moses and Jesus, and in that which was given to the prophets from their Lord, we do not make any distinction between any of them and to Him do we submit. Sura 2:135-136

And when Allah will say: O Jesus, son of Mary, did you say to men, Take me and my mother for two gods besides Allah? Sura 16:116

...and they falsely attribute to Him sons and daughters without knowledge. Sura 6:101

How could He have a son when He has no consort? Sura 16:102

Allah and the God of the Bible are not one and the same. The Bible makes this clear, as well as the Quran. Muslims do not believe in the virgin birth or that Jesus ever died on the cross, and certainly not that He is God. If fact, they believe that Christianity is polytheistic (the belief in more than one god).

Islam and Christianity are not compatible. They never will be. However, people can be compatible, regardless of their religious beliefs, if they choose to be.

Many Christians love the fact that Muslim immigrants are in America, because it exposes them to the teachings of the Bible, which is forbidden in many Muslim countries, and if they get converted in the United States they then spread that love to their family and friends still living in their countries of origin. Yes, it's true that many American churches have put in place unarmed and armed security teams because of continuing attacks by radical Islam jihadists and mentally disturbed active shooters, which is needed, but many of these same churches are praying for the Muslim nations as well. It seems to be working, because many people in these Muslim nations, including Iran, are seeing Jesus in their dreams, and coming to Him.

Christine Darg, author of *Miracles Among Muslims* stated, "There is an end-time phenomenon that is happening through dreams and visions. He (Jesus) is going into the Muslim world and revealing, particularly, the last twenty-four hours of His life – how He died on the cross, which Islam does not teach – how He was raised from the dead, which Islam also does not teach – and how He is the Son of God, risen in power."

So, the bottom line is that conservatives, especially a great many evangelical

Christians, are not "anti-Muslim" as the left so consistently claims, but they just don't want to see Muslim terrorists coming into the country. That's what President Trump has been saying all along if only people would get past the rhetoric of the 2016 presidential campaign. In case you haven't noticed by now, President Donald Trump throws out an extreme position for negotiation purposes on many issues, then he is willing to compromise leaving his opponents to feel as if they got a portion of what they wanted, but he gets the best deal possible. Hello! He wrote the book – *The Art of the Deal*. So, if keeping America safe means extreme vetting for Muslim visitors and immigrants, then so be it.

Finally, conservatives certainly do not want to entertain the idea of sharia law seeping into traditional American values by those already here as citizens, because it's not working out so great with our allies in Europe.

XENOPHOBIA

Xenophobia is another word that the left threw around, ad nauseam, during the 2016 presidential elections. No, it's not a musical instrument, but it means *the fear and distrust of foreigners*, or more specifically *immigrants*. Of course, it is not an actual medical phobia, but just one of the many political terms coined by the left. It's also a term they pinned on President Donald Trump for his strong stance against illegal immigration, which is kind of nonsensical being that the First Lady is an immigrant from Slovenia. However, many on the left know that because of Melania Trump, and his first wife Ivana Zelnickova from Czechoslovakia, that their accusation against the President is not air tight, and so they qualify their accusation by stating that it is his dislike for "Mexicans" and "Muslims" that he is a xenophobe.

Is President fearful of Mexicans and Muslims coming into the United States? Is there any truth to the accusation? Well, let's take a look at how he ended up with this negative label, and how it was also pinned on the conservative movement.

On July 1, 2015 Kathryn Steinle, a 32-year-old who worked for a medical technology development company, was enjoying a beautiful summer day with her father on Pier 14 on the bay in San Francisco. Illegal Mexican immigrant Juan Francisco Lopez-Sanchez fired three rounds from a .40 caliber pistol, and one of the bullets ricocheted off the pavement striking "Kate" in the back piercing her aorta. She screamed, collapsed, and bled on the pier. Her father performed CPR on her until the paramedics arrived, but she died two hours later in the hospital.

The gun Lopez-Sanchez had used in his crime had been stolen from a vehicle belonging to an officer of the Bureau of Land Management four days earlier. In fact, the suspect, a career criminal who had multiple felony convictions in the United States, had been deported back to Mexico five times.

The family brought a lawsuit against the federal government, run by President Obama at the time, accusing them of Kate's death for its failure to enforce immigration laws. This murder outraged the American public, the conservatives anyway, and San Francisco's "sanctuary city" policy came to light. In response to the outrage, conservative Fox News talk show host Bill O'Reilly petitioned for a law, "Kate's Law," that would impose a mandatory five-year federal prison sentence on illegal immigrants who are deported, but come back into the United States illegally.

The Democrat senators were against the proposed law, on account that it would harm existing sanctuary city policies across America. When it came to the floor Senate Majority Leader Harry Reid (Democrat) blocked Kate's Law in the Senate.

On June 29, 2017, two years after Lopez-Sanchez was in possession of the stolen gun, the law was passed by the conservative 115th Congress (H.R.3004); when President Donald Trump was in office.

Wait! You are not fully sure of what a sanctuary city is? Well, let me tell you.

A sanctuary city is one that limits its cooperation with the federal government when it comes to immigration law. For example, and let's use murderer Lopez-Sanchez as our example, if a criminal illegal immigrant is arrested in a sanctuary city the local police will not question him about his immigration status. They don't want to know. The liberal core belief is that everyone is welcome in our country, and if a dangerous criminal happens to get through the system undetected it is a small price to pay to "keep families from being separated" by immigration laws on the books. Liberals do not view sneaking into the country as breaking the law. As of 2017 there were 300 jurisdictions in the United States that claim to be sanctuary cities. In other words, they cherry pick what federal laws they wish to obey and those they wish to ignore. In a word – *lawlessness*.

Oh, and speaking of sanctuary cities in 2017, on July 17, 2017 a 65-year-old woman was in her home when a man broke in through an open window, confronted her at knife point, tied her up with scarves and socks, blindfolded and gagged her, sexually assault her, and then slammed her head into the floor. Nice guy, huh? The suspect then later assaulted another woman in a parking garage blocks away from the first victim; again, armed with a knife, sexually assault her, and kicked her in the stomach. The man the sheriff's department arrested was 31-year-old Sergio Jose Martinez. He was a Mexican national who had been deported back to Mexico 20 times. That's right! TWENTY times! Immigration and Customs Enforcement (ICE) had lodged an immigration detainer against him in December 2016 requesting local authorities to notify them before releasing Martinez. However, the feds were not notified of his release because it is "illegal for cities in Oregon to use their resources to help enforce federal immigration laws." As a result, we had these horrendous crimes.

According to a report from KGW Portland, a CBS affiliate, Sheriff Mike Reese informed the community that "the sheriff's office does not hold people in county jails on ICE detainers or conduct any immigration enforcement actions."

Well, doesn't that policy make everyone in Portland feel safe.

Who cares that Martinez had five probation violations for re-entering the United States? As long as those crimes were not committed in the greater Portland area, seems to have been the thinking. Apparently, there are no dots to be connected to his federal crimes and the accusations of burglary, armed robbery, sexual assault, felony assault, and car theft (sarcasm).

Yeah, right!

Maybe those American citizens mentioned, women, could have been spared their agony had Martinez not been given the opportunity to sneak back into the country the sixth time, or the fourteenth time, or the 20th time.

In March of 2017 the City of Portland went all the way with an actual law by declaring themselves a "sanctuary city" for "undocumented immigrants." Of course, Democrat Governor Kate Brown, the country's first openly bisexual governor, was all for the new law, for she had just issued an executive order on February 2, 2017 that forbids all state agencies and employees from helping federal immigration officials locate or apprehend "undocumented" immigrants. The word "undocumented" replaced that old nasty word "illegal." She also ordered her Attorney General to "explore legal remedies" available to "resist" in court President Trump's travel ban of seven Muslim nations that fail to properly vet travelers coming into the United States. Her MEET THE GOVERNOR biography on the official government website lays out her worldview rather clearly, and as I have been teaching you all along, "It's all about one's worldview." Find out a person's worldview, and 9 times out of 10 you'll know what issues they support, and those they don't.

Not to be outdone by Governor Kate Brown, on October 5, 2017 Governor Jerry Brown of California (Democrat) signed into law that the entire state is a "sanctuary state" in defiance of the Trump administration. California has an estimated 2.3 million illegal immigrants, many of whom commit a high percentage of crime in the state. The State Sheriff's Association opposed the law, SB 54, but what do they know? They're just law enforcement leaders. California's leftist attitude is, *so what if the 2,400 "undocumented" immigrant prisoners in California, out of a prison population of 130,000 prisoners, are doing time for homicide.*

Well, I care, because I live in the state!

The only silver lining to the illegal problem in California is that since Donald Trump became President illegal border crossing apprehensions have dropped by 53% in his first six months in office compared to when President Obama was in office. Brandon Judd, president of the National Border Patrol Council, said on C-SPAN that it was, "nothing short of miraculous."

When I was a Reserve soldier during the Obama era I served a full day along the U.S.-Mexican border with the Border Patrol in San Diego, and believe me, the morale of the Border Patrol agents I met that day was low. They were deflated. These professionals all knew that they could stem the tide of illegal immigration if they were just allowed to do their job, but their hands were tied by a government that was trying to get the American people used to the idea of "open borders." Thank God Hillary Clinton did not become President, or otherwise that could have become a reality. According to one of the 2,000 leaked emails that Wikileaks posted during the campaign, Clinton told Banco Itau in 2013, "My dream is a hemispheric common market, with open trade and open borders."

Do you really want to come face to face with one of these "undocumented" immigrant criminals? Or, somebody you care about meets up with one of them? Then why support sanctuary cities or states?

In the past, when most American lawmakers and law enforcement agencies had common sense, illegal immigrants who committed a crime would be apprehended and punished, and then deported to the country from which they came from. The only way to determine if a criminal belongs in the country or should be deported is to determine their legal status. Duh! It doesn't take a genius to figure that one out. Governments at every level in the past did not want their citizens subjected to these criminals, for the government's primary responsibility is to keep its citizens safe. If they can't even do that, then what are they there for; just to tax us? Hence, when Donald Trump took office he came down hard on sanctuary cities. The basic message he sent to them, through U.S. Attorney Jeff Sessions, was, "YOU WILL COOPERATE WITH THE FEDERAL GOVERNMENT ON IMMIGRATION LAW." Immigration law, as you know, are laws passed by Congress; the representatives of *We the People.*

Before you head on over to Cell Block 9 let me recommend another book for you to read. It's titled *The Emigrant Edge: How to Make It Big in America* by Irish immigrant Brian Buffini. He came to the United States legally at 19-years-old with $22.00 in his pocket. He didn't expect this country to give him anything, except the opportunity to make something of himself with hard work and perseverance. It is a classic rags-to-riches story. In the preface of his book he wrote, "according to a recent a survey from Harvard's Institute of Politics, more than 50 percent of Millennials no longer think the American Dream is possible at all. My advice to those folks? Go travel the world and get some perspective. Seeing how much less people in other countries have compared with us will open your eyes to how good we have it here! Take it from me, when you arrive back home you'll kiss the ground! The American Dream is still alive, and it's not nearly as difficult to achieve as you might expect."

See, that made you feel good about yourself just reading that one paragraph, didn't it? The thought of working hard and appreciating what this country has to offer is a lot better than wallowing in self-pity or blaming someone else, or even throwing a brick through a store window, isn't it?

CELL BLOCK 9

CAUSE CÉLÈBRE

DEMOCRATIC SOCIALISM

When you first came into this reeducation camp we talked about the 2016 presidential election: Donald Trump, Bernie Sanders, Hillary Clinton, and all that. I gave a rather lengthy rundown on Bernie Sanders' political history, and how he intended to implement his so-called "Democratic Socialism" to guide this great country of ours in a new bold direction. Nobody on the political right took this guy seriously at first, until we saw how many young people, by the droves, were willing to jettison our American heritage and traditional values for this Democratic Socialism. As such, for me personally, the 2016 presidential election was a real wake up call.

When I was going through middle school and high school back in the 1970s we all had to take a class called "civics." The teacher taught us about the different political systems worldwide, and then emphasized the superiority of our democratic, capitalist, system. None of my teachers ever said our system was perfect, but it was the best that the world had to offer. Contrast that to today, and many teachers are telling our youth that there's something better, and that is "socialism." And, when they praise "socialism" they mean Bernie's brand of it.

According to Wikipedia the definition of Democratic Socialism is *a political ideology that advocates political democracy **alongside** social ownership of the means of production, often with an emphasis on democratic management of enterprises* **within a socialist economic system**. In other words, "communist China."

Bernie Sanders' definition, in his own words, is "Democratic socialism means that we must create an economy that works for all, not just the very wealthy."

Now, where did I hear this term before? Hmmmm, let me think.

Ah, yes! It went something like this, "In France the Communists ally themselves with the Social-Democrats, against the conservative and radical bourgeoisie (the rich)." That is a quote from Karl Marx who wrote The Communist Manifesto first published in 1848.

Bernie Sanders just switched the words around in this term; "Social-Democrats" to "Democratic Socialism." It' didn't take a whole lot of imagination to do this, but people who don't know their history fell for it. Then the term "radical bourgeoisie" was simply changed in our time to "the 1%." The one percent are supposedly the wealthiest 1% of the people in the United States, and that derived from the Occupy Movement's slogan, "We are the 99%!"

I believe that along side the United States Constitution, The Communist Manifesto should also be mandatory reading for every red-blooded American student. They should know the U.S. Constitution by heart, because this document is what our laws are based upon, as well as the structure of our society, and it's the document that all government officials, military personnel, and law enforcement officers swear to protect against "all enemies foreign and domestic." However, the reason for learning The Communist Manifesto is for the Sun Tzu thing, *Know your enemy*. If kids read it they wouldn't be duped by the likes of Bernie Sanders and Hillary Clinton or those who will inevitably come after them.

Let me ask you a question, and be honest about it. Have you personally read The Communist Manifesto? It's not that long, because it's just a pamphlet, which you can get off of the Internet. Well, if you haven't, read it. If you have read it before, and it's been a while, then read it again. Get reacquainted with it. You ought to know fully the system you want to usher in, or that you will allow others to do for you while you sit idly by. When it comes to the politics of your own country, the very system that will rule over you, you must do your part to effect the desired change you'd like to see, be it through the ballot box or revolution. If you do nothing, then you deserve nothing.

Here is a list of the highlights of what The Communist Manifesto is all about, paraphrased in bold type, with my own opinions in regular type:

1. **There are two classes of people: the bourgeoisie** (the greedy rich) **and the proletariat** (the exploited workers). Isn't this what many progressives are saying today to foment class warfare?

2. **Today's greedy rich are cut from the same cloth as the patricians** (the wealthy elite) **of the Roman Empire and the feudal lords of the Middle Ages, and all three have failed to eliminate "class antagonism."** No, they are not the same people. People are people. Some rich people are generous and productive with their money, and some exploit others.

3. **Modern industry killed a lot of fine professions, and it oppresses people.** Modernization does indeed "kill off" many professions. So, instead of using your computer for school or work, why don't you go back to using a typewriter? Put those typewriter workers back in business. After all, modernization killed the typewriter industry. Or, better yet, let's go back before the printing press, for it was the invention of the moveable type printing press in 1454 that put a lot of

illuminated manuscript scribes out of business.

4. **Free Trade is an "unconscionable freedom," because it is "exploitation, veiled by religious and political illusions."** So, no more buying Chinese products, because "we" exploited China, and somehow did it "veiled by religious and political illusions," whatever that means. I don't think most Chinese would like to turn the clock back. I think they like prosperity a whole lot better than starving. Industrialization and innovation is the only logical way to feed over a billion people.

5. **Constant modernization is disruptive to society, and the rich take advantage of this constant modernization.** No, I think it's the other way around. Constant modernization helps society: electric cars, cell phones, medical advances, more efficient and safer passenger aircraft, computers, and so forth. What's "disruptive" is socialist leaders always trying to slap on more rules and regulations, and trying to take the incentive out of getting ahead.

6. **The rich continue to expand international commerce to control the world through distribution and dependence on their products.** It's called "supply and demand." Businesses expand because customers want their products or service. I like French wines, German cars, and Japanese electronics. What's wrong with that? Yes, I am dependent on a lot of cheap goods from China, as well as my bananas from Central and South America. So, what?

7. **Since the West created industrialization, and exported their products to the "barbarian nations," these barbarian nations have an intense obstinate hatred for Westerners having lost their own identities.** No, it was not the products that people didn't like from the West. Many foreign nations did not like European and American colonization once they were able to rule themselves. The United States had once been a colony itself. However, all former colonies benefited from European and American colonization by becoming modern.

8. **Owning private property is wrong, and the state needs to own everything.** Yes, the people can all live in housing projects while the leaders live in luxury. Wasn't that the way it was, and is, in all communist countries? What are you going to treat better? A rental car or your own car? What are you going to take more pride in? An apartment or your own house? Owning private property is the right answer.

9. **Communists must "rescue" education, and then run it.** Of course, they do. How else can they brainwash generation after generation? Who else is going to keep teaching "separation of church and state" out of context?

10. **The wives of rich men have no freedom, and are viewed upon as mere property. Therefore, traditional marriage should be abolished.** It's interesting that communism wants to destroy the very first institution of mankind, the

very foundation of human society.

11. **Rich people only have children for their own private gain. Therefore, the traditional family should be abolished, and the state should educate children.** Is it just me, or is this whole idea insane? I believe that most parents have children is because they want children to love, raise up, and have them become productive citizens. They want to have family vacations, conversations at the dinner table, and grandkids to enjoy in their golden years. I don't hear many of the young couples that I know saying, "Honey, we're really hurting for money, so let's have a few kids so we can put them to work for us." The people of today are no different than those of 1848. But, what was Karl Marx's solution? Let the state educate the children. After all, the state will be more loving and tender to the children, and teach them a superior "anti-traditional" value system.

12. **Capitalism has taken away individualism, and turned workers into mere machines.** Hmmmm, and communism gives people back their "individualism?" So, let's get this straight, a North Korean citizen can go right now and stand on a street corner in Pyongyang and start preaching the Gospel without government harassment? Anyone can hold up an anti-government sign in front of the El Capitolio, *National Capitol Building*, in Havana, Cuba without getting dragged off to a cell. Yeah, right! As far as workers becoming "mere machines," then maybe a teacher job, windsurfer instructor, or florist might be a better job for some. After all, in America you have the freedom to choose your own occupation and work towards that goal. Not all workers work in factories, and neither did they in Karl Marx's day. It was a stupid blanket statement that sounds true until you think about it for a moment or two.

13. **There should be no national differences, i.e. "no borders."** So, that way everyone can pour into our prosperous nation: people with no skills, criminals, terrorists, and those who'd want to change our very way of life.

14. **"Communism abolishes eternal truths, it abolishes all religion, and all morality." After all, "ancient religions were overcome by Christianity," and "Christian ideas succumbed in the eighteenth century to rationalist ideas."** Communism is "the most radical rupture with traditional ideas." Karl Marx hated the God of the Bible, and in his manifesto he makes that perfectly clear several times. He did not attack Islam, Buddhism, nor Hinduism, which were also world religions that existed in his day. It's no coincident that many Americans on the left today also are vehemently opposed to Christianity and its followers, and yet don't say a word about Islam when it comes to women's issues, homosexuality, "separation of church and state," i.e. sharia law. History indeed repeats itself.

15. **Nobody should get an inheritance. It should go to the state for redis-**

tribution. Why should anyone invest in a house, an estate, or save up for their children's future, if the state gets it all in the end? My question is, "Why can't there be enough to pass down to the grandchildren?"

16. **The state should control all banking.** After all, then they can get the interest on the capital instead of the banks. We all know the government will invest it wisely.

17. **The state should control all communications and transportation.** That way they can listen in on every word you say or type. And, if a train or airplane is a little late, who are you going to complain to? How well does the IRS listen to you if you disagree with them? Do you really want the government to have complete control of communications and transportation instead of corporations who are competing for your business and customer satisfaction? As for me, I like healthy business competition, which gives me choices.

18. **Equal obligation of all to work.** In other words, if you don't have a job we (the government) will give you one, and you're going to like it too. Oh yes, many communist countries choose people's occupations, as well as how much they are to get paid. You can't just quit and go find a better job with better pay if you wanted to either. How would you like to live under that kind of "freedom?" Yes, people can fail miserably in a free country, but they can just as easily succeed also.

19. **Combine agriculture and manufacturing, and distribute the population where needed.** In communist China the government forced people to work on farms, including soldiers during times of peace, known as The Great Leap Forward. By the end of 1958 700 million people had been placed in 26,578 communes. Well, what do you suppose happens when the government takes charge of something they know nothing about? Such as farming and population redistribution? I'll tell you. Despite this "revolutionary" method of agriculture that Chairman Mao insisted upon, millions starved to death, and those leaders that could not meet their food production quota were labeled as "bourgeois (rich) reactionaries," and punished. Well, don't think that bad communist ideas ever die out, because they don't. On March 16, 2012 President Barak Obama signed the Executive Order – *National Defense Resources Preparedness* in the White House. I'll let you read that one for yourself.

20. **Free education for all children in public schools, and absolutely no home schooling and no traditional parenting.** As Hillary Clinton wrote, *It Takes a Village*; as long as that "village" is socialist leaning, that is. Now, if the government wants to control everything that children learn, then how does that foster "individualism?" If they all have the same Common Core going through school, then how could there be open debate on differing ideas and methods if

they are in a "group think" environment? Why can't public schools seriously examine Judaism or Christianity? Why can't they be reintroduced to America's first textbook *The New England Primer?* Why can't grade schools be taught the benefits of capitalism? Why can't parents be given school vouchers to educate their kids at home or in a private school? Is public, *village*, education the best way?

Bernie Sanders 168 years later, basically advocated many of the same things found on this list that Karl Marx advocated. The prominent theme, if I can paraphrase it for you, is "the government needs to take from the rich and give (redistribute) it to everyone else to make everybody equal." In other words, no more first class on airplanes, because "class" is a bad word, and everybody flies economy. One of Hillary Clinton's favorite phrases she used during her presidential campaign was, "economic equality." Everyone should be equal when it comes to money. Wait! Was that going to apply to her as well? Was she going to give away her millions to be equal to the rest of us? Well, she has not done it so far.

Throughout his entire eight years in office President Obama had the same idea, but he just used a different phrase, and that was "an even playing field." So, it would be safe to say that the words "socialism" and "communism" are interchangeable in the minds of many Democrats. Marx, Obama, Clinton, Sanders – it's all the same, just different years.

The only problem with the redistribution of wealth is that it never works, and believe me, many countries have tried ever since The Communist Manifesto first came out.

Karl Marx was a Prussian (that's a German state that no longer exists) who lived between 1818 and 1883. He was a philosopher, economist, and a journalist living most of his life in London, England. The story of his Jewish ancestry, his parents raising him as a Christian, the influence of his liberal humanist teachers, and the local police raiding the school in 1832 is an interesting backdrop, but we won't go into that here. I'll cut right to the chase, and that is KARL MARX NEVER LIVED IN A COMMUNIST SOCIETY! His communism was just theory from his own imagination, and what other like-minded men were also thinking about at that time. The first constitutionally socialist state was in Russia in 1917, thirty-four years after Marx died, and we all know what a disaster Russia turned out to be under communism.

"Oh, but they didn't follow Karl Marx's theory as he envisioned it," you may be saying. "It was not pure communism," many of today's socialists protest in defense of the utopian system.

Well, what about the other self-declared socialist states that have tried and failed? Afghanistan, Albania, Angola, Belarus, Byelorussia, Benin, Bulgaria, Cambodia, Congo-Brazzaville, Czechoslovakia, Ethiopia, East Germany, Grenada, Hungary, Mongolia, Mozambique, Poland, Romania, Somalia, Ukraine, South Yemen, and Yugoslavia. What a mess that turned out to be for these 22 countries. Take a good look at what has just happened to oil-rich Venezuela over the past decade, a country President Obama had praised throughout his presidency even though they disrespected us Americans the entire time. The result of their glorious socialism, as of May 4, 2017, was that most Venezuelans went to bed hungry each night. Pets and zoo animals were being stolen and eaten so that people could survive. 15% of the people literally ate garbage, and the country lacked basic resources like medicine and toilet paper. Well, if you don't care about the people, how about their children? 11% of them suffered from malnutrition.

The countries still clinging onto communism today, in one form or another, are China, Cuba, Laos, North Korea, and Vietnam. They're not exactly countries Westerners want to go live in.

Again, Karl Marx's theory, in any form, has been tried and failed for 100 years, and counting. Even China could not adhere to "pure communism," and they had to introduce capitalistic methods to grow their economy and feed their 1.380 billion people. So, economically capitalism is superior, that much is undisputed, but politically there's reluctance from other countries to allow people the freedoms that we American's enjoy.

So, then, why is capitalism superior to socialism? To put it simply, and I love this expression, *I never got a job from a poor man.*

It's the "wealthy," the people Karl Marx and Bernie Sanders despise, that creates the jobs that everyone benefits from. Their desire to make a profit, through their hard work and ingenuity, is what fuels the economy. Governments don't manufacture things, corporations and small businesses do. Of course, some don't do it just for the money, but they are actually passionate about their work, and money is just a byproduct of that passion. Do you work only for the money? If you do, how pitiful is that? Corporations and small businesses, so criticized by the progressive left, employ people, be it designing the newest high-tech device or waiting on tables. Karl Marx hated the rich in London, but out of all the places on the planet he could have made his home, he chose one of the most prosperous cities and countries in the world at the time. What a fricken hypocrite. It's just too bad that he didn't live long enough to live in his own "utopia," in his own filth, so to speak.

Remember, my wife and her family came from the former Union of Soviet **Socialist** Republic, the USSR, and they lived the reality. Why do you think they all came to the United States? Because, it sucked over there! The majority of people who lived under that oppressive system will tell you the same.

I have one quick story for you. One day my wife, Karen, went to work during the Christmas season wearing a button that had a nativity scene on it with the words JESUS IS THE REASON FOR THE SEASON. She was a teacher at a junior college. Her supervisor asked her to remove the button stating, "separation of church and state," and all that good stuff, and my wife refused to remove it. She looked the supervisor in the eye and said, "I left the Soviet Union so that I'd have the freedom to wear a button like this."

Wow! Did that piercing statement shut that supervisor down. She was left alone to wear the button, and she did just that for many years to follow. *Good for her*, I thought. My wife recognized heavy-handed communist tactics when she saw it, because she had lived it before. Who would dare argue with her?

This reminds me, when I was the NCOIC of SECFOR, that is a Noncommissioned Officer In Charge, it's like a chief of police, of a 25-soldier Security Forces unit at Joint Forces Training Based in Southern California, I said to my soldiers on the last day of duty before our holiday break, "Merry Christmas." I said it right there on a U.S. military base at a time when the Obama administration was hostile towards Christmas, and as such there were more and more attacks by the progressive left on Christmas in the public square during his eight-year reign.

I, like my wife, was not afraid to speak up, thus exercising my First Amendment right. As an American soldier, I knew that Christmas was an official federal holiday on December 25 (5 U.S. Code 6103 – Holidays), and I didn't have any qualms in saying it out loud. The official wording of the U.S. government for this scheduled holiday is "Christmas Day." As the name implies, it is mass for Christ. It is the day Congress had set aside as a legal holiday to commemorate the birth of Jesus of Nazareth, which, as you know, Christians know as God.

There are a lot of left-leaning liberals that have declared a "War on Christmas," but that should not surprise anyone in the least. Karl Marx smeared religion every chance he got. One of his many quotes, besides calling religion "the opium of the people," is, "Religion is the impotence of the human mind to deal with occurrences it cannot understand." No, he does not mean a man's inability to achieve an erection, but he meant the first definition of the word, and that is the inability to take effective action or helplessness. Again, this guy was a moron. Some of the greatest "action takers" in history believed in Jesus of Nazareth, and I'll just mention some of those who lived in Karl Marx's century: Alessandro Volta who invented the first battery (where we get our word "Volt" from), Andre Ampere (where we get our word "Ampere" from), John

Abercrombie who was a pioneer in neuropathology, Benjamin Silliman who was the first person to distill petroleum and the founder of the American Journal of Science, William Whewell who coined many of the scientific words we use today (scientist, physicist, cathode, and more), James Forbes who brought to light discoveries about the conduction of heat and seismology, Charles Babbage who was the first to come up with the idea of a programmable computer, Andrew Pritchard who improved microscopy, Gregor Mendel who is "the father of modern genetics," Heinrich Hertz who proved the existence of electromagnetic waves, Louis Pasteur who discovered the principles of vaccination and pasteurization (you can thank him for that next bowl of cereal or ice cream being germ free), James Joule who brought forth the first law of thermodynamics (and for you Airsoft gun enthusiasts, you know all about Joules), and John Dawson who debunked Darwin's theory of evolution.

I just chose scientists of Marx's day, and left out the great God-fearing politicians, inventors, and others who helped humanity. And, let me tell you, there are a lot of them. Great men and women the world respects.

So, come Christmas time pay more attention to how many of those who embrace socialism want to do away with Christmas Day as an official American holiday, like the Freedom From Religion Foundation, who's spokesman is Ron Reagan, is trying to do (see The New York Times opinion article *Let's Observe Dec. 25, but not as Christmas* by Annie Laurie Gaylor updated April 19, 2013).

Least you forget, many American socialists are against Christmas, because they're against religion, and they're against religion because communism is against religion. In The Communist Manifesto it claims, *The charges against communism made from a religious, a philosophical, and, generally, from an ideological standpoint*, are not deserving of a serious examination. So, in other words, if you're a serious person you can't use religion, philosophy, or "generally" other ideologies. You can't even use historical precedence to argue against communism (socialism), because, *In bourgeois society, therefore, the past dominates the present; in communist society, the present dominates the past.*

"The present dominates the past!" Alright then, so what Karl Marx had many people believe is, and I paraphrase, "forget about the lessons of yesteryear, and whatever we decide today is the only thing that matters."

This is ludicrous! Yet, Americans, even many of our government leaders who call themselves progressives, are buying into this communism ideology again, even after we won the Cold War.

The last thing I need to tell you about Democratic-Socialism, socialism, communism, or whatever you want to label it, is that if they don't get their way their last resort is REVOLUTION! That's right, if it takes violence to accomplish the change, then so be it.

The last two paragraphs in The Communist Manifesto reads;

The communist disdain to conceal their views and aims. They openly declare that their ends can be attained only by the forcible overthrow of all existing social conditions. Let the ruling classes tremble at a communist revolution. The proletarians have nothing to lose but their chains. They have a world to win.

Workingmen of all countries, unite!

What are groups like Black Lives Matter and Antifa shouting in American streets? "REVOLUTION!" And, straight out of the playbook, The Communist Manifesto, there was even photos taken of a BLM protest that took place on Market Street in West Philadelphia on July 12, 2016 showing two black protestors holding a large nylon sign that read We have nothing to lose but our chains! which, as you now know, came straight out of paragraph you just read. And, what is Bernie Sander's latest book called again? Remind me. Oh, yeah, Bernie Sanders Guide to Political Revolution. Isn't he the one, with the support of Massachusetts Senator Elizabeth Warren (Democrat), leading the charge with the organization OUR REVOLUTION? Don't think that these are just idle words. They are threats. One such threat on their website states, "Our Revolution will transform American politics to make our political and economic systems once again responsive to the needs of the working families."

At least Senator Sanders changed the term from "workingmen" to "working families," least OUR REVOLUTION appeared as if they were supporters of misogyny.

AIRBRUSHING HISTORY

Yes, I know. It's an unusual subheading. It's meant to be. So, let's delve a little bit more into history as part of your reeducation, shall we.

Vladimir Lenin (1870-1924) led the revolution that turned Russia into a communist state. A close comrade of his, Leon Trotsky, had been influential in helping bring about this social change. A famous black and white photograph had been taken of Lenin giving a speech in a city square surround by throngs of people. At the foot of the platform was Trotsky.

After Lenin's death his successor, Joseph Stalin, had Trotsky exiled from the Soviet Union, and he had the famous photo altered by having Trotsky airbrushed out of the photo. Trotsky's name, and any connection to the communist revolution, was blotted out. Future Soviet generations knew nothing of Trotsky's contribution to their history.

Communist Chinese leader Mao Zedong had Qin Bangxian, one of his trusted political deputies, airbrushed out of a photo in 1935. Gone. No more.

Years later Nikolai Yezhov, the head of Stalin's secret police, had a falling out with the Russian leader and was arrested, tortured, and forced to commit suicide in 1940. A famous photograph of Stalin standing with Yezhov was also altered. Yezhov was airbrushed out of history.

Fast forward to more recent events in your lifetime. A photograph of North Korean communist dictator Kim Jong-un shaking hands with an unknown military officer was published by state-run Korean Central News Agency (KCNA). His uncle Jang Song-thaek was in the background of this photo. Song-thaek helped Kim rule the country while the dictator was still in his 20s, and in need of guidance. As such, Song-thaek was considered one of the most powerful figures in the North Korean government. Then sometime after the mentioned photo was taken Kim Jong-um had his uncle executed in 2013. It was quite a gruesome execution at that. According to a Chinese newspaper Jang Song-thaek was stripped naked and fed to a pack of hungry dogs. It came on the heels of a KCNA article stating, "Despicable human scum Jang, who was **worse than a dog**, perpetrated thrice-cursed acts of treachery in betrayal of such profound trust and warmest paternal love shown by the party and the leader for him." Why does every statement out of North Korean seem to be a Google translation? Anyway, the photograph taken before the execution resurfaced, and a British news agency discovered that the photo had been altered. Song-thaek had been Photoshopped out of it.

"So, who cares about communists airbrushing or Photoshopping people out of historical photos?" you ask.

Well, in a sense, many on the liberal left today are doing the same thing. Perhaps not with photographs, but with American history itself. So, let's connect the dots with a brief history lesson.

For two hundred plus years American school children had been taught in the classroom that Christopher Columbus, an Italian, technically a Genoese, discovered America in 1492. I still have this Columbus Day poem in my mind since childhood, "In fourteen ninety-two Columbus sailed the ocean blue. He had three ships and left from Spain; He sailed through sunshine, wind and rain. He sailed by night..." and on it goes.

Prior to 1492 Europeans did not know that the continents of North America and South America were between them and Asia, since nobody had successfully sailed west from Europe to get to Asia before. Oh sure, some say the Vikings may have touched North American shores somewhere around Canada in the

11th century, but there is sparse evidence of it, and certainly no lasting colonization. However, because it's more likely than not that it happened, October 9th is Leif Erikson Day, but it's not a federal holiday, only permanent colonization merits that. Moving on, the Europeans in Columbus' day knew that the earth was spherical, and they also knew that the "Ocean Sea," the ancient name for the Atlantic Ocean believed to separate Europe from Asia, to be a daunting task to cross that no monarchy was willing to finance. Who wants to lose expensive ships to the unknown? However, Columbus had calculated that the distance from Spain to Cipangu (Japan) was about 2,400 miles (3,862 kilometers), and by sailing 100 miles (160 kilometers) a day he could reach the Indies in 30 days. The term "Indies" came from Portuguese explorers to mean the Indian subcontinent.

Established trade routes to the east from Europe were not only long, having to go all the way around Africa and then east, but dangerous because of the many enemies and pirates along the way. Columbus presented his ideas for a western voyage twice to the king of Portugal, but twice he was denied.

However, after two years of negotiations Christopher Columbus finally convinced King Ferdinand II and Queen Isabella of Spain to finance his expedition to establish a new trade route to Asia. The purpose was to find a more efficient way to the Indies to secure enough gold and valuable spices to spend the profits "on the conquest of Jerusalem." He, like many Europeans, wanted to launch a new Crusade to take back the Holy Land from the Muslims, which also appealed greatly to the crown. After all, that very year in 1492, the Spanish had just pushed out the Muslims from the Iberian Peninsula after 781 years of occupation, and Spain was fast becoming a world superpower.

So how did he do it? How did he succeed were others had failed before?

In Columbus' own words he tells us exactly what he told the Spanish sovereigns, and that was, *"At this time I have seen and put in study to look into the Scriptures (the Bible), cosmography, histories, chronicles and philosophy and other arts, which our Lord opened to my understanding, I could sense His hand upon me, so that it became clear to me that it was feasible to navigate from here to the Indies, and He unlocked within me the determination to execute the idea."*

His "worldview," his faith in God and limited scientific knowledge, literally changed the world.

King Ferdinand and Queen Isabella agreed with his vision, and they provided him with three ships: the Pinta, the Santa Clara, and the Nina, along with all the supplies they needed. Five weeks later the explorer set foot on what is today The Bahamas, which he named "San Salvador," *Holy Savior.*

Believing that he had landed on an island in the Indies he called the indigenous people "Indios," Indians. In his diary he wrote, "They should be good servants and intelligent, for I observed that they quickly took in what was said to them, and I believe that they would easily be made Christians, as it appeared to me that they had no religion."

Before some of you have a seizure over the word "servants" that Columbus used, and condemn him, remember that all people under a monarch are "servants." There are still monarchies today in Europe, and the citizens in those nations are technically servants of the crown. That's what monarchies do, they rule over people. Of course, you American Millennials and Gen Zers don't live under a monarchy, thanks to our founding fathers, so you can't image yourself being a "servant."

Getting back to what I was saying, based upon this one sentence alone his mission was twofold: expansion of the Spanish Empire, and the spiritual conversion of all those with whom he met. In those days "colonization" was something both noble and patriotic, and leading pagan people to the Lord was the most compassionate thing one could do for anyone.

After San Salvador Christopher Columbus continued his voyage to what is today Cuba, Jamaica, Santo Domingo and other Caribbean islands, and then he and his crew returned to Spain to a thankful king and queen.

Columbus took three more voyages to "the New World" discovering Central and South America. History was forever changed.

Between 1493 and 1820, Spain sent approximately 15,585 missionaries to the Americas to convert the indigenous people to Christianity. In other words, "to save their souls from the fires of hell." Again, that was a caring thing to do, not an evil thing. For in the New Testament, Colossians 3:10-11 to be exact, it states, "and have put on the new man who is renewed in knowledge according to the image of Him who created him, where there is neither Greek, nor Jew, circumcised nor uncircumcised, barbarian, Scythian, slave nor free, but Christ is all and in all." In other words, when a person finally surrenders their life to God they are all brothers and sisters equal in the eyes of God. Race, ethnicity, and social status are no longer important in the Kingdom of God.

In the first fifteen years after the conquest of Aztecs, Mayans, Incas, and other tribes in the region, the Franciscans baptized approximately 5 million people, sometimes a thousand a day.

Were there other Spaniards and Portuguese in the mix with other agendas in mind? Of course, there were. The desire for conquest and obtaining riches by the conquistadores, *conquerors*, are also recorded, and even the search for the fabled Fountain of Youth by conquistador Juan Ponce de Leon in the 16th century.

Okay, I'm starting to get to my point. But, first, let me show you some pictures from my last vacation. What? You don't want me to bore you with family photos. Alrighty then, I'll just tell you about it.

I recently took a little trip up to the wine country in Northern California with my wife. She got what she wanted, to stay in a nice B&B, and I got what I wanted after seeing the coast of California and vineyards, and that was to stop at a couple historical sites and visit a museum or two. As you can tell, I'm a history buff.

As Karen was strolling through some shops I went into the Mission San Francisco Solano in city of Sonoma. This was the last of twenty-one missions build by the Spanish, and the only one founded under Mexican governance. The site was consecrated on July 4, 1823.

Inside the Mission there was a small museum. I walked up to a large sign, and the headline immediately caught my attention. It read, A COLLISION OF CULTURES, and not just in English, but in Spanish also, CONFLICTOS DE CULTURAS. There was a map of the State of California showing where the various Native American tribes had lived in the 1800s.

Under the map was some text explaining the history. I started reading, *During the thousands of years that Native Americans lived in the Californias their cultures evolved to coexist with the natural environment.*

My suspicions were immediately raised. The wording sounded like an environmentalist wrote it, and so I continued to read out of curiosity, *The Spanish introduced European methods of farming and ranching that drastically altered the natural environment and changed the diet of the Native Americans.*

Have you ever seen a Spanish mission? At most they're 10,000 acres, and California is vast. It's a huge state. It took me 8 hours to drive from Los Angeles to San Francisco. I thought to myself, *Oh, come on! How could a little farming and ranching 'drastically alter' the natural environment? This is ludicrous!*

Oh, and it got much deeper, as in "deeper in political correctness crap," as I read on. *The policy of the Spanish, to bring the Native Americans into the new colonial communities, was based on both Spanish religious beliefs and economic necessity. The Spanish believed that a baptized Native American would become part of their society.*

A baptized Native American did become a part of the church. That's a good thing. "There is neither Greek nor Jew..."

The Spanish also considered the Native Americans as necessary laborers, and in some instances forced them to work in the missions.

For a people that could live off the land, and had done so for thousands of years, I find it hard to believe that they couldn't have fought or run away from the mean old priests and monks "forcing" them to work (sarcasm).

Not all Native Americans were as "peace-loving and one-with-nature" as many of your peers make them out to be. In his letter to King Ferdinand and Queen Isabella of Spain, Christopher Columbus wrote, "As for monsters, I have found no trace of them except at the point in the second isle as one enters the Indies, which is inhabited by a people considered in all the isles as most ferocious, who eat human flesh." We get our word "cannibal" from Christopher Columbus' Spanish pronunciation of the indigenous tribe called the Caribs. When explorer and cartographer Amerigo Vespucci, from which we get the word "America," sailed across the Atlantic Ocean seven years after Columbus' first voyage, and he also wrote about the practice of cannibalism in his book *Mundus Novus* published in 1505. He's the guy who figured out that it was not Asia that the Spanish had been sailing to, but an entirely new continent. When the Spanish conquistadors began the conquest and colonization of New Spain in 1519 they were horrified by the widespread human sacrifice they witnessed by the Aztecs (today's Mexico). Their accounts have been verified by archaeological evidence. Their god Huitzilopochtli required nourishment, and that nourishment was human hearts. The victims were from the "ethnically inferior" neighboring Tlaxcala tribe. In fact, not only did the Aztecs sacrifice adult captives, but children as well; as did the Olmecs, Mayans, Teotihuacans, the Toltecs, and the Incas in South America, but it also occurred all the way up into North America with Cahokia, Pawnee, and Iroquois.

Then, here came the kicker as I finished reading the sign in the museum, *Diseases brought by the Spanish devastated many tribes. Native Americans living near the missions participated, often unwillingly, in the new culture and religion. Although some Native Americans assimilated into the new communities, most died.*

Boy, doesn't this all sound so bleak; "diseases, often unwillingly, most died." Any child reading this "history" would have thought that the Native Americans had no mind of their own. Although they outnumbered the Spanish, had their own way of life for thousands of years, they just gave it all up like dumb sheep.

As for diseases, I'm sure that Christopher Columbus, and those that followed him afterwards, did not say, "Come on boys! There's probably a lot of people on the other side of that ocean that we should bring our diseases to. Let's go give them our smallpox, influenza, measles and chicken pox," for a lot of left wingers accuse the Spanish of genocide of the Native Americans. However, in the 15th, 16th, and 17th centuries people didn't know how diseases came about or how they could spread. Of course, like many "historians" on the left, the full story was not explained on the sign that I read in the mission's museum. For accuracy it should have ended with, "some of Christopher Columbus's crew members brought back syphilis from the New World to Europe with them, for prior to 1492 there had been no written record of this sexually transmitted disease." But, nope! That bit of information was missing from the sign.

I know it's hard for the left to believe, but most Native Americans wanted their soul to be saved just like the Spanish did before them. Christianity was not a "Spanish" religion, but it's origins are from Israel. Spain had been a pagan nation that eventually accepted the Gospel of Jesus Christ.

Then my wife and I drove down the coast heading back home to Los Angeles, *The Angels*. We stopped at Mission San Miguel Arcangel, which was founded on July 25, 1797 by Padre Presidente Fermin Francisco de Lasuen. He chose this site because he was a friend to the Native People for 25 years. In his own words, "I have spoken the language of the local Native people. I have heard the Indians say that they desire a mission."

So, let me get this straight. A white man, thousands of miles from his own country spends twenty-five years getting to know the indigenous people, learns their language, and refers to them as friends. Then they ask him to establish a mission in their area, which he does it. This is quite a different depiction of the Spanish than the text I read up in Sonoma.

Well, I just happened to walk into the chapel when a group of people were having mass. The priest was speaking to the small congregation in Spanish. They all appeared to me to be there of their own free will. I would suspect that was also the case over 200 years ago with the Native Americans.

And, now, finally, to my point. Wait for it…

Have you ever heard of the Tongva? If you took a poll of those who live in the greater Los Angeles area, asking the same question, I doubt you could find few people that could answer you.

The Tongva were the indigenous people living in the Los Angeles Basin at the time of Spanish exploration in 1542. When Mission San Gabriel Arcangel was constructed in 1771 the Tongva population was estimated at 5,000 to 10,000.

On September 1, 2017 the Los Angeles City Council voted to replace the federal recognized holiday Columbus Day with "Indigenous Peoples Day." Oh yes, the term "Native American" is long gone in California, because "America" is named after Italian explorer Amerigo Vespucci.

Anyway, the almost four million inhabitants of the city of Los Angeles decided to follow the liberal city of Berkeley, California that did the same twenty-five years earlier. Many on the left believe that Christopher Columbus was the catalyst for the destruction of the Native American people, and the environment. Had Columbus not come to America there would have been no genocide, no global warming, and no rush hour on the 5 Freeway.

Of course, it's believed that Tongva originally came from the Nevada area, and migrated west about 3,500 years ago. When they hit LA they either absorbed or pushed out the Hokan people in the region. That's why it's called Indigenous Peoples Day instead of Tongva Day. In the minds of the radical left it doesn't matter who inhabited the area prior to the arrival of the Europeans, as long the holiday does not honor the white-rich-Christian-colonizing Columbus. It's all part of erasing American history like the Russian, Chinese, and North Korean communist did with people they disagreed with, and historical photographs that they were in.

Mark my words, the name of the city is next. Los Angeles, *The Angeles*, was named after a Spanish pueblo named El Pueblo de Nuestra Senora la Reina de los Angeles de Porciuncula, *The Town of Our Lady the Queen of the Angeles of Porciuncula* in honor of the Virgin Mary. That's a mouth full, and so they shortened it to "Los Angeles."

As of 2010 the racial composition of Los Angeles was 48.5 percent Hispanic (the majority), 28.7% white, 9.6% African American, and 11.3% Asian. If we just take those of possible European descent the percentage comes to 77.2% of the population that is in Los Angeles because of Christopher Columbus' discovery. Obviously, the blacks were impacted by this discovery as well, but under unfavorable circumstances – slavery. So, just to avoid any controversy we'll leave this percentage out of the equation. The Chinese immigrants came over in the 1800s to work on the rail road and in mines. The Native Americans certainly did not invite them over, but because of the "cheap Chinese labor" controversy we'll also leave out the Asian percentage in this equation. It's true that the following generations of blacks and Asians benefited from the result of Columbus' discovery, but why get anyone upset for the statistic I'm going to share with you. Therefore, 2,923,169 Angelenos (the name for all those who live in Los Angeles) were directly affected by Christopher Columbus discovering America. Yet, despite these incredibly high numbers of people that Christophe Columbus impacted, and the fact that 65% of the population considers themselves Christian according to the Pew Research Center in 2015, most of those sitting on the Los Angeles City Council decided to honor the "indigenous peoples," which number 54,236 in the city of Los Angeles. As of 2008 only 1,700 people identified themselves as Tongva, also known as the Gabrielino tribe. So, that raises the question, "Who are the other 52, 536?"

The Tongva tribe is not recognized by the federal government, but it is recognized by the State of California; along with the Ventureno and Fernandeno tribes. Yes, I know, they are all Spanish names, but that's beside the point. Two of these tribes want to build gaming casinos, while a third does not, and there have also been legal battles over land and water rights. As the old saying goes, *follow the money*.

Since the federal government does not recognize the Tongva tribes, could the LA City Council possibly have a beef with the federal government, and then decided to retaliate by overlapping Indigenous Peoples Day over the federal holiday we know, and love, as Columbus Day? Naaaah, they wouldn't do that, would they?

Oh, and before we go on, the federal government does recognize 104 Native American tribes in California. So, it's not like the federal government has ignored the ingenious peoples of The Golden State.

Now, I am not opposed to having an Indigenous Peoples Day in Los Angeles, or in any American town or city for that matter. The Indians, Native Americans, Indigenous People, or whatever you want to call them, are part of American history. Some are even quite respected like Pocahontas, Geronimo, Crazy Horse Lakota, Sitting Bull Lakota, and even the actor Chief Dan George. I'd support such a holiday whole heartedly, especially since I'm part Cherokee from both my mother's side and my father's side, and I even have the characteristic Cherokee jaw and chin to prove it. But, an Indigenous Peoples Day should never replace Columbus Day! There are 12 official holidays recognized by the city of Los Angeles. That means that there were 353 other available days that the Los Angeles City Council could have chosen for their new holiday, but they didn't. The council voted 14 to 1 in favor of bringing down Columbus Day like a confederate statue. The one council member opposed to the motion was Joe Buscaino who suggested that Indigenous Peoples Day fall on another day. After all, Italian-Americans celebrate Columbus Day big time.

Los Angeles has been an incorporated city since April 4, 1850, and the discovery of America by Christopher Columbus has been taught in schools since then. So, why the need now to do away with this holiday?

How long have you been in this camp now? I've been telling you all along, it's all about one's worldview. So, with a little digging I discovered that the council member who led the charge for Indigenous Peoples Day was Mitch O'Farrell, the chair of the committee.

You would think that with a name like "O'Farrell," a good Irish name, that one would have no reason to oppose admiral Christopher Columbus being honored one day out of the year, but he did. It turns out that he is a member of the Wyandotte Nation, which is a federally recognized tribe in Oklahoma. That's where Mitch O'Farrell was raised before moving to California in 1982. Okay, that sheds some light on the issue. He also lives with his partner, George Brauckman, and has established strong ties with the Los Angeles LBGT Center, Bienestar, Equality California, and other advocacy organizations – this, according to his own bio on the city's website. "Mitch has steadily maintained the visibility of the LGBT community and is working to elevate its place in mainstream society." Get the picture?

So, essentially council member O'Farrell, and thirteen others, didn't care if they insulted Americans of Italian descent, Hispanic descent, and citizens of all descent who honor Christopher Columbus for his incredible contribution to Western civilization.

We'll give O'Farrell a pass, but why would 13 other council members, who all but one had European last names, vote against their own history? The one non-European last name was Krekorian, which is Armenian, and 99.9% of the Armenians in Los Angeles identify as Armenian Orthodox Christian. The biggest common denominator is that of the 15 Los Angeles City Council members 14 of them belong to the Democratic Party. Now, I don't know what Mitchell Englander's problem is, the one Republican. I sent him an email asking if he could explain to me why he voted to replace Columbus Day, but I never got a response.

What's ironic about the decision of the Los Angeles City Council to "airbrush out" Columbus Day is that their own city seal contains the coat of arms of Castile and Leon that signifies the city's history as a Spanish colony. So, let's get this straight. Christopher Columbus is the first European to step foot on America, plants the Spanish flag in the sand, Spain colonizes North, Central, and South America as a result, the majority of those living in Los Angeles are Hispanic (of Spanish blood), and the wise politicians of LA want to erase the national holiday Columbus Day. And, the left wonders why President Donald Trump won the 2106 election, and why democrats have lost over 1,000 seats all across the nation.

I painstakingly took all this time to educate you about Los Angeles' Indigenous Peoples Day to warn you that it's not just Berkeley or Los Angeles trying to erase parts of history they don't like, but this communist tactic is spreading rapidly from coast to coast, from border to border. I have traveled to over 20 countries around the world, and I have never seen a country that loathes itself like the United States of America does; at least a sizeable amount of its people anyway.

So, if you Millennials and Gen Zers keep pulling on this Columbus Day thread, where do you think it will eventually unravel? I'll tell you. It all ends at the capital of this country, Washington, D.C.

In September 1791 the newly designated capital was named after George

Washington located in the Territory of Columbia. "Columbia," of course, was derived from Christopher Columbus, and it was the patriotic reference for the United States during the Revolutionary War. Then in 1871 the Territory of Columbia was officially renamed the District of Columbia. So, the morons who splash red paint on statues of Christopher Columbus each year on the second Monday of October or who want to overlay another holiday over his, will be the same people who will demand that the District of Columbia be renamed. And, while they're at it they also do away with the name "Washington," because he owned slaves. Well, so did pre-colonial Native Americans. Own slaves, that is. But why let history get in the way? It doesn't fit into the left's narrative.

The bottom line is not about the plight of the indigenous people. The bottom line is, and always has been, that the radical left wants to destroy Western culture, and rip up its roots – Christianity.

There you have it. You've been reeducated. Now you know why you'll never hear "Happy Indigenous Peoples Day," come from the lips of a conservative Republican unless it falls on another day of the year other than the federal holiday Columbus Day.

RIOTS TO ACHIEVE "PEACE THROUGH VIOLENCE"

First came Anonymous. They're the ones that wore that funny looking Guy Fawkes mask. You know, the white face with a pencil thin upturned black mustache, a goatee, and rosy cheeks. It originated from the DC Comic book and film *V for Vendetta*. The story is about a future United Kingdom under fascist rule where anarchists start a revolution to bring down the government. "Bring down" meaning systematic assassinations, bombings, and computer hacking.

The Anonymous movement of today is *life imitating art*, rather than other way around; *art imitating life*. The movement began in 2003 on social media where people would post things anonymously on a site called 4chan. Eventually large numbers of people would identify themselves as "Anonymous," and it made it appear as if all these postings were by one person.

Then came the trouble starting in 2004. Nameless individuals that had been using 4chan started to branch out by hacking into international businesses' servers. By 2007 Fox News KTTV in Los Angeles was the first to report the story to the American public labeling the cyber criminals as "hackers on steroids" for disrupting websites and social media sites. Some in the media were even calling them "domestic terrorists."

There was no central leadership to Anonymous, but it was a bunch of like-minded people feeding ideas to each other. It was not an "organization" per se, but rather a movement. It was the beginning of "hacktivism," which means hacking and activism together to promote social and political change. Armed with just a keyboard tucked away in their parent's house, "Not now Mom, I'm busy!" or in a tiny apartment somewhere, they hacked into government, corporate, and religious computers to disrupt day to day operations or send propaganda. This way the criminals never had to come face to face with their victims. It's kind of like what many bad guys do when they are executing people, be a street criminals or war criminals. They either have the victim turn away from them, or put a bag over their head, so they don't have to see their face when killing them. That's too personal. To do the dirty deed, they need to dehumanize the situation.

However, not everything Anonymous did was in the shadows. During public demonstrations, many members would wear the Guy Fawkes mask, or a wide variety of other masks with the purpose of remaining "anonymous." The mask was also a symbol. Of course, the mask wearing is nothing new, going back to the first Palestinian Intifada, uprising, that began in 1987. Young men, usually throwing rocks at Israeli soldiers and committing acts of vandalism, wore keffiyehs (a traditional Arab headdress wrapped about the head and face) to hide their identity. It's hard to arrest a person if he gets away from you, and you can't identify him. I was there in both Israel and the West Bank during this Intifada. Come to think of it, I witnessed the second one as well.

Anyway, Anonymous was a left-leaning movement, in case you didn't figure it out.

Then came the Occupy Movement in 2011. They had the slogan, "We are the 99%!" They hated the rich, which they called the "1%," and corporations were evil in their eyes. Therefore, the answer to society's problems was to redistribute the wealth, and change the percentages. Of course, they had to use their corporate made phones and computers to coordinate their protests, and pump the corporate refined gasoline into their corporate made cars to get to the locations, but hey! Why let reality get into the way of a good cause?

The signature of the Occupy Movement was marching around the front of various corporate headquarters, a few times on Wall Street, and camping out in front of city halls. I had a 20-something-year-old niece of mine at the time, Charlotte, join the movement. She and her unemployed boyfriend lived in a two-person tent for a week or so in front of our city hall. I'd pass by them every morning and evening on my way to work. One day I asked her to tell me her reason for protesting, and she couldn't give me any concrete details, only that they were "anti-corporation."

I responded, "So, why are you in front of city hall? Shouldn't you go camp out in front a corporate building somewhere?" After all, my city has several major corporations with their headquarters located there. "What is city hall going to do for you?" As if the city was going to tell the corporations, "Nope, we don't want your taxes anymore that keep our city afloat and provide our salaries. Close down your business, and move out you big, mean, greedy, corporations!"

Even mainstream media could not nail down what the movement was all about, because the protestors' beliefs were all over the map, and they offered no viable solutions to any of society's ills.

Then came along another group, Antifa, that made Anonymous and the Occupiers look like kindergarteners.

Most Americans never heard of Antifa until less than a month after President Trump took office, and so I am going to describe how Americans first heard about them before we go into what they are all about.

On February 1, 2017 gay conservative Breitbart News editor Milo Yiannopoulos was scheduled to give a speech about defending free speech at California's most liberal institution of higher education – the University of California Berkley founded in 1868.

Here's a fun fact. The logo of the University of California has a banner over a book with the Bible scripture LET THERE BE LIGHT. Yeap! That verse comes from the Old Testament, Genesis 1:3 *And, God said, "Let there be light," and there was light.* Now, mind you, light was created on the first day, but the sun, moon, planets, and the stars were not created until the fourth day. So, what exactly was this "light?" Jesus said in the New Testament, *"I am the light of the world. Whoever follows me will never walk in darkness, but will have the light of life." John 8:12* In fact, the official logo for all ten University of California campuses (a combined student body of 251,700 students, and 21,200 faculty members) is the same, LET THERE BE LIGHT. However, there are many on the left that would be delighted to exist under the motto LET THERE BE DARKNESS, because some of their actions would indicate this.

Instead of hearing what Milo Yiannopoulos had to say about free speech, to weigh the merits or fallacies of his arguments like any good student would, many students, and outsiders who were bused in, started to riot. Not a little riot, but a big one clashing with the police, burning things, and beating up Trump supporters. Some of the protest signs read THIS IS WAR, BECOME UNGOVERNABLE, an "X" through the name MILO, OUT OF BERKELEY NAZI SCUM, and someone even spray painted the words KILL TRUMP on the side of a building. Oh, and don't forget the anarchist "A" graffiti as well. But, rioting is hard work that makes one thirsty, so a dozen or so masked ninja looking protestors looted a closed Starbucks Coffee for refreshments; not hot coffee lattes unfortunately, but bottled drinks and muffins. So much for "free speech."

It wasn't just fascist tactics using students and outsiders that tried to shut down free speech at UC Berkley, but professors as well. Samra Halperin, a visiting assistant art professor at Mills College, told the local newspaper *Daily Californian*, "I'm outraged that Milo has been given a platform at UC Berkley, and there should be no place for him here. He should be scared that people aren't going to stand for this."

I thought higher education was hearing different perspectives, pondering ideas, and engaging in healthy debate? That's the way it used to be. That's the way it ought to be. I've sat in on plenty of lectures in my higher education days listening to people I didn't agree with. I was also never one for backing down from a good argument, but it was always in a respectful, courteous, manner. Certainly, the thought of trying to keep a visitor or speaker from visiting my campus or rioting never crossed my mind, or the minds of my fellow alumni. Plus, nobody ever thought of hiding their identity with a mask. When facing an opponent one looked him or her in the eye and stated their name for the record. Things were much more civilized back in the 1980s.

In defense of the UC Berkley's administration, they did publicly condemn the violence that occurred on their campus. However, they blamed the mayhem on "outsiders." Kind of like a parent blaming other kids for their child's mischievous behavior.

So, who were these "outsiders?" They were an extreme leftist group called Antifa, pronounce *ann-tee-fah*. The name derives from the German acronym *Antifaschistische Aktion*, meaning anti-fascist action. The original grouped formed in 1932 with the Communist Party of Germany, and thus why their logo includes the red communist flag to this day. Although fascist Germany and Italy were had been defeated by the capitalist United States of America in World War II, the group resurfaced in modern times to resist German neo-Nazism and Britain's skinheads who were seen as anti-immigration.

In the United States Antifa was always a small, little-known, group. They caused trouble here in there, but the University of Berkeley riot put them on everybody's radar.

Although there are no fascist governments in the world today, the American Antifa members believe that President Donald Trump is a fascist akin to Adolf Hitler's Nazi Germany. Why? Because they believe, and their banners often say it, RESIST PATRIARCHY WAR & COROPRATE RULE.

"What the hell does that mean?" some of you not involved in Antifa are questioning, as you scratch your heads.

RESIST means to resist hate and racism. Apparently, President Trumps' attempts at keeping radical Islamic terrorists out of our country are considered

"Islamophobe," and thus racist and anti-immigration. Antifa never speaks out against the threat of radical Islam; not even when there are attacks on our own soil by the likes of Sayfullo Habibullaevich Saipov, an immigrant from Uzbekistan, who mowed over 19 people in Lower Manhattan with a rented pick-up truck. If Antifa so much as thinks that someone is anti-multiculturalism, then watch out! You're on their harassment list.

PATRIARCHY WAR means to do away with Judeo-Christian values. Remember, their core belief is rooted in communism, and communism doctrine hates God. So, ultimately, they hate our American values and system.

CORPORATE RULE means just that. They hate corporations. Yes, they love their corporate made hoodies, and they use corporate made spray paints to do their graffiti, and communicate on their corporate cell phones, but they'd rather have the almighty state be in control of all commerce like the former Soviet Union was. Then they'll be happy driving around in their state manufactured Yugos (look up *Yugo Is One of the Worst Cars Ever Made*).

One of the driving goals of ANTIFA is to have "a one world government." The belief is that all nations united under one leadership can erase all the borders, and put an end to racism. Funny, because we are going to talk about a one world government in this very Cell Block. A lot of people want it, you know.

October 2, 2017 was the deadliest active shooter massacre in U.S. history in Las Vegas, Nevada. 64-year-old Stephen Paddock was held up in his room on the 32nd floor of the Mandalay Bay hotel on the famous Las Vegas Strip, broke out the windows so he'd have two fields of fire, and then shot at 22,000 people below at street level who were attending the country music Route 91 Harvest Festival. One of the 16 weapons he had used in his deadly attack was a fully automatic assault rifle (using a bump fire stock) that spits out up to 880 bullets a minute, each ripping through human flesh at supersonic speeds. In 15 minutes he had killed 59 people, and wounded 527. When police were breaching the hotel room he committed suicide. President Donald Trump called the mass shooting, "an act of pure evil."

Just hours after the shooting, while people were still expiring in hospitals, and others were undergoing surgery to have their horrendous wounds repaired, Hayley Geftman-Gold, one of the top attorneys for the CBS network, and a vice-president no less, posted on her Facebook, "I'm actually not even sympathetic" to the victims of the shooting because "country music fans often are Republican gun toters."

At least CBS did the right thing by immediately firing her for her callous comment.

So here we have a highly educated, upper class, white, Jewish woman who was incapable of compassion for 59 fellow American citizens murdered, and 527 wounded, because they were assumed to be Republicans; as if only Republicans listen to country music. Unfortunately, she's not the only heart of stone that leftist progressivism has produced.

I brought her up because it's not just black-clad Molotov cocktail throwing youths who think violence is the answer to ousting the Republican Party from power, but educated, upper class, professionals as well.

The one thing that the election of Donald J. Trump has clearly demonstrated to those on the right is that many on the left will resort to violence and destruction to disrupt social order to ultimately achieve their goals. These scary occurrences have not been lost on many conservatives. Whereas Antifa, and many on the left, want "revolution," many on the right are seriously wondering if they ought to be preparing for a "civil war" for the not so distant future.

Of course, Bernie Sanders can get away with using the word "revolution," but imagine if conservatives started using the words "civil war" for new political organizations, T-shirts, and banners. How would they take it?

You just can't get over the words "civil war" can you, as if somehow, I just crossed a forbidden line. But, let me tell you, there is a civil war occurring in America right now. It's only considered a cultural civil war at this time by the right, but it's an actual shooting war from the left. Not an all-out war, thank God, but guerrilla warfare. Which, brings up an important issue – *the deep state*.

The "deep state," as defined by Wikipedia, is *an alleged entity that coordinates efforts by government employees and others to influence state policy without regard for democratically elected leadership.* I'll make it simpler for you. It is the left, in government positions, trying to subvert traditional American values and system. Bingo!

I'll give you a couple of examples to make it more tangible. When the rioters were tearing up UC Berkley the police did a pathetic job. When 150 rioters were destroying property the University of California Berkeley Police took a "hands-off approach," and allowed things to get out of control. After it was all over, and despite $100,000 of damage, only one person was arrested.

It was not the police officers on the front line who made the decision not to arrest rioters, for several officers fired paint-ball guns to mark rioters for detention and possible arrest, but it was their supervisors. Ultimately, the chain of command goes up to mayor level. Berkley Police Sergeant Sabrina Reich made the lame excuse, "It was a crowd-control situation," adding, "We steered clear of individual action."

This sounds a lot like the lame excuses coming from Democrat government officials on justifying "sanctuary cities."

The truth is, as the American people move ever increasingly to the left so do government officials; including the police.

When I had left the federal government I was looking to get back into municipal law enforcement again a few years later. This was in 2004. The Los Angeles Police Department was hiring a ton of police officers, and having been a police officer with up to date state credentials, I applied as a lateral candidate. I passed the written test, the physical abilities test, the medical examination, and even the background examination. I was good to go, until the final step was to write a paragraph on what I thought about "homosexuality."

I knew exactly why they were requesting my opinion, and that was because homosexual acts had been illegal for most of my law enforcement career, and even considered as a mental disorder by the American Psychiatric Association in 1974. Now that the climate had changed, and homosexuality was considered normal, they wanted to see where I stood on the issue.

I could have easily written the words that they wanted to see, but I didn't. I wrote something like this:

For 6,000 years of mankind's recorded history homosexuality was considered immoral and illegal. Recently, the State of California has deemed sodomy and other homosexual acts, between consenting adults, as legal. As a peace officer of the State of California, should I be hired by this agency, I would enforce all laws equally, regardless of a citizen's sex, race, ethnicity, religion, or sexual orientation.

If the Los Angeles Police Department no longer wanted me to arrest people engaging in homosexual acts, which I had never caught any anyway, then fine by me. However, I'm pretty sure the decision makers looking at that sheet of paper, on which I had just written on, were not too thrilled with my opening sentence. But, whether it was because of this paragraph, or for other reasons, I did not get the job. I knew immediately after writing it that I wouldn't be serving with the Los Angeles Police Department. As a Christian I was offended that they would even ask my opinion on homosexuality knowing that my eligibility probably depended upon the answer given. They certainly had to have known that all the major religions of the world are against it. That is an example of the deep state, and it was in the Los Angeles Police Department long before Donald Trump was elected President of the United States of America.

Is the deep state a leftist conspiracy or organized sabotage? Yes and no. It is like-minded people who tend to take the same actions, either subconsciously or consciously, like what had happened to me at the LAPD. Then there are outright cases of destroying conservatives (religious or non-religious) in a coordinated manner. Take the IRS for example. On February 3, 2014 President Barak Obama (Democrat) stated before the American people, in an interview with Fox News' Bill O'Reilly, that there was "Not even a smidgen of corruption" with the Internal Revenue Service that had denied numerous conservative political nonprofit organizations of Section 501(c)(4) tax-exemption. You may recall the name Lois Lerner (Democrat). She's the one who delayed the process for many conservative groups that resulted in them not being able to take part in the 2012 election. How convenient for the Democrats. She eventually resigned over the controversy. Finally, on October 25, 2017, long after the Democrats had lost their power, the IRS admitted that they targeted the Tea Party and other conservative groups during the Obama era. So much for "Not even a smidgen of corruption."

I guess U.S. Representative Joe Wilson had it right the first time when he interrupted a speech by President Obama addressing the joint session of Congress by shouting "You lie!" And, that was in 2009, just eight months after the man had been elected.

CLIMATE CHANGE

I don't know where Millennials got the idea from that conservatives and corporations want to destroy the earth by polluting it? Actually, I do know where Millennials got the idea from. It's propaganda from the left.

If you must know, it was big business in 1953 that founded Keep America Beautiful. Founding members included Coca-Cola, PepsiCo, Anheuser-Busch, Philip Morris, along with nonprofit organizations and some government agencies. They're the ones who coined the term "litterbug" and had the ad campaign, that everyone in my generation remembers, featuring Native American Iron Eyes Cody, known as the "Crying Indian," with the headline GET INVOLVED NOW. POLLUTION HURTS ALL OF US. They were the one really pushing for litter prevention and recycling. That's right – CORPORATIONS.

When I was a kid in the 1960s many scientists were saying that we were entering another ice age. At the same time Americans became aware of the dangerous effects of pollution, because of organizations like Keep America Beautiful. As such, it was President Richard M. Nixon, a Republican, who proposed the establishment of the United States Environmental Protection Agency (EPA) on December 2, 1970. It's funny how Republicans establish worthwhile causes, and then the eventually liberals take credit for it – like protecting the environment through the EPA or the Republicans freeing the slaves.

Then in the 1990s the so-called scientists reversed course, and they insisted that the planet was heating up. They came up with an obvious name for this phenomenon – "global warming."

When temperatures seemed to have stabilized in the early 2000s, supported by historical recordings that indicated that the weather of the planet followed cycles, and some places were actually experiencing a cooling trend or more precipitation, the term was then changed to "climate change." It was embarrassing for liberal news reporters to be citing "global warming" as the cause of the weather phenomena while standing in a snow storm.

What an ambiguous term, "climate change." Duuuuuhhhh! The weather changes every day all over this God's green Earth. So, when is it a normal cycle or caused by humans?

Anyway, even though half the scientists today say that the weather is normal, and just doing its thing, the other half are saying the poles are melting, the ozone layer is disappearing, and it's all the fault of my Chevy, Silverado, 8-cylinder, gas guzzling pick-up truck leaving its energy-wasting carbon footprint.

Climate change, was just another excuse for the Democrats to seize another sector of the economy, like they had done to health care under the Obama administration, and that my friend translates into real political power. In 2015 health care spending was 17.8 percent of the Gross Domestic Product (GDP), which means $3.2 trillion dollars, which means $9,990 per every person in the United States according to CMS.gov (Centers for Medicare & Medicaid Services).

When the Republicans took control of the White House, the Senate, and the House of Representatives in 2017 they wisely pressed on the brake of spending when it came to climate change. On May 17, 2017 Environmental Protection Agency (EPA) Director Scott Pruitt announced that the United States was withdrawing from the Paris Agreement. It was basically a plan for the West to get off of petroleum and coal by 2040 in order to keep the planet from permanently warming by 2100. Well, that sounds like a noble goal, but the problem was that there was no binding enforcement mechanism. In other words, if China, India, Iran, or North Korea didn't follow the agreement, then oh well! So, we'd do our part, and spend trillions doing so, but half the world would cheat, and cheat they would. Therefore, Director Pruitt was right in saying, "Paris represents an agreement that puts America last... Paris represented a situation where China and India went ahead and didn't take any steps to address CO2 reductions, while we front loaded our cost, contracting our economy 2.5 trillion dollars in domestic product over a 10-year period."

After our withdrawal the left was convinced that President Trump didn't give a hoot about the environment. From European governments all the way down to Hollywood celebrities, the President got a lot of flak. Actor Leonardo DiCaprio, and he is really a great actor, said, "Today, our planet suffered. It's more important than ever to take action." Well, he was absolutely correct. Not about the planet suffering, but that "action" needs to be taken. I'll tell you where the first action should be taken, but not one peep was heard from the tree-huggers.

OK, that term was a little mean. I apologize. A tree-hugger is a derogatory term for someone who campaigns for the environment. I for one love nature, and I do my part: I don't litter, I recycle, and when a Tesla car cost less that putting a kid through an ivy league school for four years then I might buy one.

The first action by those concerned about climate change should have been having one protest after another to pressure North Korea into dismantling their nuclear weapons program. Do you know how much environmental damage can be done with one hydrogen bomb?

Time after time North Korea threatened to nuke the USA, Japan, and Guam, and even detonate a hydrogen bomb over the Pacific Ocean just for the hell of it, but that didn't get the left all riled up at all, but President Trump pulling out of an agreement that only a handful of countries would follow anyway got the reaction "our planet suffered."

Nobody on the left is screaming about Iran's ambitions to develop nuclear weapons, along with ICBMs, and their repeated threats "Israel must be wiped out," even painting this slogan on their long-range rockets. Nope, that does not seem to bother the environmentalists one bit. Forget the fact that Israel is believed to have a stockpile of 300 plus nuclear weapons, and would be forced to use them if they felt their survival was at stake.

Of course, launching nuclear tipped warheads is not just a one-sided venture only for smaller countries. The United States, if it had to retaliate, alone has 14 ballistic missile submarines (SSBN) and 4 guided missile submarines (SSGN) that have a combined arsenal of 336 Trident II nuclear missiles, and 616 Tomahawk cruise missiles.

Just those nuclear weapons that are currently deployed, i.e. on launch pads ready to use now, and not those sitting on the shelves in storage, are: United States 1,800, Russia 1,950, United Kingdom 120, France 280, China. Well, who knows? They're a bit secretive.

The sad thing is that these nuclear weapons are not going to go away - ever. What country that possesses them would give them up? That would be like Americans willing to give up their Second Amendment right, and letting the criminals know that their homes and businesses are GUN FREE ZONES.

So, I think that my gas guzzling pick-up truck is much less of a threat to the environment than weapons that can fry the earth many times over. At least with good old capitalism, and American ingenuity, we're developing vehicles that will eventually replace fossil fuels.

Now, moving on. Right after back-to-back hurricanes Harvey and Irma hit the states of Texas, Louisiana, and Florida in September 2017, which were two of the most destructive hurricanes in American history, the climate change pushers stating, "See! We told you so! The climate is changing! It's all because of the carbon emitting factories and cars."

I'm probably going to say something here that is going to shock you, but I, and most conservative evangelical Christians are not climate change deniers. Nope, quite the opposite. We're in agreement with the liberals on this one. I believe the climate is indeed changing around the world, and it is getting worse and worse. Hello! All someone has to do is look at the data. However, it's the right data you have to look at.

So, let's quickly take a look at the available data, shall we?

Hurricanes do not prove climate change one way or another. The climatological statistics of storms and hurricanes affecting the United States, since scientific records were first kept in the 1850s, shows a very cyclic pattern. In the 1880s the number of storms increased, and by 1900 they decreased. A decade later the numbers were up, and by the 1920s they went down. The hard hitters increased until the 1940s, and from the 1950s to the 1970s they had decreased even less than the 1850s. Up again by the 1980s, and down by the 1990s. The roller coast then started to go back up again in the 2010s. This decade seems to be quite a rise in major storm and hurricane activity. So, again, storms and hurricanes are not a good indicator of climate change. If anything, the statistics support normal planet activity.

Now let's have a look at sea level rise. After all, Al Gore and his bunch claim that the polar caps are melting and causing the sea level to rise globally. So, who do we go to for accurate information? How about NASA, the National Aeronautics & Space Administration.

NASA, with all of their fancy computers and multimillion dollar satellites in space, have studied "ice melt fingerprints" to determine global patterns through a program called GRACE, Gravity Recovery and Climate Experiment, which has something to do with looking at Earth's changing gravitational field, stuff that all goes over my head, and have concluded that "for a variety of reasons, sea level does not change at the same pace everywhere at the same time," this according to Philip Thompson, Associate Director of the University of Hawaii Sea Level Center in the School of Ocean and Earth Science and Technology, and members of NASA's Jet Propulsion Laboratory, or as everyone calls them,

"JPL."

Now, here's something weird. NASA discovered that sea level drops around melting glaciers instead of rising. See, I told you it was weird, because it does not seem logical. Well, it turns out that "the loss of ice mass reduces the glacier's gravitational influence, causing nearby ocean water to migrate away. But far from the glacier, the water it has added to the ocean causing the sea level to rise at a much greater rate." Those expensive satellites are worth every penny.

NASA, using a bunch of modeling tools, believes that during the 20th century (1900-2000) the global average sea level rose 6.7 inches (17 centimeters). So, yes, the sea level is rising a little bit each year. On the other hand, NASA's official website also states, "According to the new analysis of satellite data, the Antarctic ice sheet showed a net gain of 112 billion tons of ice a year from 1992 to 2001. That net gain slowed to 82 billion tons of ice per year between 2003 and 2008." In layman's terms, the snow and iced is replacing the ice that is melting into the ocean. This research challenges the Intergovernmental Panel on Climate Change's (IPCC) 2013 report, which states that Antarctica is overall losing land ice. No wonder why President "Donald Trump doesn't think much of climate change," according to CNN. Various government research and reports at his disposal have yet to conclusively determine if we are simply seeing natural earth cycles or actual "global warming" caused by man and his machines. Venice, Italy and Miami, Florida are not under water yet, and it does not appear that they will to be under water any time soon.

What about tornados? Do they prove climate change? Let's look at the facts.

"Much of the early work on tornado climatology in the United States was done by John Park Finley in his book Tornadoes, published in 1887," according to the National Oceanic and Atmospheric Administration (NOAA).

In the days before the invention of radar a tornado had to be observed in order for it to have been recorded. Today we can confirm tornado activity through NOAA's Doppler weather radar. This means that both weak and great tornadoes can be recorded and charted.

Like the major storms and hurricane charts the tornado charts are cyclic. For U.S. Annual Count of EF-1+ Tornadoes, 1954 through 2014, we see up and down trends. There were just over 400 tornadoes in 1954 that steadily increased to 900 until 1973. Then there was a downward trend until 1978. It climbed until 1982, and then back down again until 1987. Up and down, up and down, and then a climb back up in 2011 with almost 900 tornadoes. Guess what? Back down by 2012. We see the same thing with the most violent tornadoes on NOAA's U.S. Annual Count of Strong to Violent Tornadoes (F3+), 1954 through 2014. In 1954 F3+ tornadoes were at 46, and in 1957 close to a hundred of them. Then a drop in deadly tornadoes, and up again in 1961. Then a big jump in 1974, almost 140 of them, and a drop again. For thirty-six years there were under 70 killer tornadoes per year, and then a jump to 84 of them in 2011, and back down the following year. Most tornado activity seems to be in the month of May.

So, tornadoes don't seem to offer any good proof for climate change.

How about looking at actual temperatures over time in the United States. For that we need to look at the U.S. Climate Atlas by NOAA. It' easy to do on their website.

The temperatures in January of 1895 are much the same 100 years later in 1985. In 2015, overall there was a warming trend. Yet, in January of 2016, the following year, it got colder again in some parts of the country, like the Pacific North West, and the drought that had plagued California for years saw abundant rain and snow fall.

Using the same records, the summer of 1985, July to be specific, was overall warmer than a hundred years earlier (1885). Then twenty years later, in 2015, there is not much difference, except with the Southeast United Sates, but nothing alarming. The following year was slightly warmer in some parts of the mid-section of the country. However, those living in the northern states from coast to coast in 1885 would not have noticed any difference in the weather than those that their descendants experienced in 2016. The weather for the 4th of July holiday would have had the same feel upon skin in either century. Therefore, temperature alone does not prove global warming. Oh, sorry, I forgot. It's now "climate change." I've got to break myself of that old habit.

As we have seen, the weather goes in cycles, thus the weather always changes, but the term climate change is a political one, not a scientific one. Of course, once you convince enough people that climate change is scientific then you can pass laws to control the petroleum companies, the energy sector, the car manufacturers, and even levy an extra tax if people want their chicken sandwich heated, because, after all, heating a chicken sandwich, which could be eaten cold, leaves a "carbon footprint." It takes energy to heat that chicken sandwich. Oh yeah, I had to pay this tax in England. I ordered a chicken sandwich from a sandwich shop, and the sandwich maker asked me, "Do you want it cold or toasted." I replied, "Toasted, please." She said, "Then there is a tax for heating it."

Then I got the whole "saving the environment speech" after I said, "You're kidding me?"

I paid the tax, but I rolled my eyes when I handed her my British pounds. I was gutted.

And, speaking of "toasted," and getting back to why many born-again Christians do believe in climate change, Revelation 16:8-9 describes what will happen when mankind continues its rebellion against God. *Next, the fourth angel poured out his bowl on the sun, and it was given power to scorch the people with fire. And the people were scorched by intense heat, and they cursed the name of God, who had authority over these plagues; yet they did not repent and give Him glory.*

I guess the term "global warming" is correct after all. The weather is not going to change due to our factories and cars burning fossil fuels, but God is going to turn up the heat.

Most of you are rolling your eyes, and making snide remarks. You refuse to believe God is somehow involved in climate change, and detached from His own creation, and are convinced that I am a complete lunatic for even suggesting such an outlandish thing. Well, I guess you're probably the ones this scripture is talking about then, if you're still around to see it, "and they cursed the name of God, who had authority over these plagues." Since you will not give Him the glory, and admit that this weather phenomenon to come is a "plague," you will have no choice but to stick to your story "it's because of the carbon emitting gases that we are producing that is causing the climate change." You'll have to blame it on something beyond your control.

This event mentioned in the New Testament is going to take place after the great war in the Middle East, but we'll discuss this a little bit later.

EVILUTION

Let's continue to talk about science. After all, any good education requires units in the sciences, as does your reeducation.

We were all taught evolution in school, from the Baby Boomers on down. I know I was.

In my day, public schools called it "the theory of evolution." Do you know why they dared not call it "science?" No, it's not because the majority of Americans believed in God at the time, and the liberals were afraid of the backlash if they said anything.

First, let me give you a little statistic. According to GALLUP Poll in 1980, that's when I graduated from high school, 40% of Americans believed that "the Bible is the actual word of God, and is to be taken literally, word for word," whereas in 2017 that number had dropped to 24%.

The reason my teachers called it "the theory of evolution" was because of the definition of science, which is *the intellectual and practical activity encompassing the systematic study of the structure and behavior of the physical and natural world through **observation** and **experiment**.* Evolution did not fit the definition of science.

Was anyone around to **observe** the "Big Bang?" That's supposedly when there was an explosion in space 13.8 billion years ago that formed our universe. That's right, a gigantic explosion created the stars, the sun, moon and earth, and all that you see in the sky. Now, in the military I saw, or **observed** if you will, plenty of things get blown up with explosives, and it only resulted in destruction. But, hey! Who am I? I'm not a scientist. I just recorded in my brain what I saw. But, I do know one thing, and that is you need explosives, a detonator, a power source, and an operator to create an explosion.

When I was in grade school the science teachers told me that a bolt of lightning, the power source, hit a mud puddle, and this high intensity energy somehow jumpstarted some protein floating around in a goo that created life. After all, you need water to have life. The "simple single-cell" that was formed from inorganic material eventually divided into other living cells to form multi-cell creatures and sea plants. Somewhere there was a split between the animals and plants, or was it the other way around? Anyway, over billions of years the seas were teaming with life. One day a fish sprouted little legs and walked up onto the beach. However, it only left the water for as long as it could hold its breath, because it would take a few billion more years for its descendants to developed lungs from gills capable of breathing air. Well, once that evolutionary hurdle was jumped, the next generation formed into reptiles, who in turn formed into dinosaurs, and from there new creatures galore came about. It's quite impressive, and you can see the development of all this life yourself on Charles Darwin's Tree of Life graph, which has lots of branches that starts with just an itty-bitty dot called the "Origin of Life." We don't know exactly what that looked like, so a dot represents our beginning. One branch became birds, another branch became mammals, and from that offshoot came primates (monkeys and apes), and from them we humans shed our fur, stood upright, and became mankind. TADA! Well, because we had shed our fur, we had to find some clothes to put on to stay warm, and to indicate our social status. Thus, was born the fashion industry.

Since Darwin's book *On the Origin of Species*, published in 1859, more sophisticated graphs for school walls have been updated and published, like the *Phylogenetic Tree of Life* in 2009, which is based on rRNA genes, and the 2016 metagenomic representation of the tree of life. You can order them all from Amazon.

So, in a nutshell, evolution, should you ever have to write a term paper about it, is FROM NOTHING CAME EVERYTHING. Of course, it took "billions of years" for it all to happen. It ain't easy getting the ball rolling from nothing.

Somehow time changes the complex DNA code. Naturally, there is a scientific name for FROM NOTHING CAME EVERYTHING, and that is *abiogenesis.* Evolutionists had to name it something to make the absurd sound legitimate, right?

The definition of abiogenesis is *the original evolution of life or living organisms from inorganic or inanimate substances.* Some like to call it the "primordial soup," a chemical environment that had the right combination of inorganic molecules that when some sort of natural force acted upon it, POOF! life was formed. I like what Charles Darwin first called it in 1871, and that was a "warm little pond." I don't know how he knew the little pond was "warm," but he did. He even drew a graph to prove it.

You're smart, and you knew exactly where I was headed with this, didn't you? Yeap, up until the late 1800s American schools, including public schools, exclusively taught creation. Again, this was a time before all the noise about "separation of church and state."

In the beginning, God created the heavens and the earth.   Genesis 1:1

If you want, you can call it "the theory of creation," for none of us, not even our top scientists, were there to **observe** God making the universe, and there are no **experiments** that we can do to prove it one way or another. We just know that somehow it all came about. "I think, therefore I am." Just like nobody has observed evolution, and no **experiments** prove that we started from goo, progressed into a zoo, and became you.

It's interesting that the word used for "create" found in the first sentence of the Bible is the Hebrew word *bara*, which means to create something from nothing. In fact, this first sentence is just loaded with revealing information. Let's parse it.

In beginning is more how the Hebrew reads instead of *In the beginning* like the English translation. They mean the same thing, but God, the angels, and eternal heaven were already in existence before we humans came along. Therefore, when it comes to God's plan for mankind He begins His project.

In beginning God, stop right there! The word *God* is the Hebrew word *Elohim.* An "im" ending on a Hebrew word makes it plural. In fact, further along in the story of creation, twenty-five verses later to be exact, it reads, "Then God (Elohim) said, 'Let us make man in our image.'" What? "us" and "our." What's that all about? Isn't there only one God? The answer is yes. Both Jews and Christians reading this passage acknowledge that this word is referring to one singular God, and not many. Christians believe God used this plural form intentionally right from the start to introduce Himself as the Father, the Son, and the Holy Spirit, and we already talked about the concept of the Trinity earlier. Don't worry, nobody can fully wrap their mind around this, because we are finite beings, and God is omnipresent – at all places at all times. Even Satan is finite, because he is a created being. He can only be at one place at a time. Therefore, he is not the opposite of God.

You've heard of the term "meme" (pronounced *meem*) before, haven't you? It's an idea that spreads from person to person in a culture, and it is replicated. An Internet meme, sent through social media, is typically an image with a message or hashtag; also known as an image macro. Well, it was Richard Dawkins who came up with the term meme. He's only one of the most famous professors in the world on the subject of evolutionary biology. He was also an assistant professor of zoology at the University of California, Berkley, that's a red flag, and a professor at Oxford University. He has half a dozen books on the market today including *The God Delusion* published in 2006. It's wasn't enough just to be a world-renowned scientist, but Professor Dawkins goes after religion of all types. In fact, he prides himself on his "atheist pride." However, when Ben Stein ("Anyone, anyone!" Only one of the funniest classroom scenes ever filmed in the 1986 movie *Ferris Bueller's Day Off*) pressed him to explain the mechanism to which life evolved on planet Earth, he couldn't. He, like many scientists, have switched their view to the theory of panspermia. That's the belief that life from outer space "seeded" our planet, and from that colonization life developed, because it couldn't happen on its own from a bunch of rocks. Professor Dawkins even went as far as saying, "And I suppose it's possible that you might find evidence for that (panspermia) if you look at the details of biochemistry, molecular biology, you might find a signature of some sort of designer."

So, for years many students and academia have hung their hat on Professor Dawkins' "scientific" explanation of evolution, believing in the Tree of Life graph, which he knows full well is an impossibility based upon mounting evidence, and yet he entertains the idea of an extraterrestrial "designer." As long as that designer is not God, then it's okay. Why do you suppose that is? It's because if God exists, especially if He is the God of the Bible, then we would be accountable to Him, because it says that God is very much involved in his creation on a day to day basis even to the point of knowing the "number of hairs on your head" and "every thought" you think. Being "seeded" means that we could just do what we want, because whatever, or whoever, "seeded" the planet is no longer tending the garden.

I quoted to you "Let us make man in our own image." Well, later in the account of how man was made, and subsequently how he rebelled against God, the whole eating the apple thing, bad, the Bible records:

By the sweat of your brow you will eat your food until you return to the ground, since from it you were taken; for dust you are and to dust you will return. Genesis 3:19

This is astonishing! Don't you see it? It says, "from it you were taken." From what? From the dust. The very first human being created, that was Adam, was not made from heavenly mystical elements like star dust, but from plain ol' dirt. The same stuff under your feet.

Now, this is astonishing because Genesis was written by the hand of Moses, inspired by God (so we Jews and Christians believe), around the year 1445 B.C., which makes it almost 3,500 years ago. It wasn't until the 19th century that scientists discovered that there are 11 elements in the human body that come from the 92 elements that occur naturally on Earth.

The top 4 elements in the human body are oxygen, hydrogen, carbon, and nitrogen. It makes sense that oxygen and hydrogen tops the list, because those molecules are mainly water in our body (H_2O), and 50% to 70% of the body is made up of water. Together these 4 elements make up 96.2% of your bodyweight. There's no life without water. The other 7 elements are calcium, phosphorus, potassium, sodium, chlorine, magnesium, and sulfur. There are also trace elements in the human body (less than 0.01%), and they are boron, cadmium, chromium, cobalt, copper, fluorine, iodine, iron, manganese, molybdenum, selenium, silicon, tin, vanadium, and zinc.

So, let's consider just the four most abundant elements in our bodies for a moment. The first chemical analyses of carbon were not made until the 18th century. It was Antoine Lavoisier who listed it as an "element" in 1789. Then in 1793 he named hydrogen as an element. However, Lavoisier was building upon the scientific discovery made by Henry Cavendish in the year 1500. Daniel Rutherford discovered nitrogen, based on the gases expelled by animals in 1772, and Lavoisier named it in 1775. Although scientists had been breathing air all their lives, they didn't know what air really was made of until experiments in 1771 made by Carl Wilheim Scheele, who didn't publish his findings until 1777. However, it was Antoine Lavoisier who first recognized oxygen as a true element and named it, and now it's forever on the Periodic Table. That Lavoisier was on the ball. Unfortunately, the new socialist French government became his demise. Although he had made so many wonderful discoveries in the field of science, and even was instrumental in establishing the metric system, the government went after the rich to seize their money, goods, and estates to fund the state. "Non aux 1%!" was the cry. Well, not really, I made that quote up just now, but the same socialist crap people are spewing today is nothing new. Antoine Lavoisier was both rich and successful, and for that he became an enemy of the state. Forget the fact that he was a genius, or that he improved street lighting, or improve air quality that people breathed in the big cities, or that he tried to improve the living conditions in prisons, they chopped his head off anyway. At the age of 50 he was executed by way of the guillotine during the French Reign of Terror, and that's where we eventually got the words "terrorism" and "terrorist" from. The French Revolution was not like the American Revolution. Okay, in the long run eventually democracy came about, but the first few years were a blood bath, and God help you if you were not part of the 99%. They should make a movie about Antoine-Laurent de Lavoisier.

Anyway, back to dust. The Earth's crust is primarily made up of 49.5% oxygen, 25.7% silicon, 9.2% other elements, 7.5% aluminum, 4.7% iron, and 3.4% calcium.

We need oxygen for breathing and our metabolism. All of the cells of our body are oxidized. Hydrogen and chlorine are necessary for digestion, and many chemical reactions that make life possible involve the hydrogen ion. Practically every part of the body is based on the carbon chain of molecules. The body turns nitrogen into energy.

To summarize, the Bible emphatically stated that humans originally came from dust, and over 3,000 years later scientists discover that we have some of the same elements in us that is found in the dirt. Either Moses was either a super scientist or he got the information from someone else.

Eventually you are going to return to the dust, whether you are buried, cremated, or lost at sea. Here's one scientific fact you can count on. 1 out of every 1 person who is born, dies. But, to put it into computer terms, your body is only the hardware. Fortunately, the programmer, the "designer," keeps a copy of the software, and He can upload it into better hardware.

"But, wait! What about the dinosaurs? Don't they prove the theory of evolution?" you may be asking.

I don't know. Do they? Let's take a looksee.

Let me start by asking you a question. "When an animal dies on land, or in the sea, what happens to its remains?"

That's right, decomposition. Organic substances (animals, insects, plants, and people) are broken down into simple matter. In other words, they return to the dust.

Let's say that dear Uncle Mike dies. He is buried six-feet deep in ordinary soil without a coffin. Since we couldn't afford a coffin we certainly couldn't afford embalming him either. He just goes into the ground au natural. It will take 10 to 12 years for Uncle Mike to decompose down to the skeleton. If left undisturbed the bones will be fully decomposed, turned to dust, in about 300 years.

So, why is it then that we have thousands of animal bones (dinosaurs), little creepy crawlers, and plant life that are fossilized, supposedly that died millions of years ago, found all over the planet? Dinosaur fossils have even been found in Antarctica.

The only way animals, bugs, and plants could have been preserved through fossilization is by way of sedimentary rock. In other words, mud suddenly covered up these once living organisms, depriving the ground the ability to decompose them, and after drying over time it turned to rock. Marine fossils have even been found on the tallest mountain in the world – Mount Everest. The jawbone of a whale was discovered below this great mountain in the foothills of the Himalayas. That can only mean one thing. Mount Everest was once under sea water. Okay, but then how was the whale preserved. When whales die they decompose on the ocean floor or on a beach somewhere. This whale was buried in a sedimentary layer. How did mud bury a whale?

In our hemisphere whale fossils, along with other marine animals, have also been found in the Andes. That means that they too were buried rapidly with mud. Oh, and did I forget to mention, fossilized land animals were also found embedded in the rock layer. Keep in mind that even sea shells decompose, and the only reason we have fossilized seashells all over the globe is because they are in sedimentary rock. They were buried – suddenly.

Petrified wood is a fossil. It is plant material that was buried by sediment. You can visit the Petrified Forest National Park in Arizona and see tree trunks that were once 200-foot conifers.

73% of the Earth's surface is sedimentary rock. That means water, and lots of it. The rest of the surface is igneous rock, formed by cooling magma, and metamorphic rock, formed by temperature and pressure changes.

So, back to our super scientist Moshe, or in English *Moses*. When he was alive, back almost 3,500 years ago, just after the pyramids were built, he had never traveled more than 906 kilometers. I used kilometers in honor of Antoine Lavoisier. That's 563 miles. So, within a 563-mile radius that is all Moses knew about the earth. He had never seen a jungle, he had never seen the polar ice caps, he had never climbed the Himalayas or the Andes in South America. His knowledge of geography and geology was rather limited. The most advanced technology of his day was the wheel. Yet, in the book of Genesis he wrote, "The waters rose and increased greatly on the earth, and the ark floated on the surface of the water. They rose greatly on the earth, and all the high mountains under the entire heavens were covered. The waters rose and covered the mountains to a depth of more than fifteen cubits (20 feet, 6.9 meters). Every living thing that moved on earth perished – birds, livestock, wild animals, all the creatures that swarm over the earth, and all mankind. Everything on dry land that had breath; men and animals and the creatures that move along the ground and the birds of the air were wiped from the earth. Only Noah was left, and those with him in the ark. The waters flooded the earth for a hundred and fifty days." Genesis 7:18-23

You can choose to believe this Biblical account of the flood or not, but one thing is certain, Moses wrote down that the "highest mountains" were covered with 20 feet of water, and there are fossils on Mount Everest and the Andes proving it. Go up there yourself if you don't believe it.

"Oh, but scientists say that Mount Everest was once the sea floor, and it was pushed up to the height that it is today," some of you evolutionists claim.

Either way, Moses knew that every mountain on earth had been covered by water at one time. He said the earth was covered for 150 days, and scientists say millions of years. The point is, Moses knew.

It wasn't until 875 years later that ancient Greek philosopher Xenophanes (570-480 BC) wrote about fossils of marine animals that he had discovered deducting that his land had once been under water. Other Greek philosophers that followed in history came to the same conclusion, and that was that Greece may have been under water at one time. It wasn't until the Islamic Golden Age, 2,475 years after Moses, that Ibn Sina, the writer of *The Book of Healing*, who also studied geology, wrote about how the mountains themselves could have been formed by water. Of course, he only knew his corner of the world – Persia. About 60 years later, and two countries away, Chinese naturalist Shen Kuo (1031-1095 AD) brought forward the idea of climate change based on some petrified bamboo he had discovered. Petrified wood, as we had discussed, is formed by rapid burial by mud. In Europe it wasn't until the 1600s that scientists started to seriously study fossils. In 1665 a Catholic priest named Athanasius Kircher, considered the father of Egyptology, wrote a scientific textbook titled Mundus Subterraneus, *Underground World*, in which he inaccurately describes dinosaur bones as an extinct race of human giants. Keep in mind that the Mayflower had just landed at Plymouth only 45 years earlier; the European colonization of the future United States of America. However, that same year English scientist Robert Hooke, the man who coined the word "cell," wrote a book called *Micrographia* where he explained the microscopic structure of fossil wood compared to ordinary wood. Johann Jakob Scheuchezer, a Swiss scholar, published three works that linked fossils to the deluge, the great flood, as recorded in the Bible: *Complaints and Claims of the Fishes* (1708), The *Herbarium of the Deluge*

(1709), and *The Museum of the Deluge* (1716). In 1822 the word "paleontology" was coined by the editor of the *Journal de Physique*, Henri Marie Ducrotay de Blainville, who was a student of Georges Cuvier, considered the "father of paleontology."

If evolution were true, and fossils were created by many different flood events over millions of years as most paleontologists theorize, then there should be evidence of creatures evolving in the fossil record. We should have evidence of "transitional forms," but we don't. On the other hand, the Bible said that it rained for forty days and forty nights.

"But, wait! It is impossible for rain to last that long?" you're thinking. And, you would be correct.

According to Genesis there had been a water layer that surrounded the earth above the stratosphere at the beginning of world history, and it all came pouring down. How else could it have rained globally for that many days? This would also explain why Adam lived to be 930-years-old, and some of his descendants lived even longer than that until the flood came upon the Earth. The water that enveloped the planet prevented harmful radiation from penetrating the atmosphere, and thus less radiation bombarding the surface of the planet resulting in a very slow rate of cellular breakdown in organisms. However, after the flood the Bible charts a dramatic drop in human life span in a relatively short period of time, until it is where we are today. This would also explain the abundant, and sometimes very large, plant life found in the fossil record. The world was like a giant mild green house, and this is a proven fact. Professor Jane Francis of the University of Leeds spent ten seasons in Antarctica studying and collecting fossil pants, and even received the Polar Medal from Queen Elizabeth in 2002 for her work. "I still find the idea that Antarctica was once forested absolutely mind-boggling," Professor Francis said in a BBC interview. "We take it for granted that Antarctica has always been a frozen wilderness, but the ice caps only appeared relatively recently in geological history."

"Well, how long?" you may be asking. "How long ago was the flood of Noah, and why did it happen?"

Excellent questions. I'm glad you're curious. However, I'm going to be brief, because I must get you out of Cell Block 9 and into 10 very soon.

Now, keep an open mind to what I am about to tell you, because it is opposite to everything taught in most schools, both public and private. According to the Bible the world was created almost 6,000 years ago. That's right, it ain't millions or billions of years old. Just take a look at what year it is right now on the Jewish calendar. I don't know if it is exact, but it's got to be close.

The Bible takes great pains to give us the genealogy from Adam, the first man, to Jesus Christ, the Messiah. Since we know exactly when Jesus was crucified by the Romans, we just tack on today's date to that, and we arrive at the sum of mankind's history.

When the Bible says that God created everything in six days, and rested on the seventh, that's exactly what it means. Six 24-hour days. The Hebrew word for day is *yom*, and it is the same word used today by Israelis daily to keep track of time. Besides that, the Bible gives us a timetable that goes exactly like this, "When Adam had lived 130 years, he had a son in his own likeness, in his own image; and named him Seth. After Seth was born, Adam live 800 years and had other sons and daughters. Altogether, Adam lived 930 years, and then he died. When Seth had lived 105 years, he became the father of Enosh, and after he..." and on it goes until the list comes to Noah, the one who built the ark, which must have seemed absurd in his time, because vegetation was watered from the ground up, and not from the sky down - rain. 726 years after the death of Adam the worldwide flood came. This would have been 1,656 years from when Adam was created. Since Adam was created on the 6th day of creation the precise date would have been 1,656 years and 5 days since the Big Bang. God thought it, and BANG! it happened.

Abraham (revered by Jews, Christians, and Muslims alike) was born 1,936 after creation, which means 280 years after the flood. That may not seem like a long time just by looking at that number, but if you were to compare that 280-year time span to today there was no such nation as the United States of America. It was still only thirteen colonies, and independence was still many years away. A lot of history has happened in our country in 280 years. The population in the Colonies in 1740 was 889,000 people. The population of the country today is approximately 324 million. So, yes, a lot can happen in 280 years.

Moving on, Abraham was 20-years-old when Noah died. When Noah's ark came to rest on Mount Ararat the world population was 8. That's right, just eight people: Noah, his wife, his three sons, and their three wives. Eight survivors from the millions that had once walked the earth. By the time Abraham was 20-years-old mankind had repopulated and spread their civilizations as far north as Magog (today's Russia), as far west as Javan (today's Greece), as far south as Sabtah (Yemen and Somalia), and as far east as Elam (today's Iran).

So, using today's Gregoran calendar, Abram is believed to have been born in the year 1996 BC. Add 280 years (with BC you have to add, not subtract) and the flood that covered the entire earth took place in 2276 BC. Add today's date to that, and the flood was over 4,000 years ago (4,294 years to be exact in 2018). Add the years before the flood (1,656 years) going back to Adam, and you come really close to 6,000 years since creation. There's not going to be a 7,000th year, not under man's rule anyway, but that's another study we don't have time for now.

I'm not saying that these numbers I gave you are 100% accurate, because not every single person's life span was recorded in Jesus' genealogy, but from Abraham on we have fairly accurate numbers based upon Babylonian and Egyptian history, and we must rely on the Biblical account prior to Abraham. The Old Testament gives the genealogy from Adam to Abraham (20 generations), and the New Testament gives the genealogy from Abraham to Jesus Christ (42 generations). How far back can you trace your family tree? Certainly not 62 generations. The Bible did give us a sense of when creation happened. If you were just to take the average life span of today, which is 79 years, and multiply it by 62 generations, you have a total of 4,898 years. Now, if the average life span was for a much longer period, up until the flood (the 19 generations before Abraham), then getting to 6,000 years is not a problem.

Because you have been told your entire life that the earth is "billions of years old" you find it hard even contemplating that the earth is only almost 6,000 years old, as if either number makes any difference to you; there was a beginning at some point. We were all told that it took "millions of years" for the Grand Canyon to form by the Colorado River. Heck, even the American government tells us the same thing. On the National Park Service website on the Grand Canyon it states, "The Canyon's mile-high walls display a largely undisturbed cross section of the Earth's crust extending back some two billion years. Three 'Granite Gorges' expose crystalline rocks formed during the early-to middle Proterozoic Era."

Billions of years to form the Grand Canyon was the common secular explanation until something big happened on May 18, 1980 to change the mind of many scientists – the eruption of Mount St. Helens.

Mount St. Helens, a volcano, had been dormant since the 1850s, and then several small earthquakes rocked the area on March 15, 1980. Ten days later things really began to shake. Within a two-day period there were 174 tremors of a magnitude of 2.6 or greater. Pretty soon there were five earthquakes per day with a magnitude of 4. In April steam and small rocks were ejected from the crater, and Governor Dixy Lee Ray declared a state of emergency. Then on Monday, May 18th, as I was already thirty-minutes into my first period class preparing to graduate from high school, KABOOM! The volcano erupted; BIG TIME! No, I couldn't feel in in Los Angeles, but it certainly was all over the news that night.

The event was cataclysmic. Part of the summit dome gave way creating the largest landslide in recorded history. The mass slid down the west slope at 155 miles per hour (249 kilometers per hour) filling the valley below with 600 feet (180 meters) of avalanche debris over a 24-square mile area. Then came a 20-megaton vertical eruption column, just like you'd see in a natural disaster Hollywood film. 57 people were killed, $1.1 billion in property damage, and ash was deposited in 11 states and 5 Canadian provinces.

To everyone's surprise the eruption and destruction had created a "mini Grand Canyon." The rockslide had displaced the water in Spirit Lake pushing waves up to 850 feet high at the north shore. The rapid erosion formed cliff features and canyons as deep as 100 feet (30 meters) that looked like the Grand Canyon in Arizona; features that had not been there before.

The conclusion that we can draw from Mount St. Helens is that extreme erosion need not take millions of years, but it can happen in hours.

Yes, the scientists are right. The tallest mountains on earth were pushed up. The Bible is also right, the earth had once been covered by water. The pressure that pushed up mountain ranges could have easily been formed by trillions of tons of added water to the surface of the earth. The Bible states that not only large amounts of water fell to the earth, the protective water layer that once enveloped the Earth, but water gushed up from the ground as well.

In the six hundredth year of Noah's life, on the seventeenth day of the second month, on that day all the springs of the great deep burst forth, and the floodgates of the heavens were opened. Genesis 7:11

Did you catch that? "all the springs of the great deep burst forth." How did Moses know that on the ocean floors that there were "springs" of water? Springs in the ocean are also mentioned in the book of Job (pronounced *jobe*). "Have you journeyed to the springs of the sea or walked in the recesses of the deep?" Job 38:16

It wasn't until the invention of scuba equipment in 1942 by Jacques-Yves Cousteau and Emile Gagnan, coupled with reports from Mexican abalone divers in the 1960s, that scientists discovered shallow-water hot springs along the coast of Baja California. However, only submarines that can withstand three-tons-per-square-inch pressure could actually explore the ocean floors. In 1973 the first observation of deep sea springs was made by Project FAMOUS off the Mid-Atlantic Ridge. Then in 1977 hot springs were discovered in the Pacific Ocean on the Galapagos Rift by the submarine ALVIN. This same submarine also explored the hot springs of the East Pacific Rise south of the Gulf of California in 1979. So, again, how did two writers of the Bible know that there were springs in the deep? Nobody else knew this until the 20th century. They didn't have scuba gear or submarines 3,500 years ago. You know that answer, but you're just afraid to admit it, because it changes everything.

The water that had covered the earth, and the extreme pressures that pushed the mountain ranges upwards eventually ran off into the lakes and oceans that we have today. As these waters receded they carved out the Grand Canyon; not over millions of years, but over days, perhaps weeks. The Colorado River now keeps the water erosion process going in the Grand Canyon, but nothing compared to the great flood. Plants and animals got caught up in this catastrophic flood and were buried under mud and became fossilized. There are fossil fields on all seven continents, and even on islands. There are fossils in the Arctic Circle, and on Antarctica. All of this is evidence of a global flood.

Besides impressive fossils in rock, do you know what many of the buried plants also became? The answer is, oil. That's right, crude oil. Or, if you prefer, petroleum, and this word is actually comprised of two Greek words: *petra* – rock, and *oleum* – oil.

You've heard the term "fossil fuels" before. Well, that's because petroleum is fossilized organic materials that was transformed into a liquid state by sediment under heat, pressure, and anoxic conditions (that's a fancy term for groundwater that has been depleted of dissolved oxygen). Mankind, being very intelligent, has used petroleum products in one form or another since the Tower of Babel. There were oil pits near ancient Babylon. Asphalt was used in construction, and pitch was used to waterproof boats. Noah, your great, great, great, great, great… grandfather, used pitch (tar) in the construction of the ark to waterproof it.

Of course, just as there are fossils found on every continent, there are also oil reserves on every continent. And, since there is a lot of oil underground, that means there were lots and lots of plants on the surface at one time. That makes sense if the entire world had been subtropical due to the greenhouse conditions, and no axis tilt at the time.

It's also interesting that 65.5% of the world's oil reserves are in Iraq, Iran, and the Arabian Peninsula since the Bible states that the Garden of Eden had been located "in the east," which is always a Biblical reference to mean east of Jerusalem. The Book of Genesis is even more specific in pin pointing the garden's location by naming four rivers that flowed from the garden: Pishon, Havilah, Tigris and the Euphrates. The last two rivers are still part of today's topography. Draw a straight line on a map eastward from Jerusalem, and it intersects roughly in the middle of the richest concentrations of oil fields in the Middle East extending from Mosul in the north all the way down to Oman in the south.

The flood of Noah's day, the global flood, buried the Garden of Eden with trillions of tons of mud, and several millennia later you have oil – lots of oil. Coincidence? I think not. Oil was not discovered in Persia (Iran) until 1908, and then in Saudi Arabia and the other Persian Gulf states in 1938.

The area is not only where mankind first rebelled against God through Adam and Eve, but after the flood it is also where men built the Tower of Babel to continue their rebellion against God. This is why God guided Abraham out of the area, and to the land of Canaan (today's Israel) and eventually making Jerusalem the spiritual capital of the world saying, *Leave your country, your people and your father's household, and go to the land I will show you. Genesis 12:1*

Now, back to the dinosaurs. A fascinating book that you should read is *Evolution Impossible* by Dr. John F. Ashton. He discredits the theory of evolution based on DNA, deoxyribonucleic acid, evidence. Scientists have been telling us for years that the fossils are "millions of years old," and yet soft tissue DNA, which doesn't last very long, has been found in both plant and dinosaur fossils. "These biomolecules break down naturally fairly rapidly in the environment and cannot survive for millions of years. For example, based on current research observations, if the average rock temperature was 10 degrees Celsius, DNA would not be detectable after 20,000 years. If the average temperature was 20 degrees Celsius, the DNA would have completely broken down and not be detectable after about 2,500 years, and collagen would not be detectable after 20,000 years," said Dr. Ashton.

Dr. Carl Werner (biology, medicine), author of *Evolution: The Grand Experiment*, visited 60 natural history museums, and found that none of them display any of the 430 mammal species that were found in the same dinosaur fossil layers. It was as if they were trying push the false narrative that mammals did not live side by side with dinosaurs, and that the mammals and birds "came later in history." Why is that? Yet, the Bible describes what can only be two different types of dinosaurs living at the same time as man, after the Great Flood.

In the Book of Job, a book in the Old Testament, there is a description of what sounds like a Brontosaurus or some other type of Sauropoda. *Behold now, Behemoth, which I made as well as you; he eats grass like an ox. Behold now, his strength in his loins and his power in the muscles of his belly. He bends his tail like a cedar; the sinews of his thighs are knit together. His bones are tubes of bronze; his limbs are like bars of iron.* Then the description continues, *If a river rages, he is not alarmed; he is confident, though the Jordan rushes to his mouth. Can anyone capture him when he is on watch, with barbs can anyone pierce his nose?" Job 40:16-24*

The second creature described in the Book of Job is similar to the descriptions of a medieval dragon. *Can you draw out Leviathan with a fishhook? Or press down his tongue with a cord? Can you put a rope in his nose or pierce his jaw with a hook?* Then the description continues with, *I will not keep silence con-*

cerning his limbs, or his mighty strength, or his orderly frame. Who can strip off his outer armor? Who can come within his double mail? Who can open the door of his face? Around his teeth there is terror. His strong scales are his pride, shut up as with a tight seal. One is so near to another that no air can come between them. They are joined one to another; the clasp each other and cannot be separated. His sneezes flash forth light, and his eyes are like the eyelids of the morning. Out of his mouth go burning torches, sparks of fire leap forth. Out of his nostrils smoke goes forth as from a boiling pot and burning rushes. His breath kindles coals, and a flame goes forth from his mouth. Job 41:1-21

There are many examples of ancient civilizations having encounters with "dragons," all the way up to the Middle Ages. We have many stories, and works of art, from all kinds of cultures depicting dragons from Europe to the Orient. Even petroglyphs in North America made by the indigenous peoples before the arrival of the Europeans depict what look like dinosaurs. Look up the word "Unktehi" or "horned serpent."

Now, I could go on and on about scientific statements in the Bible that have eventually been authenticated by scientists. I could talk about how the ancient "God-fearing conservatives" knew that the earth free-floats in space, or how they knew that light could be divided, how Matthew Maury (the father of ocean-ography) discovered the "paths of the seas" in the 19th century based upon the Bible verse Psalm 8:8, or how they knew that there was an infinite amount of stars (even though the naked eye can only count 5,000 of them), or that they knew about the Second Law of Thermodynamics, plus many more fascinating facts. Nope, there's no time for that. You can find out all of this on your own. Your reeducation only covers evolution, and the impossibility of the theory. Hopefully, you can wrap your head around the possibility of creation based on a book like no other – the Bible.

Thanks to modern science we can rule out evolution. Evolution is political, and we have already discussed, ad nauseam, that socialism, communism, and fascists all hate religion, especially Judaism and Christianity. Just like Pharaoh wanted all the Hebrew baby boys thrown into the Nile River and drowned (the Egyptian form of "Planned Parenthood," just like founder Margaret Sanger pro-moted during her lifetime), and just like King Herod wanted all baby boys two-years-old and under put to death by the sword in hopes of killing the Messiah, so too most political systems on this planet do not want the God of the Bible ruling and reigning in people's lives. They want the state to be god; the all-powerful benevolent state. What better way to make this happen than to keep teaching children and college students that they evolved from a mud puddle, or were seeded from outer space, and that they were not created in the image of God.

BOYCOT ISRAEL

Israel. It seems that the whole world is against this nation. Well, in fact, the world literally is against them. Since the creation of the he United Nations Human Rights Council in 2006 the Council has resolved more resolutions condemning Israel than the rest of the world combined; amazing, considering Israel only has a population of 8,299,706 - 74.8% of which are Jewish, as of November 6, 2017 according to the Central Intelligence Agency's *The World Factbook.* That's just under the population of Switzerland. In other words, a tiny country.

Since the birth of the modern State of Israel on May 14, 1948 the United States government has recognized the Jewish government. To prove it, here are the words of the President of the United States:

This Government has been informed that a Jewish state has been proclaimed in Palestine, and recognition has been requested by the provisional Government thereof.

The United States recognizes the provisional government as the de facto authority of the new State of Israel.

(signed) Harry Truman

Approved,
May 14, 1948

Since that date the American government has strongly supported the Jewish State of Israel: culturally, economically, and militarily. However, over the years the political left in this country has been increasing hostile towards Israel culminating with the Obama administration. President Barak Hussein Obama was the very first president to double-cross Israel by having U.S. Ambassador to the United Nations Samantha Power (Democrat), and the same woman who is believed to have illegally "unmasked," *requesting the intelligence community to provide the identification of individuals,* hundreds of American citizens while in office, abstained from voting against Security Council Resolution 2334 that condemned Israeli settlement expansion in Samaria (known to the rest of the world as the West Bank), and even in the Jewish capital of East Jerusalem. Although Donald Trump had won the election before the resolution came up, and was only a month away from being sworn in, President Obama took this parting shot at Israel. Failure to veto the resolution resulted in a 14-0 vote on December 23, 2016. This action had been the complete opposite position of established American policy for decades, and Israeli Ambassador Danny Danon made this known publicly by stating, "It was to be expected that Israel's greatest ally would act in accordance with the values that we share, and that they would have vetoed this disgraceful resolution." House Speaker Paul Ryan (Republican) also spoke out clearly, "This is absolutely shameful. Today's vote is a blow to peace that sets a dangerous precedent for further diplomatic efforts to isolate and demonize Israel."

Television talk show host of CBN News, Gordon Robertson, wisely once said, "If you don't understand the history [of Israel], you can't understand today's headlines," and how true that is.

Do you understand what's happening today in Israel, and why the region is a potential powder keg that the whole world is concerned about? You need to know what's going on there, because World War III may very start over this tiny nation.

Now, I'm not going to take you through a three-thousand-year history lesson on how the Jews were in the land before the Arabs, Turks, or the Europeans, starting with Joshua conquering Canaan (which is today's Israel) around 1406 BC, or the rich Jewish history underneath the very soil there, but I'm going to start with BDS.

"What is 'BDS?'" some of you are asking. Well, it is the acronym for Boycott, Divestment, Sanctions. Israeli Prime Minister Benjamin Netanyahu called it *Bigotry, Dishonesty, Shame.*

BDS is a boycott of all Israeli products in hopes of applying stiff economic pressure on Israeli in order to achieve an "end to the occupation of Palestinian lands, dismantle the walls that separate Jewish and Arab villages, full equality for Palestinian citizens living in Israel, and the rights of Palestinian refugees to be repatriated.

BDS started on July 9, 2005 as a call to "people of conscience" all around the world to draw attention to the plight of the Palestinian people, and eventually a lot of Americans, both young and old, jumped on board this boycott. Of course, most Americans know little of ancient history or Middle East history of the past 100 years, and therefore have no appreciation of the complexities of the situation in that region. Yet, what you Millennials and Gen Zers do appreciate is your cell phones and other devices. You really love them, don't you? You couldn't hardly get through the day without them.

"What does that have to do with BDS or Israel?" you ask dumfounded. Well, let me tell you, by starting off with a story I found on the website *Dr. Naomi on*

Israel that was posted on September 18, 2014.

During the recent cease-fire, the leader of the Palestinian terrorist organization HAMAS, Khaled Mashal, sent a gift to the Prime Minister of Israel, Benjamin Netanyahu, in an elaborate box with a note. After having the box checked for safety reasons, Prime Minister Benjamin Netanyahu opened the box and saw that the content was human feces.

He opened the note, handwritten in Arabic by Mr. Mashal, which said, "For you and the proud people of the Zionist Entity."

Mr. Netanyahu, literate in Arabic, pondered the note and decided how best to reciprocate.

He quickly did so by sending the HAMAS leader a very pretty package with a personal note. Mr. Mashal and the other leaders of HAMAS were very surprised to receive the parcel and opened it very carefully suspecting that it might contain a bomb. But to their surprise they saw that it contained a tiny computer chip.

The chip was rechargeable with solar energy, had a 1.8 terabyte memory and could output a 3D hologram display capable of functioning in any type of cellular phone, tablet, or laptop. It was one of the world's most advanced technologies, with a tiny label, "Invented and produced in Israel."

Mr. Netanyahu's note, personally handwritten in Arabic, Hebrew, French, and English, stated very courteously...

"Every leader gives the best his people can produce."

In case you didn't know, HAMAS (an Arabic acronym for Islamic Resistance Movement) is the organization that rules the Palestinian territory of Gaza (a strip of land bordering southwest Israel), which had been a part of Egypt up until 1967. The seal of HAMAS shows the entire State of Israel under Palestinian control, two crossed Arabian looking swords, and the Dome of the Rock shrine. They are about as anti-Zionist and anti-Semitic as they come; just read their HAMAS Covenant. According to Article 2 they are "one of the branches" of the Egyptian group Muslim Brotherhood, which is considered a terrorist organization by the Russians, Egyptians, Arab Emirates, and several other nations. Does it ring a bell yet? They're the group that had been invited to the White House numerous times by President Obama. Yeap, the same ones who wrote a 1991 internal memorandum, discovered by the FBI and CIA, which outlined their strategy for the United States that involved "eliminating and destroying the Western civilization from within." Ummmmm, that's you, your family, and friends. Don't you find that offensive? I certainly do.

President Obama was disappointment when the Egyptian people rose up against the Muslim Brotherhood, who had ruled the country from 2011 to 2013, and took their country back. Now Egypt and the United States are best buddies again, thanks to President Trump.

Anyway, back to cell phones and devices.

I quoted you the story of Prime Minister Benjamin Netanyahu's gift of an advanced computer chip to HAMAS leader Khaled Mashal because it illustrates the point that Israel is a technological giant, and you are reaping the benefits. Yes, you! The first benefit you enjoy, probably without even knowing it, is that of your cell phone. Mobile phone technology was developed in Israel, and it was the first place they were manufactured. How about texting? Do you text? You can thank the Israelis for that modern miracle.

Do you still want to boycott Israeli products? Then make sure your computer, laptop, or notebook does not have an Intell Pentium or Celeron computer processor chip inside it, because those were either developed or manufactured in Israel. The new Ivy Bridge processor is manufactured in Israel, so if you are running Windows operating systems then stop using it if you insist on the boycott. After all, Microsoft is reliant on Israeli research and development. So, the question must now be asked, "Do you really want to hurt an American company that also provides you with wonderful products by insisting on a boycott of Israeli products?"

Do you ever send emails? That was developed at the Ben Gurion University in Be'er-Sheva in 1980. Have you ever used a USB flash drive to store or transfer data – yeap, Israeli. If your doctor needs to literally see inside your bladder, lungs, joints, colon, or other internal organs then they'll most likely use a flexible endoscope outfitted with the world's smallest video camera designed by Medigus – Israeli. Or, you might even be swallowing the first endoscopic PillCam (pill camera) one day to monitor your health – Israeli. However, to make transistors that small they need nanowires – Israeli. Do you know anyone with multiple sclerosis? They might be receiving treatment with the Copaxone immunomodulator drug – Israeli. Is anyone in your family taking the drug Velcade for Myeloma? - Israeli. Do you live in an arid part of the country, and water is scarce? Then your farmers are using drip irrigation – Israeli. Have you ever typed on a laser projection keyboard? If you have then – yes, Israeli. Anyone trained in tactical medicine (soldiers, police officers, paramedics) has slapped on a First Care Emergency Bandage on a serious wound – Israeli, and it still referred to by many as the "Israeli bandage." It's the same product that saved Arizona senator Gabriella Giffords (Democrat) after she was shot in the head. For you women, have you ever used an EpiLady to remove unwanted hair?

Yessiree, Israeli. Do you like cherry tomatoes in your salad – Israeli genetics company. Worried about SIDS, *Sudden Infant Death Syndrome*, in the middle of the night? BabySense monitors the baby's breathing through the mattress while they sleep – Israeli. It has only helped to protect more than 600,000 babies around the world. Do you text while driving, even though it is against the law, and a stupid thing to do? Mobileye in your car will alert you of driving hazards in front of you – Israeli. Are you afraid that one day you may be stuck in a skyscraper and no way down in an emergency? Just put on the Skysaver, and go down the fire-resistant cord – Israeli. Do you plan on buying an electric car to save the environment? Then you had better think twice, because chances are high that an Israeli battery or charging mat may be inside it.

I could go on and on about Israeli products, but I think you get the picture. Moving on.

There are a lot of countries that want to literally wipe Israel out – destroy them. The Iranian military often paints the words ISRAEL MUST BE WIPED OUT on their long-range Qadr missiles. So, let me get this straight, we want to boycott or wipe out a country that has given us so many incredible products that we use every day, has the highest number of university degrees per capita in the world, has the largest number of startup companies in the world in proportion to its population, is ranked #2 in the world for venture capital funds right behind the United States, has the largest number of companies listed on the NASDAQ after the USA and Canada, has the highest average living standards in the Middle East, has the world's second highest supply of new books per capita, more museums per capita than any country on earth, and has been a close ally of ours in one of the most volatile places on earth? I just don't get it.

I just had some Italian friends stay at my house for a week recently. I asked him, "Why do so many Italians hate the Jews?" His answer was, "Because they're greedy. They love money."

That's not the first time I've heard this. I even have some family members and American friends who have answered the same thing. So, my response is always, "So, being successful and making money is wrong? Why is nobody condemning the Chinese? They are making money hand over fist. Why is nobody condemning the oil rich countries? Why the Jews?"

Once you get past the money issue the next criticism that inevitably surfaces is, "Because they control the media," or "Because they control the banks and government."

Then I come back, "Really? The estimated world Jewish population of 13.9 million, around 0.2% of the world population, has that much control and influence over everyone else? Even if they did, are they helping people or harming people? I enjoy Steve Spielberg movies. Sergy Brin's Google is very useful to me. I use Mark Zuckerberg's Facebook daily. So, what's your point?"

Of course, once you get beyond this absurdity most "gentiles" really don't have a valid reason for hating the Jews. So, then the attack is directed to the Israelis; the Jews who live in Israel. "Well, they're occupying Arab land! They're cruel to them! They're oppressors!" and the list of transgressions go on.

Now, having been to Israel a few times, and many police and military units have adopted my self-defense system when it comes to surviving knife attacks (the Jim Wagner Reality-Based Personal Protection system), I'll be first to say that the Israelis are not perfect. What people are? But, I can tell you that American mainstream media puts out a lot of misinformation when it comes to Israel. They try to compare it to the former white-ruled country of South Africa that created apartheid, a country I have also worked in, and the two histories and current situation in Israel are not even close.

I could use leftist progressive reasoning on you to justify Israel's existence, and persuade you to support her. For example, do you think we, the United States, should give back our land to the Indians? If so, then Israel ought to go back to the Jews. There are no more Canaanites, the original indigenous people, to give the land to, and thus by default the land ought to go back to the Jews who lived in the land after the Canaanites.

How about an evolutionary argument for supporting today's Israel? Let's use Darwin's theory of "survival of the fittest." The Israelis seized the land by force, some of it anyway, and the victor takes all. Hasn't most countries in the world done the same thing throughout history? The United Nations is not demanding that Argentina give the land back to Spain. Argentina is a good example, because like the Spanish in South America, the Palestinians were not the ingenious people of today's Israel, and neither were the Dutch, Portuguese, English, or French the indigenous people of the rest of South America. Strangely, the United Nations is not on the backs of Argentina, Bolivia, Brazil, Ecuador, French Guiana, Mexico, Peru, or Venezuela even though some of the indigenous people there would like to see this happen. If anyone has a legitimate gripe about getting their land back it is those people before European colonization. But, let's face it, no country is willing to do that. Many Mexican-Americans want California back, because it belonged to Mexico for 27 years (1821-1848). I know this, because every year in my home state there are demonstrations, editorials, and petitions demanding that California be "returned" to Mexico. Yet, the Spanish had claim to it for 329 years (1492-1821). Not even the 109 federally recognized Indian tribes in California are demanding California back. If they did, can you imagine the confusion that would ensue? There are 100 distinct languages with over 300 dialects. Heck! We can't even agree on English as the official national language. They certainly would not go back to indigenous architecture, technology, or even ancient religions since most are Christians today.

So, when it comes to Israel, rather than getting into the Balfour Declaration of 1917, the Oslo Accords of 1993 where the Israelis were willing to give Palestinian leader Yassir Arafat 90% of what his government was asking for but refused the deal in the end, or even going over the finer points of the numerous wars and two intifadas (Arabic for *to shake off* as in *shake off the dust of one's sandals*) that galvanized the current positions, I'm going to cut to the chase and give you the evangelical Christian's point of view of Israel so you can better understand why, once again, Donald Trump was elected President of the United States. After all, a lot of evangelical Christians are pro-Israel, and this was one of the major issues that brought record number of Christians to the voting booths so that they could cast their ballots for the Republican ticket.

If I had to sum up in just one word why the Bible is undeniably the true Word of God it would have to be the word "Israel." That's right, the country of Israel.

I always carry a small silver coin in my wallet. It is the Israeli Sheqel with the name "Israel" engraved upon it in Hebrew, English, and Arabic. The last time I was in Israel, training the Israel Defense Force, I grabbed as many of these coins as I could and brought them home with me. On my pastor's recent trip to Israel I also had him grab me a bunch of them to bring them back to me. Whenever I find myself in a conversation with someone who is truly seeking the answers to life, and questioning the validity of the Bible, I give them a Sheqel to keep. Then when I get home I place another one in my wallet for the next person I come across. I tell them, "If you ever doubt the authenticity of the Bible take out this coin, hold it in your hand and look at it, and in so doing you have tangible proof that the Bible is true."

So, why do I do this? How can a coin prove that the Bible is the only spiritual truth on earth? It's easy. The Israel Sheqel is tangible proof that the Old Testament book of Ezekiel, chapter 37 specifically, has come to pass in the Baby Boomer era, and at this point of history you Millennials and Gen Zers are about to see chapter 38 happen. I kid you not.

Let me paraphrase what theses chapters are all about to save time, but I encourage you to read the passages yourself when you have the time. In fact, do yourself a favor and read the entire Bible so you can better understand Western culture.

Ezekiel was a Hebrew prophet when Babylon was the world's first superpower (718-539 BC). Israel and Judah (the Jews had been divided into two separate countries) had been conquered by King Nebuchadnezzar, and the surviving Hebrews were forcibly disbursed throughout the empire. While Ezekiel was in captivity in Babylon God gave him a vision; a vision of the future.

In the vision Ezekiel found himself in the middle of a valley filled with the bones of dead people, lots of dead people. The bones upon the floor of the valley were "very dry," meaning they had been there a very long, long, time.

God asked Ezekiel, "Son of man, can these bones live?'

How do you answer that one? Ezekiel gave a pretty good answer under the circumstances, "O Sovereign Lord, you alone know." In today's vernacular, "Lord, you tell me."

After a command was given to the corpses the bones began to rattle, and they started to come together and assemble. Soon whole skeletons lay upon the ground. Then muscles formed upon them, and finally skin covered them all. However, there was no life in them.

God then put breath into the bodies, bringing them to life, and they "stood up on their feet – a vast army."

God said to Ezekiel, "Son of man, these bones are the whole house of Israel," and then He goes on to say, "O my people, I am going to open your graves and bring you up from them; I will bring you back to the land of Israel."

Woe! Stop right there! God indicated in this passage, represented by many dry bones, that the nation of Israel was going to be dead for a very long time. Has that ever happened? Yes, of course it did. The year was 70 A.D.

As the result of the Jewish Revolt that began in 66 A.D. Emperor Vespasian sent his son, General Titus, to wage war against the Jews. The Romans not only killed the rebels, but also an estimated 1.1 million non-combatants, which brought an end to the ancient Jewish state.

Proof of this war can be seen today in the center of Rome, Italy. It's the Arch of Titus, an ancient war memorial. I know this for a fact, because I've been there, and I took a lot of awesome photos of it before getting a pizza on Via dell'Archetto. The Arch of Titus, erected in 82 A.D., depicts Roman soldiers carrying off artifacts from the 2nd Jewish Temple as booty in a victory procession. In fact, the Jewish menorah that they are carting away was the model used for the official seal of the modern State of Israel.

In addition, if you go to Jerusalem today you can see further proof of the Bible's accuracy. There is a big pile of debris, huge carved stones, at the bottom of the Temple Mount that had been excavated by archeologists. These stones had once been the very building blocks of the Jewish Temple that the Romans tore down stone by stone and pushed over the side. And, yes, like the Arch of Titus I've seen these stones as well with my very own eyes. So, you can say that I've done my homework. It's interesting that around 33 A.D. Jesus said to His disciples, who were marveling at the beauty and immensity of the Temple they were beholding, "Do you see all these things? Truly I tell you, not one stone will be left on another; every one will be thrown down." Matthew 24:2 Quite a statement considering the Temple took 20 years to build.

After Rome's victory the surviving 97,000 Jews were dispersed throughout the empire as slaves, and for almost 2,000 year the Jews were without a nation. Yet, without a nation they maintained their identity throughout the ages. There is no parallel in human history.

Ezekiel, a man who lived over 2,600 years ago wrote, inspired by God, "I will take the Israelites out of the nations where they have gone. I will gather them back into their own land. I will make them one nation in the land, on the mountains of Israel. There will be one king over all of them and they will never again be two nations or be divided into two kingdoms." Ezekiel 37:21-22 Then on May 14, 1948 the British occupation of Palestine ended, and the Jews declared Israel a nation; a nation that was born in one day. Funny, because the prophet Isaiah, a contemporary of Ezekiel, also wrote, "Who has ever heard of such things? Who has ever seen things like this? Can a country **be born in a day** or a nation be brought forth in a moment?"

Regardless of what you think about the Bible, this prophecy has come true. If you don't believe me then buy an airline ticket to Israel and go walk around there. While you're at it, keep the change they give you when you purchase things with cash, and come back and hand out your own Sheqels to people you come across. Then, the next time you see a story, or read a story, about Israel remember that Ezekiel chapter 37 has come true. Now, if Ezekiel 37 has come true, then that means the rest of the Bible is true as well: Heaven, Hell, Judgement Day, creation, sins, miracles, the Second Coming, the whole enchilada.

"So then, what is Ezekiel chapter 38 all about?" You've got to be wondering. Well, let me tell you, things on earth really go down hill fast when this happens. We're already seeing the preparations happening today.

Ezekiel chapter 38 talks about, well, let me just give it to you. I'll just put the modern names of countries next to the ancient names. Here goes:

The word of the Lord came to me: "Son of man, set your face against Gog, the land of Magog (Russia), the chief prince of Meshech and Tubal (some countries from the former Soviet Union); prophesy against him and say: 'This is what the Sovereign Lord says: I will turn you around, put hooks into your jaws and bring you out with your whole army – your horses, your horsemen fully armed, and a great horde with large and small shields, all of them brandishing swords. Persia (Iran), Cush (Ethiopia-Sudan region), Put (Libya) will be with them, all with shields and helmets, also Gomer (Turkey) with all its troops, and Beth Togarmah (the Caucasus region) from the far north (draw a line northward from Jerusalem and see what countries it intersects) with all its troops – many nations with you."

The scriptures go on to say that these nations will invade Israel "whose people were gathered from many nations." The people of Sheba and Dedan (Saudi Arabia and the United Arab Emirates) protest the invasion (naturally, because they probably think they're next to be targeted, because of their vast oil reserves), as well as the merchants of Tarshish (peoples to the west, possibly the European Union); for it disrupts the global economy. Remember, I laid out the reason before you as to how important Israeli innovations and products are to the world.

Despite being outnumbered and outgunned, Israel wins the war with the help of God. Oh, and it is going to be a very bloody war. From the Biblical descriptions it sounds like there's going to be a limited nuclear exchange. It's going to take months for the Israelis to bury the dead enemy soldiers.

So, ask yourself, "Are the countries mentioned in the Bible hostile to Israel today?" You know what the answer will be. "Yes."

According to Wikipedia "currently Russia acts as both an economic and a military benefactor to Iran."

On August 30, 2017 Israeli Prime Minister Benjamin Netanyahu warned the world, "Iran is busy turning Syria into a base of military entrenchment, and it wants to use Syria and Lebanon as war fronts in its declared goal to eradicate Israel." Of course, Russia has warned the United States and Israel that they will "respond with force" if their own "red lines" are crossed in Syria. As you know, Syria shares a border with the State of Israel. Therefore, you have Russian and Iranian troops literally at the door of Israel. Oh, and did I forget to mention that Russia has deployed advanced S-300PMU-2 long-range surface-to-air missile batteries around the Fordow nuclear site located 60 miles south of Tehran. This is not just rumor, but it was reported by Iranian state media. Russian Deputy Foreign Minister Gennady Gatilov warned, "Of course, any possible military scenario against Iran will be catastrophic for the region, and for the whole system of international relations." In other words, if Israel tries to take out Iran's nuclear program Russian will come to Iran's aid – "hooks in your jaws and bring you out."

I have been visiting and working in Europe for over thirty years, and for many years I'd argue with my Europeans colleagues and friends that "Turkey will never be a part of the European Union." I even said this before the European Union was founded on November 1, 1993. Before 1993 it used to be the European Economic Community.

Many in the EU were certain that this country would be admitted into the organization, but I knew the Bible scriptures, and I stuck to them. Then came along Turkish President Recept Tayyip Erdogan on August 28, 2014 who moved the country away from being a secular state and towards a more fundamentalist Islamic state. They once had strong ties with Israel, but President Erdogan all but severed them. He even stated on May 17, 2017 that Turkey might consider joining the Chinese Shanghai Cooperation Organization instead of the European Union.

Just as Jesus said, as we get closer to the "End Times," major events prophesied in the Bible would be "like labor pains" happening more frequently, and closer together. On November 22, 2017 diplomats from Russia, Iran, and Turkey met in Antalya to form a unique alliance in the Middle East after the defeat of ISIS. Again, Ezekiel 38.

And, speaking of China, the Bible mentions "the kings from the East." *The sixth angel poured out his bowl on the great river Euphrates, and its water dried up to prepare the way for the kings from the East. Revelation 16:12*

Are the "kings from the East the Chinese?" The number of troops they field to move into the Middle East mentioned in the Bible would seem to indicate so.

It's interesting that on October 18, 2017 Chinese President Xi Jinping laid out his vision for a "new era" for China. The government let the world know that it wants to turn China into the leading "global power by 2050" while at the same time maintaining their communist strong hold.

Anyway, war in the Middle East is only the beginning of "the birth pains" referred to in Matthew 24.

Nation will rise against nation, and kingdom against kingdom. There will be famines and earthquakes in various places. All these things are the beginning of birth pains. Then they will hand you over to be persecuted and killed, and you will be hated by all nations on account of My name. Whose name? The name of Jesus Christ.

The Greek word for "nation" used is *ethnos* or *ethnic groups*. So, read it like this, "Ethnic groups will rise against ethnic groups." Are we seeing that today? You bet we are. "White privilege" accusations, the Catalan independence movement in Spain, Brexit, the Kurds, and a whole host of tensions worldwide. Do we see kingdoms (basileia) against kingdoms? Keep in mind that when the Bible was written there was no such thing as countries ruled by democratic elections. You either had a king or a queen. According to the Mirror on August 9, 2017 there are "22 conflicts around the globe that threaten to erupt into major military standoff."

If you are living in the middle of Kansas these conflicts probably do not concern you very much. But if you are living in Anchorage, Seattle, or Los Angeles you're probably a little uncomfortable with the thought of the North Korean government threatening to nuke the West Coast.

Oh, and the mention of "earthquakes in various places." That's been happening. Even the mainstream media has noticed it. In 2014 NBC News wrote a story titled *Worldwide Surge in 'Great' Earthquakes Seen in Past 10 Years.*

Since 1900 there have been more than 10,000 "strong" earthquakes with magnitudes of 6 or greater around the world, according to the U.S. Geological Survey. Major earthquakes, greater than magnitude 7, happen more than once per month, and all around the world.

I know what you are thinking, and that is, "You're rabbit trailing! You still have not answered the main question, which is, 'Why do many Christians support the State of Israel? Forget the economic or strategic military interests, that's all well and good, but tell us why spiritually it is important to support the Jews?'"

Okay, I will. Our reason for supporting the Jews, which includes the State of Israel, pretty much boils down to Genesis 12:3. God spoke to Abraham, a gentile as I mentioned, who became the very first Jew, and today is revered as the patriarch of Judaism, Christianity, and Islam, and He (God) said to him, "I will bless them who bless you, and curse him that curses you, and in you all the families of the earth will be blessed."

Just take a historical look at every group or nation that have mistreated the Jews or the State of Israel. Bad things came to those people and nations. And, since God's law is just as sure as the law of gravity there are consequences when you go against it. As long as the United States of America supports the Jews and the State of Israel God will continue to bless our nation. As long as there are God-fearing men and women running our government the blessings will be poured out upon us.

President Richard M. Nixon (Republican) understood this concept very well when he was leader of our country. In October of 1973 the Egyptians, Syrians, Iraqis, Moroccans, Algerians, Tunisians, Jordanians, and Cubans, supported with weapons and a massive resupply effort by the powerful Soviet Union, wanted to wipe out the nation of Israel. In fact, the Arabs called it the War of Annihilation, whereas the Israelis called it the Yom Kippur War, because it happened on one of their holy days.

President Nixon had remembered his mother, Hannah Nixon a devout Quaker, telling him early on in his political career that if he ever found himself in a position to help the Jews and Israel that he was to do it. So, when Israeli Prime Minister Godda Meir telephoned President Nixon at 3:00 a.m. requesting urgent help from the United States the President remembered his mother's words, and capitulated.

Here's what is written on a plaque in the Richard M. Nixon Library in Yorba Linda, California. I took a picture of it. "With Israeli troops seriously outnumbered and facing possible defeat at the hands of the Soviet-backed Arabs, Nixon ordered an emergency airlift of supplies. 'Send everything that will fly,' he ordered. The American airlift enabled Israel to launch a decisive counterattack that pushed the Egyptians back across the Suez Canal."

Donald Trump understood this Biblical principle as well, because he had surrounded himself with devoted Jews and Christians. During his presidential campaign he boldly proclaimed that he would support the Jews and the State of Israel. Yes, he was a flawed candidate, but he won the election as a result of Jews and Christians sending "everything that will fly" – their prayers and their votes. Then when President Trump took power he acted upon his promise and announced to the world the United States' unequivocal support for the State of Israel.

Then on June 8, 2017 U.S. Ambassador to the United Nations Nikki Haley announced to the world from Jerusalem, "I have never taken kindly to bullies. And the U.N. has blamed Israel for a very long time. And we're not going to let that happen anymore."

As a direct result of our support of Israel blessings have indeed been poured upon our nation once again: a lower unemployment rate, a strong Stock Market, and fewer illegal border crossings. If only this country would completely turn back to IN GOD WE TRUST then even more blessings would be poured out, and evil purged from our land. *Let God be true, and everyman a liar; as it is written. Romans 3:4*

Interesting enough, it's not just many insightful Christians supporting Jews, but also Jews supporting the pro-Israel Christian community. On October 15, 2017 Benjamin Netanyahu, the Prime Minister of Israel, addressed the Christian Media Summit at the Israel museum in Jerusalem, and stated in perfect English, "I want to welcome you to Jerusalem, the eternal capital of the Jewish people," which coincided with the 50th anniversary of the unification of the city. He then said, "Israel has no better friend, I mean that, no better friend in the world than the Christian communities around the world. And Israel is the one country in a vast region where Christians not only survive, they thrive."

Now you are well informed on Israel.

NEW WORLD ORDER

It's not just many governments that desire a "one world government," which will ultimately resemble socialism or communism, but even corporations are willfully, or ignorantly, edging towards that direction. After all, the rich keep getting richer, and the poor are stuck at the bottom. It's the middle class in America that is fast disappearing, which happens to be the biggest block of conservatives. The majority of the rich and the poor in America tend to lean left more and more. Hopefully, your reeducation here will reverse that trend.

Mark Zuckerberg alluded to his own leanings towards a new world order movement at the 1st Facebook Communities Summit in Chicago on June 22, 2017. This event marked the Facebook "community" reaching 2 billion users. He said at this event, "Now, the thing that I think we all need to do right now is, is, work to bring people closer together. And, I think that is actually so important that we're going to change Facebook's whole mission as a company in order to focus on this. So, for the last decade or so, ah, we've been focusing on making the world more open and connected. And, we're not done with this yet. We're always going to do this. Ah, but, I used to think that if we just gave people a voice, and, and helped some people connect that, that would make the world a lot better all by itself. And, and in a lot of ways it has. But, today when we look around our society is still very divided. Alright, so, now I believe we have a responsibility to do even more. Not just simply connect the world, but also work to bring the world closer together."

The PowerPoint presentation that was projected onto the screen behind him revealed the new direction that he was talking about. It read, "Our mission: Bring the world closer together."

Mark Zuckerberg went on to explain, "That mission reflects, that this is something that we can't do by ourselves. Alright, the only way that we can do this is by empowering people around the world to build community, just like all of you are, and to bring people closer together."

It's subtle, but he used the word "community" instead of "communities."

And, let me ask you Millennials and Gen Zers, what does it mean "to bring the world closer together?" Isn't the world tied together economically? I can use my Visa card in Los Angeles or London to purchase things. Hasn't the Internet brought the world closer together? I can have Skype or Facetime meetings with my business partners all over the world. I can see them on the screen in real time as if they were sitting in my office in California. No, when people say that they want "to bring the world closer together" it means "to be of the same mind." They believe that if people would just talk to each other more, and listen, that political and religious issues will be resolved, that somehow there will finally be peace on the globe. However, I'm telling you right now that it is never, and

I mean "never," going to happen. Freedom and oppression are not compatible. Capitalism and communism are not compatible. Birth and abortion are not compatible. Criminals and law & order are not compatible. The God of the Bible is not compatible with the other world religions. The "narrow minded" Christians are not going change, because Jesus Christ Himself said that the way to God is to, "Enter through the **narrow** gate. For wide is the gate and broad is the way that leads to destruction, and many enter through it. But small is the gate and **narrow is the way** that leads to life, and only a few find it." Matthew 7:14 Jesus also said, "I am **the way** and **the truth** and **the life**. No one comes to the Father except through me." You can't get any narrower than that. Therefore, does Mark Zuckerberg believe that Jesus is the only way that the world will truly come together as a "community." If he does he's certainly not saying so. Is the United Nations delegates pleading with the citizens of the world to repent and not repeat the same mistake of our ancestors who built the Tower of Babel, and then defiantly proclaimed, *"Come, let us build ourselves a city, with a tower that reaches to the heavens* (a one world political and religious system that does not glorify God), *so that we may make a name for ourselves* (our ways and morality above God's), *otherwise we will be scattered over the face of the whole earth* (thus losing centralized government, and keep in mind technology back then was not like it is today)." Are Americans in one voice crying out, "Let's return to our Judeo-Christian roots! Let's put the New England Primer back into the public schools! Let's once again display the Ten Commandments on our public walls, and in front of each courthouse throughout the land! Let's stop killing our fellow Americans in the womb, and bring them forth to build our economy, and teach them to be true patriots for the security of our country; "One nation under God!" No, this is not the "community" most Americans, or the rest of the world for that matter, are seeking after. Yet, because the Bible is the true Word of God it does give us a glimpse into the future, and it states that the world will indeed get their One World Government that they want so desperately. Jesus Himself warned us about it, "I have come in my Father's name, and you did not accept me; but if someone else comes in his own name, you will receive him." He was speaking about the Antichrist who will seek to unite the world, and rule it supremely. The problem will be that his charm is going to turn real nasty, real soon. You can read all about him, along with his connection to Saul Alinsky's Lucifer, and his rise to power in the New Testament found in Revelation chapter 13.

Now, I'm not going to get into how the Bible describes the procedure on how to deal with dead bodies contaminated by what appears to be nuclear radiation in the upcoming war, which happens to follow the U.S. Army's Field Manual on how to deal with radioactive corpses, or how the world economy will be switching over to a cashless monetary system to eliminate the black market and force rogue countries to capitulate, or how the world will be able to see events happening live on the other side of the world during this time (technology you take for granted today, but it didn't exist when the Bible was written). Nope! You can do your own homework on this time period if you are interested. The only thing I am going to tell you is NEVER TAKE A MARK ON YOUR RIGHT HAND OR FOREHEAD BY ANY GOVERNMENT! Don't do it! Believe me, you'll remember this warning when the times comes – if you're still around, that is. Yeah, they're going to execute you if you don't take the mark, but the alternative is even worse. Store this tidbit of advice in your memory.

No, it's not the end of your stay here! You still have one more cell block to stay in before your release.

CELL BLOCK 10

YOUR RELEASE

PATRIOTISM

Well, well, well. You've come to the end of your stay at the Reeducation Camp for Liberal Millennials & GEN Z. You're almost ready to live under a Republican administration. Yeah, I know, you've already been doing it involuntarily for a while, but now you can do it voluntarily, from the heart, when you walk out of that gate; the gate that has a mezuzah attached to the gate post, and a flag pole out front with the Stars and Stripes hoisted high and proud.

(In hushed tones, and this paragraph is only for you die hard liberals) Yeah, I know, some of you were just in this camp only to gather some intelligence on us, "the enemy." You're liberal, you'll never change, and you're doing what General Sun Tzu suggested that you ought to do, and that is "Know your enemy." At least you learned that much while you were here. You learned all about us conservatives. But, know this, you are going up against a lot of people that have hearts like lions, and a "nation under God."

(Back to the rest of the detainees with a normal volume to my voice). So, my new American conservatives, the first thing that you should do before receiving your pardon is to recite The Pledge of Allegiance. I use the word "should," because in 1943 the U.S. Supreme Court ruled that no child should be compelled to recite the pledge based upon a case brought forth by the Jehovah's Witnesses having the belief that a flag is a "graven image." All right, so if you are a JW you're off the hook. Now, when do this, you are giving an oath, a pledge. It is your word, your bond, and you must keep your word. Are you ready? Place your right hand over your heart. If you are a veteran the law allows you to salute it in pain clothes. Look at the flag and repeat after me:

I pledge allegiance to the flag of the United States of America, and to the republic for which it stands, one nation under God, indivisible, with liberty and justice for all.

So, any time you see our flag, Old Glory, remember your pledge. Your pledge is not just to a piece of cloth, but to the very principles and ideas of the republic - the U.S. Constitution.

This pledge was written in 1892 by former ordained Baptist minister Francis Bellamy, who preached in churches in New York and Boston, and then at 37-years-old he went to work for Youth's Companion, a family magazine with a readership of a half million subscribers. He worked in the promotion department, and his job was to arrange a patriotic program for schools to participate in the opening ceremonies for the Columbian Exposition of 1892, which was the 400th anniversary of Christopher Columbus' discovery of the New World.

The American Civil War had only ended 27 years earlier, and Bellamy wrote the pledge so that the loyalty of the youth in his day would be towards the United States of America, and never again would there be a desire to split the Union like it had been done by the Southern States. The original Pledge of Allegiance Bellamy wrote went like this:

I pledge allegiance to my flag and the Republic for which it stands-one Nation indivisible-with liberty and justice for all.

Millions of school children recited the pledge on October 21, 1892, and because of this stirring moment it caught on in schools across America.

In 1923 the American Legion and the Daughters of the American Revolution were able to get the words "the flag of the United States" added to the pledge, and the following year the words "of America" were added so that school children would never be in doubt as to which flag they were pledging to. After all, some states considered their own state flag to be more revered than the Stars and Stripes.

In 1942, on the 50th anniversary of the Pledge of Allegiance, Congress made it a part of the United States Flag Code. Yes, there are federal laws governing the display and care of the national flag, although the penalty for failure to comply is never enforced. Oh, and by the way, according to 4 U.S. Code 4 "veterans may render the military salute in the manner provided for persons in uniform." I already mentioned this, but now I'm giving you the authority that allows it. So, for you 99% who have never served in the U.S. Armed Forces, if you see a civilian saluting the flag while everyone else is placing their hand over their heart, know that this person served in the United States Armed Forces in defense of our freedom. HOOAH!

Atheistic communism was a threat to Western Civilization after World War II, and the Knights of Columbus, a Catholic organization, lobbied Congress to approve the words "under God" to be inserted into the pledge. On June 14, 1954

President Dwight Eisenhower signed the bill into law. Of course, he did. The President was baptized in the Presbyterian Church in 1953. If you ever drive on any interstate highway it's because President Eisenhower convinced Congress to build it in order to move equipment and supplies quickly across the country if we were invaded by another country and went to war. The highway system also served to grow the economy.

Once the Soviet Union had dissolved, and the threat of communism subsided, American atheist Michael Newdow filed a law suit against the Elk Grove Unified School District in 2000 on his "daughter's behalf," because the Pledge of Allegiance was recited in her classroom each morning, and that, in his opinion, and the opinion of the liberal U.S. Court of Appeals for the Ninth Circuit in California, was an "endorsement of religion." However, the U.S. Supreme Court held that Newdow did not have standing to bring the suit on his daughter's behalf since the mother had sole legal custody of the daughter.

In 2002 Sandy Banning, the mother of Michael Newdow's daughter, appeared on Fox News Channel to give an exclusive interview. In the interview she said, "Well, I'm speaking out because my daughter is being raised in a Christian home. We are not atheists, and I need to communicate to the American people that my daughter's not being harmed by reciting the Pledge of Allegiance." She then went on to emphasis their belief in God and that "American history is founded on the belief of God." Of course, she was right.

In 2005 full-steam-ahead-Newdow appeared on Fox New's Neil Cavuto and stated that he also wanted "In God We Trust" removed from our money, and he compared having these words on our currency to "racial segregation." In 2006 a judge rejected his lawsuit.

In 2009 Newdow sued Chief Justice John Roberts for saying "so help me God" during President Barak Obama's inauguration in 2008. This case was dismissed.

In 2010 another Newdow lawsuit came before the court, on behalf of three unnamed parents and their children, requesting that the words "under God" be removed from the Pledge of Allegiance, but that too was shot down as well. It was the Ninth Circuit that upheld the words "under God" this time, because they did not want to be slapped again by the U.S. Supreme Court.

The bottom line is that "under God" remains in the Pledge of Allegiance, and it does so because the U.S. Supreme Court recognizes it as part of our history, and nobody is obligated to recite it, and therefore it is not an "endorsement of religion." It is an acknowledgement of our American heritage.

SUPPORT CAPITALISM

When you were a child did you ever set up a lemonade stand? Did you ever deliver newspapers on your bicycle? Did a neighbor ever have you mow their lawn or shovel show from their driveway for a few bucks? Did you ever babysit? If you did, then that was your first introduction to capitalism, and boy did it feel good to earn that pocket money. It had a lot more value than just getting allowance handed to you by your parents for chores you should have been doing for free anyway as a member of the household who was not helping pay the rent or mortgage. A lot of self-esteem was developed when you struck the deal, provided the service, and got paid for it. Allowance without actually working for it was the equivalent to getting welfare. It was an entitlement.

For years I couldn't understand why so many Millennials had distain for capitalism, and were willing to embrace socialism. Then it occurred to me one day that most people in this country have 9 to 5 jobs, because most Americans are middle class. They show up to work, punch the time clock, work their eight hours, sometimes put in a little overtime, and then go home and have the evening and weekends to themselves. Thank God it's Friday! Then Monday morning rolls around, and the routine starts all over again. Since most people work for others, or for the government, they have no idea what it's like to be the owner of a business. They don't appreciate the risk the owner, or a corporation, took during the start up phase. Most new business go under within five years of starting. Time card punchers don't realize that when they get to go home at a certain time each day the owner may have to work through the night or weekends to keep the business afloat. There's payroll to worry about, bankers to deal with, legal issues, taxes, personnel problems, threatening competition, and a whole host of details that must be handled or everyone in the organization suffers. However, despite the problems that arise being one's own boss, the rewards are fantastic when the business is on the upswing. When a business is profitable, then the owner deserves the all the perks that come with it.

Since most people take the safe route in life when it comes to earning money, by being an employee, they come to think that government is an extension of their employer, and that it runs the same way. Since their job provides for their needs, then so must the government. They develop the *cradle to grave* mentality.

While going through high school I did odd jobs here and there, and I got a taste of what it was like to be an employee, as well as what it was like to be an entrepreneur. I say "entrepreneur" because I have always had God-given artistic abilities, and when Christmas time rolled around each year I went door to door showing my neighbors and small businesses sketches of my work asking them if they wanted a colorful Christmas scene painted on their windows like department stores did back in the day. Both the rejections and the commissions helped to not only building my knowledge of capitalism, but my character as well. Rejection makes one tougher, and reward makes one want to achieve more.

As an adult I've worked plenty of 9 to 5 jobs, some of them just above minimum wage, and some of them well paying. I've worked for a city government, a county government, the state government, and the federal government. I've also owned four different businesses. Through a couple of these business I've had the opportunity to work in a dozen countries obeying their rules and regulations, and pay taxes on my earnings on both sides of the ocean. With my businesses I've lost a lot of money, and I've made a lot of money. And, it's because of this business experience that I support American capitalism above all other earthly systems. Do you realize how fast and easy it is to start a small mom and pop Internet business in the United States, and then immediately start selling goods on it? It's easy, and I did it for many years. Try doing the same thing in Germany. Good luck! My German friends know what I am talking about.

No matter what your age is, or what your background is, if you have never started your own business before, then do it now. Find something you enjoy doing that could possibly make some money if people were to find out about it, and start a small business. Whether you fail or succeed you will come to appreciate the entrepreneurial spirit, how much work it takes to run a business, and come to appreciate capitalism. Capitalism takes hard work! Even if you are too busy, or too timid, to start a small business, then at least go to a stockbroker, slap down a few thousand dollars, and tell them to invest it wisely for you. You'll get to see firsthand how the stock market works. It's fun, or it can be nerve racking, watching your own stock perform. It's like watching your own horse in a horse race. Investing in the New York Stock Exchange or the NASDAQ will help you appreciate our system. It's a lot more productive for America, win or lose, then gambling it away in a casino, provided you invest in American companies. Remember, "America first," as President Donald Trump would say.

JOIN "THE" PARTY

Are you registered to vote? If not, then go to your local U.S. Post Office, Department of Motor Vehicles, or Armed Services recruitment center and pick up a Voter Registration Application form. It's just one page you must fill out, and then send it in.

To legally vote you must:
1. Be a United States citizen 18-year-old on or before Election Day, or older.
2. You must meet eligibility requirements of your state.

271

You can also go online with the U.S. Election Assistance Commission at www. eac.gov and fill out the Registration Application form.

When you are asked on the form to select the political party you want to be in, although you are not required to, in which case you'd write down "no party" and be listed as UNDECLARED, write down proudly "Republican."

If you are currently a Democrat, it is now time to change sides.

Although we have given you countless reasons for being a God-fearing conservative, the Republican Party is the best party for the United States of America, I'll give you one more very important reason to shun the Democratic Party.

On September 13, 2017 Hillary Clinton was interviewed by CNN's Anderson Cooper. In her book *What Happened*, released after the 2016 Presidential election, she referred to the Electoral College on page 386 as "the God forsaken Electoral College." She doubled down on her distain of it by stating to Cooper in the interview, "I said that in 2000 after what happen to, ah, the 2000 election with Al Gore."

Hillary Clinton then praised the French elections that took place in May of 2017, and the coup de grace was, "We've moved toward one person one vote. That's how we select winners. I was amused after the French elections when I was listening to an interview with a French electoral expert, and he said, 'Well unlike your country the person who wins the most votes wins.' So, I think it (the Electoral College) needs to be, ah, eliminated. I'd like to see us move beyond it, yes."

Have you ever seen Broadway's hit musical *Hamilton* by Lin-Manuel Miranda? Oh yeah, it's pretty cool. Great music! Even President Barak Obama gave a standing ovation when he attended it with his daughters Malia and Sasha. Well, concerning the Electoral College Alexander Hamilton himself said "if the manner of it be not perfect, it is at least excellent."

There's a reason our founding fathers formed the Electoral College at the Constitutional Convention of 1787. When it came to how we select the President of the United States some wanted popular elections, "one person one vote," while others wanted Congress to make the choice without public input. Our genius founding fathers compromised between the two ideas and decided that the President of United States would be indirectly elected by *We the People* through a "college of electors" that would be chosen before each election, and then disbanded after their duties were fulfilled after the election. The popular vote prevented just the big cities, or the most populous states, from always deciding the direction of the country, and it prevented Congress from deciding alone who would be President, thus keeping the real power in the hands of the people; all of the people, including those living in the small rural city of McCook, Nebraska with a population of 7,526. Besides that, throughout our history Constitutional amendments have improved the Electoral College, and the Electoral College has endured through 56 Presidential elections. The system works. Then along comes Hillary Clinton of the Democratic Party, and she says to the American people, straight-faced, that it "needs to be, ah, eliminated."

What? Is she serious? Unbelievable! After 229 years of an "excellent" system, this woman, the most powerful person in the Democratic Party until recently, decides it's time to do away with the framework that our founding fathers had set up for us! Because she lost, and Al Gore lost, both of whom are Democrats, it's now time to throw the Electoral College in the garbage heap of history, the very system we have improved over two centuries! Is there more wisdom in Hillary Clinton's 69+ years of life than the two centuries of combined effort of many? *E pluribus unum.*

What's just as astonishing about this CNN interview is that well-known "professional" journalist Anderson Cooper gets one of the most controversial answers in news history, from one of the most powerful politicians in U.S. history, and he just let it slide. He, the press, is supposed to be the watchdog protecting the United States Constitution. Yet, he didn't challenge the frontal assault on the U.S. Constitution by Hillary Clinton. At least that's how CNN edited the interview to make it appear. Maybe his reaction was deleted. I don't know, for immediately after her un-American comment the interview went right into how many women didn't vote for her.

Why didn't former President Obama (Democrat) put forth a statement about her egregious comment about the Electoral College? After all, wasn't he a constitutional law professor? Nope, silence from him.

Why didn't the Democratic National Committee (DNC) immediately put out a press release distancing themselves from her inflammatory comments? Could it be because Tom Perez was the chair of the DNC at the time she made them? For you who may not know who Tom Perez is, he was President Obama's former U.S. Secretary of Labor, and immediately following the 2016 Presidential election he claimed that "January 21st" was the day that the "resistance took over," referring to the protests against President Trump that took place all across the nation. Perez fomented, "They marched all over the world and said, 'Donald Trump you don't stand for our values!' That's what they said. 'Donald Trump, you didn't win the election.'"

In other words, according to DNC Chair Perez, President Donald Trump didn't win the popular vote. He won the Electoral College, and that does not count.

Hamilton was rolling in his grave after that ignorant comment.

Could it be any clearer? To vote Democratic is to vote for a party that is opposed to the Electoral College, our very foundation for electing a president. Think about this, should they, the Democrats, ever take the White House again, and become the majority in Congress, what other parts of the U.S. Constitution are going to be "eliminated?" It's not hard to predict where this road will eventually lead us if the ass regains control. It will pull that destructive cart down the road with you in it, and everyone you care about, in it as well.

BELIEVE IN GOD

Do you remember in Cell Block 8 that I told you that you should always know where the end of a road leads you? I even just mentioned it a minute ago. Why do you think so many on the left want to erase Christopher Columbus Day as was done by the City Council of Los Angeles? Why do so many in academia want to do away with mandatory reading of classic English "white authors" as they do in Yale? Why do so many on the left want to take down George Washington and Thomas Jefferson statues? You've figured it out by now. It's not only to do away with our American heritage and the United States Constitution, but the end of the road is to ultimately to do away with Jesus Christ. "No, not Him! Give us Barabbas!" **All roads of the radical left lead away from the God of the Bible.** Adolph Hitler's socialism and Karl Marx's communism made that perfectly clear. Hillary Clinton's and Bernie Sanders' American progressive political agendas reemphasized it. We have come full circle back to the Tower of Babel. Now that you have this knowledge, what are you going to do with it? Continue to go down the road to disaster or repent? There's no middle road when you come to a fork in the road. Jesus said, "Whoever is not with me is against me, and whoever does not gather with me scatters." Our society today is so scattered, like never before.

THE SINNER'S PRAYER

Forget about politics right now. The most important subject on Earth is – your eternal soul. When you take your very last breath on Earth, and that day will surely come, you will have sealed your fate – your destiny. You will not cease to exist, be reincarnated (who would want to come back anyway), or become part of the cosmos as some proclaim. There are only two possibilities where your soul will go: Heaven or Hell. It's either going to be united with our Maker through the act of surrendering to Him (cease the rebellion), or be cast into the burning lake of fire by a buffed out angel: a place of outer darkness, gnashing of teeth, never to experience love, laughter, or peace again. It's over. Really over.

Therefore, if you truly want to be saved from damnation, and enjoy the Father's warm embrace (read the story of the prodigal son in the New Testament in the book of Luke 15:11-32) forever, then I'm going to ask you to say the following prayer. Remember, there is no such thing as "proxy salvation." Meaning, you do not automatically get into Heaven because of the faith of your parents, or because you were born in America, or because you are a "good person." No, you have to do it yourself, so if you are ready, say these words out loud:

Lord Jesus I know that you bled and died for me on the cross. I am the one condemned to death, but you took my place. I know that you stand at the door of my heart and knock right now. I now surrender my life to you, and I ask You to enter my heart. Please forgive me of my all my sins, and save my eternal soul from damnation. Have mercy on me. Now, as one of your children teach me the way I should go from here on out. I pray this prayer in the name of the Father, the Son, and the Holy Spirit. Amen (so be it).

If you prayed this prayer, or anything like it in your own words, for there are no set words one must recite, and you truly believe it in your heart that this is true, that Jesus Christ died for you, then you are saved. You're a Christian. You are "born again." As such, you will go to Heaven to be with God for all of eternity, and it won't be just sitting on a cloud playing a harp. That's a bit boring, unless you are a harp player. It is going to be fantastic, and beyond your wildest imagination.

There is nothing more you can do for your salvation. It is finished. The price to get you out of Hell was already paid for on the cross with His blood. He is the unblemished sacrificial lamb spoken about in the Bible. The symbols of the Old Testament have become the reality.

Over time the Holy Spirit will change you to make you more like Him, because He is now in you. Oh sure, you'll stumble and sin from time to time, maybe even a lot, but you'll soon find that it will grieve you to sin each time you do it, and you will "put away childish things." Sins are like toys of your childhood. Eventually, or suddenly, you outgrow them. They will lose their appeal.

As a Christian, you should read the Bible or listen to it on a device, for it is His "love letters" to you, and the "owner's manual" of your life, all bound together in one book.

The Bible is actually a collection of 66 books in three different languages by 40 different authors, who were all inspired by God, written over a 1,300-year span. I prefer to read the New King James version of the Bible myself, which is based upon the King James Bible that has served as the English translation of the original Hebrew and Greek texts since 1604. The New King James Bible just gets rid of all of the "thous" and "thees." Oh, and if you ever get the chance, when you are in Washington, D.C. go visit the Museum of the Bible a block away from the Smithsonian Institute.

Second, you should be baptized with water, for it is a symbol of your sinful body dying, going into the grave, only to be resurrected as "a new creature" when you come out of the water, or after the water flows off your head; different churches do it different ways, and it really makes no difference how it is done since it is merely a symbol of your transformation – from death to life. There are two methods of baptism, and either one is fine; total immersion, or water poured over the head (by cupped hands or from a vessel). If you don't ever get baptized, due to circumstance beyond your control, then don't worry. All is not lost. One of the thieves on the cross next to Jesus repented of his sins, and asked Him, "Jesus, remember me when you come into your kingdom." This was a strange thing to request of a man also dying from execution. How could a condemned criminal bleeding out "come into" a kingdom? The Roman Empire ruled supremely. Yet, this was not a strange request of a man who was not a political figure. The thief recognized Jesus as God in the flesh. Hanging on a cross with nails driven through his feet and hands himself, just like Jesus, the thief making this request was in no position to give to the poor, do good to others, go get baptized, have communion, or anything else physical. He was immobile, and his time was up. The only thing the man could do was simply believe in the Messiah as foretold in the scriptures. Yet, that is all it took for his salvation, for Jesus answered this man, "Truly, I say to you, today you will be with me in paradise." A few hours later, when this man died on the cross, his last breath on Earth was his first breath in Heaven. So, it can be the same for you. All you must do is believe, and God will do the rest.

BACKSLIDDEN CHRISITANS

Are you a Christians that has "gone back into the world?" Have you lost "your first love?" You're miserable in this state, aren't you? Well, then, turn back to God. Rededicate your life to Jesus Christ, and serve Him. You know very well that this universe is one day going to burn up, and all that is in it. *But the day of the Lord will come like a thief. The heavens will pass away with a roar and the elements will be destroyed with intense heat, and the earth and its works will be burned up. 2 Peter 3:10* What you do in His name will last for eternity.

You already know how to pray, so in your own words pray right now to God, and let him, once again, be the Lord of your life.

GOD AND POLITICS

Being a Christian does not mean that you are automatically a conservative Republican, just in case you thought that. However, when it comes to politics you need to support the party, or the politician, that most closely lines up with God's Word – the Holy Bible. Take the time to know a party's platform (a formal set of principal goals that are supported by the party, "a contract with the people" if you will), and where each candidate stands on the issues most important to you. If you want to be an Independent, then that's fine, but just remember that you will not be allowed to vote in a primary (a specific party's election) unless your state has an open primary (not required to be affiliated with a political party). If you cannot vote in a primary, then you'll be allowed to vote in the general election.

Oh, sure, you can withdraw from politics without any retribution from God, and hope that those who rule over you do not become tyrannical. As Edmund Burke said, "The only thing necessary for the triumph of evil is for good men to do nothing." He was in the British government in England who supported the American Revolution at the time it was happening.

For me personally, you already know where I stand. I'm a Christian first, an American second (God & country, in that order), and a Republican third (unless the Party go sideways one day, then I'll bail on them in a heartbeat).

You can download a copy of the Republican Platform 2016 from www.gop.com and read it for yourself (the next one does not come out until the 2020 election). On page 9, within the first paragraph, it states:

We are the party of the Declaration of Independence and the Constitution. The Declaration sets forth the fundamental precepts of American Government: that God bestows certain inalienable rights on every individual, thus producing human equality; that government exists first and foremost to protect those inalienable rights; that man-made law must be consistent with God-given, natural rights; and that if God-given, natural, inalienable rights come in conflict with government, court, or human-granted rights, God-given, natural, inalienable rights always prevail;

The document goes on to say that Republicans will defend "marriage between one man and one woman," "religious liberty," "public display of the Ten Commandments as a reflection of our history and our country's Judeo-Christian heritage," "our right to keep and bear arms," "free speech," "that the unborn child has a fundamental right to life which cannot be infringed," "protecting private property," and a lot about not tolerating racism. Yes, Judeo-Christian-based conservatives get involved in politics. Where do liberals get off telling us that God-fearing citizens cannot run for office or participate in the American political process? If that were the case, the United States Constitution would never have been written, nor a Revolutionary War to secure those freedoms. It was God-fearing people that pressed hard, and many risked their lives, to get the slaves freed. Getting involved in politics is not a commandment of God, but to maintain a place for God in our system it is one's duty to push back against the evil so prevalent in our society today.

Then take a good look at the 2016 Democratic Party Platform, found on www.democrats.org for it reads like a mix of The Communist Manifesto, an anti-NRA rally, and the Black Lives Matter website all rolled up into one. There's no mention of "God shed His grace on thee." Oh, but it does mention how the Democrats were going to "defeat ISIS's stronghold in Iraq and Syria," even though they did not do it under President Barak Obama who pulled out our troops from there when we had stability despite the advice of our top generals not to. However, I do recall that within six months of President Trump taking office ISIS was hammered mercilessly by Iraqi and American troops, and forced out of Iraq. The last stronghold of these butchers was in Mosul, a city that ISIS controlled for three long years, until it fell in June of 2017. Then ISIS was completely defeated in Syria several months later.

"Airborne!"

That is a good war cry to end my little speech, since the U.S. Army 82nd Airborne Division helped liberate the city of Mosul.

THE SHAMAH

For you liberal Jews who have decided that it is time to return to the traditions of your fathers, and to take a conservative path in life, you can recite the Shama here, or the next time you touch the mezuzah if you prefer. Don't just read the words like a school paper in front of the class, but live it. The byproduct of your commitment will undoubtedly strengthen America.

Hear, O Israel! The Lord is our G-d, the Lord is one! You shall love the Lord your G-d with all your heart and with all your soul and with all your might. These words, which I am commanding you today, shall be on your heart. You shall teach them diligently to your sons and shall talk of them when you sit in your house and when you walk by the way and when you lie down and when you rise up. You shall bind them as a sign on your hand and they shall be as frontals on your forehead. You shall write them on the doorposts of your house and on your gates. Deuteronomy 6:4-9

And it shall come to pass, if you shall hearken diligently to my commandments which I command you this day, to love the Lord your G-d, and serve Him with all your heart and with all your soul, that I will give you the rain to your land in its season, the former rain and the latter rain, that you may gather in your corn, and your wine, and your oil. And I will give grass in your fields for your cattle, and you will eat and be satisfied. Take heed to yourself, lest your heart be deceived, and you turn aside, and serve other gods, and worship them, and the anger of the Lord be kindled against you, and He shut up the heaven, so that there shall be no rain, and the ground shall not yield her fruit, and you perish quickly from off the good land which the Lord gives you. Therefore, you will lay up these My word in your heart and soul, and you shall bind them for a sign upon your hand, and they shall be for frontlets between your eyes. And you will teach them to your children, talking of them, when you sit in your house, and when you walk by the way, and when you lie down, and when you rise up. And you will write them upon the doorpost of your house, and upon your gates, that your days may be multiplied, and the days of your children, upon the land which the Lord swore unto your fathers to give them, as the days of the heavens above the earth. Deuteronomy 11:13-21

ALL OTHERS

For those of you who serve different gods, or no gods at all, do not be offended that I have not included any of your prayers to recite, or gave you atheists a moment of silence, or whatever it is you do, because America was founded on Judeo-Christian beliefs; a fact I, we, have established during your stay here in this camp. Thus, this is the direction that we at the camp point people towards through reeducation. That said, not being God-fearing does not exclude you from joining the Republic Party. If the Republican Platform appeals to you, then by all means, join the Party.

With our diversity we all say, "Make America Great Again." Don't we all want that?

You have been reeducated. Congratulations! You are free to go. And when I say "free," I mean FREE!

Then you will know the truth, and the truth will set you free. John 8:32

For those of you who just did what you had to do just to get out of this camp, only to "do a Sun Tzu on us" when you're on the outside, then we'll see you on the battle field, and ultimately on Judgment Day.

CONSERVATIVE RESOURCES

Now that you are a convert to conservatism you'll need a few good resources that will strengthen your stance. So, I've come up with a small list of organizations that I endorse, and their websites for you to go to.

When it comes to conservative news I watch, and read, daily **Fox News** (www.foxnews.com).

To get a Christian perspective on the news I watch, and read, daily the **Christian Broadcast Network** (www1.cbn.com/cbnnews.com).

If you want to know how current issues line up with the U.S. Constitution then there is no better commentator than **Mark Levin** (www.crtv.com).

To do the Sun Tzu thing, *Know the enemy*, I do occasionally listen to the "fake news," mainstream media, to get the left's perspective on issues, and sometimes they even get some of the stories right.

When I'm in my truck driving I like to listen to **The Rush Limbaugh Show** on the radio. The left has hated this guy for decades, and that's because he's a true patriot that exposes the left's agenda five days a week (www.rushlimbaugh.com).

A good conservative magazine I like to read, when I have the time, is the **National Review** (www.nationalreview.com).

To know what is really happening in Israel I read The Jerusalem Post (www.jpost.com).

To get the latest scientist discoveries that disprove evolution, or prove creation, depending how you want to look at it, I get a lot of good information from the **Christian Research Institute (CRI)** (www.equip.org).

For issues dealing with marriage and parenting **Focus on the Family** puts out a lot of good material (www.focusonthefamily.com), and **Dr. James Dobson's** *Family Talk* is phenomenal in this area as well (www.drjamesdobson.org).

To really understand what the Second Amendment is all about, and get expert firearms training from qualified instructors, the **National Rifle Association (NRA)** are the experts to turn to (www.nr.org).

There's a lot of liberal universities in this country brainwashing young people to detest our American heritage and culture, but there's one university that will develop your worldview based entirely on reality, and that's **PragerU**, and it's

FREE. Watch the many great short videos that will make it effortless for you to be smarter! (www.prageru.com).

Do you want to listen to what a good Bible-believing pastor sounds like? Then try listening to Charles Stanly of **In Touch Ministries**. I listen to him every Sunday before I head off to my own church (www.intouch.org). Are you a new Christian? Then listening to evangelical preacher **Greg Laurie** for a good place to start (www.harvest.org). Do you want someone a little more laid back, and with a good sense of humor, then give **Pastor Jon Courson** of *Search Light* a try (www.joncourson.com). How about a man of God who's not going to sug- ar coat the Gospel, and give it to you straight? Then download sermons from **Pastor Barry Stagner** (www.cctustin.org/teachings/archive). Do you want to know more about the End Times that we are living in, and how some of today's news headlines are connected? **Don Stewart's** *Breaking News* on *His Channel* is what will keep you updated. **The Hal Lindsey Report** also scours the news for signs of the End Times. Plus, on *His Channel* you'll find a lot of other good ministers to listen to (www.hischannel.com). *So then faith comes by hearting, and hearing by the word of God. Romans 10:17*

Do you want to help the poor, sick, and suffering around the world? Then a good organization that you can be sure that your donations will actually go to those who need it is *Samaritan's Purse* led by **Franklin Graham** (www.samar- itanspurse.org).

Do you want to help strengthen Israel, then go check out America's Pro-Israel Lobby **American Israel Public Affairs Committe (AIPAC)** (www.aipac.org).

There is another museum you must visit to learn more about creation, and to see a life-size replica of Noah's Ark, and that is the **Ark Encounter** in William- stown, Kentucky (https://arkencounter.com)

After you have registered to vote as a Republican, the next thing you can do is to strengthen the Republican Party by joining a team. You Millennials and Gen Zers can even gain leadership experience through the **Republican Leadership Initiative**. If you want to be an activist, then be an activist on the "right" side (www.gop.com). On this website you can purchase an official MAKE AMERI- CA GREAT AGAIN red baseball cap and proudly display it in your dorm room, your abode, or on your desk at work. That will certainly get a lively conversa- tion going. Be careful though, it may also get you a punch in the nose by a peace loving, tolerant, liberal.

Oh, and I almost forgot. Tell all of your liberal progressive friends about this camp, and how much you learned when you were an inmate, and how great it is now to breath the air of freedom both politcally and spiritually.

God bless you, and God bless the United States of America.

JIM WAGNER

www.ingramcontent.com/pod-product-compliance
Lightning Source LLC
Chambersburg PA
CBHW050109280326
41933CB00010B/1033